Twenty Four Hours From Tulsa

Twenty Four Hours From Tulsa

David McGrath

Waterside Productions

Waterside Productions
2055 Oxford Ave
Cardiff, CA 92007
www.waterside.com

Disclaimer

This book is a work of historical fiction. It is the fictional backstory to the Burt Bacharach-Hal David song "Twenty Four Hours From Tulsa" that was a huge hit for Gene Pitney in 1963.

Any references to historical events, real people, or real places are used fictitiously. Other names, characters, places, and events are products of the author's imagination, and any resemblance to actual events, places, or persons, living or dead, is entirely coincidental.

Yup, I made it all up!

Thanks Burt, Hal, and Gene for the inspiration.

Chapter One

Hal Douglas was the biggest pop star in the USA in 1967. He had even surpassed his idol — Gene Pitney — in popularity. His career was sailing along on the pop jet stream of hit records, sell-out tours, and a movie career getting ready to launch. The 19-year-old pop star sat at the desk — with pen in hand — in the damp, tiny room at the semi-seedy Don's Starry Starry Night Motel near Newark, New Jersey.

Jessie James — the sultry blonde bombshell singer who shared the top of the pop charts with Hal — was sound asleep in the room's double bed. Naked. Former Miss California. Miss America runner-up. She was exhausted from a surprising night of surprising passion.

The two pop stars had shared a night of unsophisticated yet genuinely blissful sex. Hal had learned a lot this night. He now knew every square inch of Jessie's exquisite body, and he learned how she wanted him to love it and her. Jessie James was a peerless teacher. Hal turned out to be both an eager and an attentive student.

Hal was now writing to his fiancée, Mallory McCoy, back in Tulsa, Oklahoma.

My darling Mallory, I am writing to say that I won't be coming home. Something happened to me; well, I fell in love with someone else. I am so sorry.

The life that he knew was over; the life that he had dreamed about was in high gear.

Chapter Two

He was Hal Douglas. BMOC — Big Man On Campus — at Messmer High School in Milwaukee. Quarterback and captain of the football team; singer and actor in all the school plays. He was so handsome that he made Ricky Nelson look like Quasimodo, the Hunchback of Notre Dame.

She was Mallory McCoy. Prom queen and captain of the Messmer High School cheerleading squad. Cute as Christmas was Mallory. Actually, the blonde-haired, blue-eyed, sun-kissed all-American girl was a stunning beauty. Had she lived in California she would have been a legendary surfer girl. She would have been the inspiration for one Beach Boys hit after another.

Their worlds couldn't be farther apart.

Mallory McCoy's nickname at school was "Sloopy." She didn't know why, but she thought it was cute. Hal called her "my gal pal Mal." And, at Messmer High, they were known to one and all as Hal and Mal.

Hal loved music. Actually, Hal was consumed by music. He was a breathtaking singer with perfect pitch. He could play guitar, piano, and drums. He performed in ALL of the school musicals and talent shows. Since he could remember, he wanted to be a star. He wanted to be another Frank Sinatra; if that was shooting too high, he figured he would settle for being the next Johnnie Ray or Gene Pitney.

Sinatra and Ray were idols of his parents' generation. Hal's idol was Gene Pitney.

Hal was obsessed with Gene Pitney. He loved everything about him: his voice, his songs, his looks, his hair, his aura and mystique — and — the fact that Gene was an international star and knew all the pop stars of the day — American and British. While Hal could only have a crush on Dusty Springfield, Jackie DeShannon, Petula Clark, and Lulu from a distance, Gene knew them. Gene spent days and weeks out on tour with them.

Gene Pitney was on *American Bandstand, Where The Action Is, Shindig, Hullabaloo,* and, Hal's favorite TV show, *Starr Power*. Gene was on the cover of *Hit Parader* and *16 Magazine*. Every weekend Hal would make his way to a specialty magazine and bookstore in downtown Milwaukee that carried international newspapers and magazines. Gene would invariably be on the covers of music magazines like *Fab208* from Europe's Radio Luxembourg, *Melody Maker,* and *New Musical Express,* both from England. Hal would read about Gene's UK tours and all the British TV and radio shows that Gene appeared on. "What a fabulous life," Hal would think to himself when he read about Gene's exploits. The specialty shop was also where he would pick up "the Bible" of the music industry, *Billboard*. He read it cover to cover. He wanted — no — he needed to know everything there was to know about the music business.

Hal also adored Broadway musicals, but his real love was Top 40 music. The British Invasion occurred during his sophomore year in high school. Hal knew the names and biographies of every member of The Beatles, The Rolling Stones, The Searchers, The Hollies, The Fortunes, Herman's Hermits, etc. He read and collected *Hit Parader* and *16 Magazine* for the song lyrics and photos of his favorite stars.

Hal was also adept at mimicking the voices of all of his favorite stars. He could sound like anyone: Gene Pitney, Frank Sinatra, Johnnie Ray, Elvis, Paul Anka, Frankie Avalon, Bobby Rydell, Dion, Buddy Holly, Bobby Vee, Del Shannon, and many others. It was just one more musical gift he had.

Just for fun, in his senior year, Hal formed his own band to utilize his talents and earn a little spending money. Hal's Pals became a very popular local band in Milwaukee. At weekend dances, they played all the hits that the kids heard on The Mighty 92/WOKY Radio. Unlike all the other local Milwaukee bands like The Legends and The Robbs, Hal's Pals specialized in Gene Pitney songs because Hal was the only local singer who had a voice that could come close to matching Pitney's.

Hal had his sights set on becoming a peer of Gene Pitney and all those stars he knew.

Mal was the only child of a wealthy Milwaukee couple, Mitchell and Maureen McCoy. Both were born with silver spoons in their mouths. He was a Harvard-educated millionaire attorney. She was a stay-at-home mom who occasionally did substitute teaching at Saints Peter and Paul Catholic School. Teaching was her joy.

They were an attractive couple. Maureen could have been Marilyn Monroe's twin sister; Mitchell was as physically chiseled and handsome as Paul Newman. But, both seemed so prim and proper — and Catholic — that their friends were convinced they never saw each other naked and never had sex with each other. Where Mallory had come from was the behind-the-back joke of their friends. The McCoys were a very happy little family. They really were Ozzie and Harriet (without David and Ricky). No scandals, private or public. No skeletons in the closet, personal or professional. Unless you counted Maureen's ex-lover, star network TV newsman Walter Watson!

The housekeeper kept the McCoy mini-mansion, located on the city's exclusive Lake Drive, spotless. She also made sure dinner was always ready at six o'clock precisely. Mitchell and Maureen liked to watch Walter Watson on The *GBS Evening News* every night before dinner. Maureen had dated Watson in 1942 while he was a radio announcer at WHA Radio in Madison. It was a quick summer fling, and Maureen never spilled the beans on Walter's sexual prowess except in a diary entry: "That stupid mustache tickled me in places where I shouldn't be tickled."

She lost track of him until she saw him on TV, anchoring the national political conventions on the fledgling Giant Broadcasting System in 1952. She never let on to Mitchell why she had to watch Walter Watson every night on the news. He thought she was just smitten with him as a newscaster as most other Americans were.

On weekends, the McCoys lived by family traditions. Saturday morning breakfast at the art deco Schroeder Hotel on Wisconsin Avenue in downtown Milwaukee; Saturday evenings at the Milwaukee Symphony or a play. Sunday morning it was Mass at Saints Peter and Paul Catholic Church on Milwaukee's East Side, then a family lunch at home with any friend or relative who decided to drop by for the noon feast. The Green Bay Packers football game was allowed on the TV, but at 3 p.m. it was family quiet time. The visitors left, the TV was turned off, and music was turned on. But, it was only classical music or opera in the McCoy house.

"None of that rock 'n' roll trash in this house," Mitchell McCoy was fond of saying. So, teenaged Mallory knew all about Leontyne Price but had no idea about Lloyd Price. Nor did she care.

Hal's parents were simple, working class people, Frank and Rita Douglas really loved each other. High school sweethearts themselves. Frank was a union truck driver. He worked for Continental Baking Company, the baker of Wonder Bread and all the Hostess products like Cupcakes, Snowballs, and Twinkies; Rita worked in a bank.

But, as Gene Pitney sang, true love never runs smooth.

Frank, a WWII vet, drank too much too often. Was he trying to deaden the pain from the debilitating leg injury he suffered at the hands of a Nazi machine gunner at Normandy — or — just trying to cope with the overwhelming responsibilities that accompanied being the father of eight? No one was sure.

What everyone did know was that his work ethic was stronger than his drinking problem. He never missed a day of work for any reason: the painful leg, the nightly drinking, or his eight kids. He respected authority and demanded that his kids did, too. But, he wasn't emotionally equipped to know how to truly and deeply love his wife and children. His hardscrabble Depression-era childhood simply wasn't a great time or place to learn how to live for life. He knew what he knew; he didn't know any more or any better.

Rita worked hard to keep heart and soul — and the Douglas family — together. She instilled manners, respect, and love of family in her children. Money was stretched thin because of the large Catholic family, but the kids didn't realize it. Frank and Rita did not share their financial concerns with the kids; they just tried to make it all work. Rita suffered through constant verbal fights and battles with her husband — and — countless alcohol-fueled public embarrassments. Nonetheless, she did her level best to always make a sunny, happy, and positive home for her kids. It worked until each one of the kids figured out the reality of the situation at his/her own speed.

Music was Hal's escape from the tensions between his parents and his socially limited lifestyle. At home, he listened to his records or the radio, and that helped him to live another life separate from the one he was born to. He dreamed of being on stage — like his idol Gene Pitney — singing his hit records to crowds of crazed fans. He dreamed of traveling the world — like Gene Pitney — doing concerts and hobnobbing with the other stars of the day. That was what he dreamed about all through high school.

When Hal had to hang out at The North Oak Inn tavern to keep an eye on his dad, he would use his paper route money to buy orange soda and play the jukebox. He wanted and needed music around him all the time. It took him away from the desperate realities of his life.

Mal's only dream was to grow up to be just like her mom. She wanted to be married to a rich, successful man with a lot of rich and successful friends. She wanted a nice big house with a white picket fence around it. But, unlike her parents, she wanted to have a large family. Maybe eight kids. Like Hal's family. She didn't like being an only child. She wanted a big brother to watch over her and a kid sister to be best friends with.

Hal and Mal graduated from Messmer High School in June 1966. Mal's eighteenth birthday was on the 4th of July. They had sex to celebrate the occasion. But, there were no sexual fireworks on the fireworks-filled holiday. She was the first woman he had ever seen naked and had sex with; he was the first man she had ever seen naked and had sex with. They didn't make love; neither knew how. They had sex. Or, rather, they tried to have some sort of sex. The fumbling was awkward; the silence was uncomfortable; both were more than a bit embarrassed. But their teenage romance had been consummated. And they made their pledge of everlasting love to each other that night.

But, just one week later, their world came tumbling down. Mitchell McCoy made an announcement to his wife and daughter at dinner one night that changed everybody's lives.

"I have decided to become a senior partner at the law firm of Christopher, David, & Todd in Tulsa, Oklahoma," he said very matter-of-factly. "They want me to start and build their franchising division. Franchises are the next big thing of the future. They want to be pioneers. And, I'm their man."

Maureen McCoy, always supportive of her husband and his legal career, just wanted to know when they were leaving Milwaukee. Mallory just looked at him in stunned disbelief.

"I met some of the senior partners at that legal conference I went to in San Francisco last month, and we just got talking," he explained further. "They want to move fast. The law firm will buy this house from us, arrange our move to Tulsa, and pay all of our moving expenses," he said quite proudly. "They want me to get there and get started right away. We leave in one week."

The next day, Mallory broke the news to Hal. "He can't do that," said the very naïve seventeen-year-old Hal Douglas. "He can't break us up just like that."

"Yes he can," said Mallory, on the verge of tears. "And he did. The moving company started to pack up our stuff this morning. Hal, what are we going to do?"

"I love you, Mallory," he said. "I want to spend the rest of my life with you. Obviously, we can't get married right now because we're too young, so why don't we do the next best thing. Let's get engaged."

"How do we do that?" she asked, somewhat incredulous at the spur-of-the-moment decision by her first-ever boyfriend.

Hal got down on one knee, took Mallory's hand in his, smiled and asked, "Will you marry me, Mallory McCoy? I promise to take care of you and make you happy for the rest of your life."

"I will marry you, Hal Douglas," said Mallory with a grin as wide as the ocean. "And I make the same promise to you. The miles may keep us apart, but love will keep us together."

Hal smiled through his adolescent tears and said, "No matter what happens now, Mal; no matter where we live, Mal; we are now engaged. One day we will be Mr. and Mrs. Hal Douglas. How does that sound?"

"Well, I was going to say that I can't wait," Mal squealed, "but I guess I'll have to. I'll wait as long as I have to for you, Hal."

Chapter Three

After Mallory's family left Milwaukee, Hal kept himself busy all summer long with his band, Hal's Pals, to keep his mind off her. A twist of fate put Hal on the road he hoped would lead to his sought-after stardom. *The 1966 Rick Starr Cavalcade of Stars* rock 'n' roll show was set to play Milwaukee's Arena on a hot August night in 1966. But, the tour bus was running late — very late. Starr, who produced and hosted the hottest teen music TV show in the country, *Starr Power*, had called ahead to warn the promoter and suggest that a local band play until the tour bus got there.

Hal's Pals was playing a medley of Gene Pitney hits when Rick Starr and the stars of his tour finally arrived at the theater. Billy Joe Royal was one of the headliners on the tour. Billy Joe's 1965 Top 10 hit "Down In The Boondocks" sounded just like a Gene Pitney record. Like Hal, Pitney was Royal's idol, too. Backstage, Royal's jaw dropped when he heard Hal Douglas singing songs like "Town Without Pity" and "Only Love Can Break A Heart."

He quickly called his co-headliners Tommy Roe and Bobby Vee, as well as Rick Starr, over to the side of the stage to watch Hal's Pals perform. "And this guy is not a star, why?" Vee asked. "He sings better than anyone on this bus!"

In his pleasant Southern drawl, Royal added jokingly, "Whoever that is singing those Pitney songs, get him outta here now! That's my act!"

When Hal's Pals came off stage, Billy Joe walked over and introduced himself to Hal. "Hey man, nice show. I'm Billy Joe Royal. This tour has been all over the country, and we've never seen a local act as good as you. You guys were great."

Hal was dumbfounded that a star as big as Billy Joe Royal would talk to a nobody like him. Billy Joe Royal had hit records. Billy Joe Royal was a star. Stars didn't talk to a nobody — did they?

"It's very nice of you to say that, Mr. Royal," Hal said very shyly. "I have all of your records."

"Call me Billy Joe," Royal said to him. Then he pummeled Hal with questions. "How old are you? How long have you been singing? Have you made any records? Man, I can't believe how much you sound like Gene Pitney."

"My parents wouldn't like that," Hal replied.

"Your mom and dad don't want you to make records?"

"No, my mom and dad wouldn't like my calling you by your first name," Hal explained. "They taught me to respect adults."

"Hal, I'm only twenty four years old. I could be your big brother. You can call me Billy Joe."

"If it's all the same to you, Mr. Royal, I'd rather stick to calling you Mr. Royal. You are an adult, and you are a star. I have great respect for both of those things. To answer your questions, I'm seventeen years old, and I haven't made any records, but it would be a dream come true."

Royal's career had already peaked, and he was struggling to get another hit record for himself. Hal's talent wowed him, and he found Hal's gentleness very endearing. He wanted to help Hal make his dreams come true. Just like singer-songwriter-producer Joe South had helped him. "I don't go on stage for another forty five minutes. Let's go talk to Rick Starr."

Starr, who had his fingers in all kinds of pies, including record companies and music publishing, was always looking for the "next big thing." Many of the artists on the *1966 Cavalcade of Stars* tour would be yesterday's heroes in 1967. Starr was always looking for new blood. He had watched Hal's Pals finish their show and had made a decision.

Starr was in the tour bus counting cash from ticket sales when Billy Joe and Hal walked in. "Rick, I want you to meet Hal Douglas. His band saved our butts tonight. They were on when we got here, remember? They played a great sixty-minute set until we got into town."

Starr stood up, shook Hal's hand, and said with a chuckle, "Yup, I saw Gene Pitney III here on stage. You were great."

Hal had a puzzled look on his face reacting to the Gene Pitney reference. Starr saw it and explained, "I refer to my friend here, Billy Joe Royal, as Gene Pitney, Junior. It's a compliment."

"I appreciate that very much, Mr. Starr," said Hal. Unlike Royal, Rick Starr didn't suggest in a friendly way that Hal call him by his first name. "I watch *Starr Power* all the time, Sir. It's a great show."

"I think he could make hit records," said Billy Joe.

"I knew that about a half-hour ago," said Starr with a smile. "Look, Hal, we're leaving Milwaukee tonight right after the show to drive to Chicago. We have a show there tomorrow night. I can get you a record deal, but we have to do the deal tonight. Give me your phone number so I can talk to your parents."

Hal was dumbfounded again. Rick Starr — a huge TV star — was talking to him, calling him Hal, offering to get him a record deal, and wanting to talk to his parents. Could this all really be happening? Could his dreams be coming true? Could Rick Starr get him a hit record? Could people hear his hits on radio stations all across the country? Could he go out on tour like Billy Joe Royal and Gene Pitney and sing his songs to big audiences around the country? Could this be the start of something big for Hal Douglas?

As Hal was nervously scribbling his phone number on a piece of paper, Billy Joe invited him to watch Bobby Vee's part of the show from the wings of the stage. As they climbed up to the stage, Vee was singing "Rubber Ball," a song written by Gene Pitney.

"Mr. Royal, do you know Gene Pitney?"

"Never met him, but I hear he's a great guy and a great businessman. I hope we both get to meet him some day."

Thirty minutes later, as Billy Joe Royal was on stage singing his huge hit, "Down In The Boondocks," in front of close to ten thousand screaming teenaged fans, Rick Starr was on the phone telling Frank and Rita Douglas everything he was going to do for their son. He told them how Hal Douglas was going to be the next teen idol. He also told them how it was going to get done. He promised them that he would take care of Hal. Just as he was ending the call, Billy Joe Royal and what appeared to be his new pet, walked in from the stage. Rick handed the phone to Hal, who spoke to his mom and dad for about five minutes.

Moments later, Hal shook hands with Rick Starr, his new manager, agent and record producer. Hal and the man he would forever call Mr. Starr had a deal where they would split any and all profits from records, tours, TV shows, and movies fifty/fifty after expenses.

Starr told Hal that their handshake deal would be formalized with a written contract after Starr got back to LA.

"Or, when I get around to it," Starr said under his breath to himself.

Starr wasn't big on putting things in writing when he was dealing with naïve kids. It was easier for the kids to instigate legal action against him if contractual terms and conditions were actually spelled out, and then he actually had to live up to them.

"How'd that go with your mom and dad?" Starr asked Hal.

"My mom and dad said they were very proud of me, and they also said that you would take good care of me," Hal replied. "Mr. Starr, will you help me take care of them? If I make any money I'd like to buy them a new car and a new house. Would you help me do that, Mr. Starr? Also, do you think I could get an autographed picture for them?"

"I think I can do all of that, Hal. They seemed like very nice people. I have your phone number. I'll be calling you in a few days. Hope you're ready to be a star."

Hal was numb. It all happened so fast. He was packing up his guitar and getting ready to leave when Billy Joe Royal came around. "How'd it go, Hal?" he asked.

"Mr. Starr talked with my parents, and we made a deal for him to be my manager, agent, and record producer. He said he would call me in a few days."

"I hope it's a good deal for you," Royal said as he turned towards the tour bus.

"If I get to make records and do shows like you do, it's a good deal for me," Hal told him.

Chapter Four

One month later, Hal Douglas — without his Pals — was in a recording studio in New York. He was Rick Starr's newest protégé. Hal was recording six songs — all but two published by Starr's publishing company Starr Songs — for Starr Records. Starr had a fifty one percent stake in the record label. One of the songs Hal recorded that day would go on to become both a teen anthem and one of the biggest American hits of the British Invasion era.

Just like Billy Joe Royal, Hal Douglas adopted a Gene Pitney "sound" on a song called "My Only Girl." He felt like he was honoring his idol by doing so. He also felt like he was honoring Mallory with this song. He thought of her every time he sang it.

Hal loved the way he sounded when he imitated Pitney. "My Only Girl" was released in early October and soared to #1 in America in November 1966. Ironically, Gene Pitney's biggest US chart record that year, "Just One Smile," struggled to make it to #55.

"My Only Girl" stayed on the American charts for an unheard of thirty six weeks. Seizing the moment to sell records and tickets, Starr hastily added Hal Douglas to the final dates of the *1966 Cavalcade of Stars* tour.

Hal joined the tour in Salt Lake City as it was heading back to the West Coast. The first one to greet him at the hotel was Billy Joe Royal. "Where in blazes did you find that song?" Royal asked as he was pumping Hal's hand. "That is a drop dead gorgeous song. Gene Pitney and I both would have killed for that song."

"Mr. Starr found it for me," said Hal. "A guy named Brian Frederick wrote it. He works at Starr Songs Publishing. He had a hit record back in 1961. Do you remember 'Stuck Up'? That was his one and only hit record as a singer."

"Yeah, I do remember 'Stuck Up,'" Royal said. "Wasn't one of my favorites, but 'My Only Girl' is a beauty. I've gotta find me a song like that."

Chapter Five

After Salt Lake City, the tour headed north to Boise, Seattle, and Portland before heading back down the coast to Eugene, Oregon, and finally on to San Francisco and Los Angeles. By the time the *1966 Cavalcade of Stars* hit Portland, Rick Starr had moved Hal up to headliner status.

It was Starr's tour, and Hal was his artist, so he really could do what he wanted. And, he always did. Hal was very uncomfortable when Starr announced the move to him after the show in Seattle. He questioned the decision.

"Mr. Starr, I appreciate your confidence in me, but I don't think it's fair to Billy Joe. This is his tour. He's the star."

Rick Starr did not like to be questioned — by anyone. He was not the sentimental sort, either. He was known to kick acts off his tour, sometimes for good reason, sometimes on a whim. Some of the biggest hit makers in the country had gotten on Starr's wrong side and felt his wrath. And it cost them money.

But, Starr knew he had to handle Hal Douglas with kid gloves. First, Hal was still very new to show business and very wet behind the ears. Hal didn't know how the business worked. Second, Starr's plan to groom Hal to be a triple threat on records, on tours, and in the movies certainly needed Hal's cooperation. So, Starr had to handle the situation patiently instead of with one of his usual stinging one-liners.

"Hal, first of all, this is my tour, not Billy Joe's tour," Starr said smugly. "Secondly,

I already discussed this with Billy Joe. He's OK with this, and he's happy for you."

It was only half the truth. He had talked to Billy Joe Royal, and Billy Joe was happy for Hal's success. Billy Joe found Hal to be one of the nicest, most engaging performers he had ever met. However, Billy Joe was not happy with being forced out of headliner status with just a few shows left on the tour. He was both personally and professionally humiliated. But, he wanted the work and the money. He knew that, and so did Rick Starr. There really had been no "discussion." Billy Joe didn't have a say in the matter.

"My Only Girl" had hit #1 in November and could not be budged from the Top 10. Hal had the hottest record in the USA. He was all over the teen magazines, and he was scheduled to make unprecedented back-to-back appearances on *Starr Power* for the Christmas and New Year TV specials when he hit LA. It looked like "My Only Girl" was going to be the biggest hit of the year. No one doubted that Hal was now the biggest star on the tour and that he was the reason the shows were selling out. As a matter of fact, shows had to be added in Portland, Eugene, San Francisco, and Los Angeles to accommodate ticket demand. Hal Douglas was now an authentic American Teen Idol.

Hal was too caught up in all the hoopla surrounding his massive hit record, the tour, and his long dreamed-of career to realize that Rick Starr never brought a written contract to his attention to sign. He was just having the time of his life.

Then, in early 1967 "My Only Girl" became an international hit after Mick Jagger from The Rolling Stones heard it while on tour in the US and suggested that a British DJ friend of his play it. It went to #1 in England as fast as any Beatles song ever did. Barely six months out of high school, Hal Douglas was now an international singing sensation.

And, Rick Starr was getting richer.

Back at her new home in Tulsa, Oklahoma, Mallory didn't get it. Oh, she knew that Hal was now famous and his song was on the radio. But, because of her parents' aversion to rock 'n' roll, the only way she could hear it was at her friends' houses or on the jukebox at her favorite diner in Tulsa. So, she missed all the accompanying frenzy of Hal's huge hit. She couldn't watch *Shindig, Hullabaloo,* or *Starr Power* at home — so — she never saw her fiancé on TV. She also didn't see the girls fawning all over him. She didn't read the teen magazines so she wasn't aware of how big a star Hal really was. He was as big as The Beatles for this moment in time. She just wanted him to come back, marry her, buy a house, have children, and live happily ever after in Milwaukee or even Tulsa, Oklahoma.

Most of the fame and fortune was lost on Hal, too. In his mind, he was just a kid from Milwaukee who got lucky. He felt bad that his buddies in Hal's Pals weren't along for the ride. But, Mr. Starr, as he still reverently called Rick Starr, was managing his career and calling every shot from way behind the scenes. Starr said that Hal didn't need his Pals.

"Mr. Starr should know what he's doing," was how Hal justified the break up to himself and anyone else who asked. He felt horrible about the whole situation, but he felt that his hands were tied. Starr told Hal that he didn't like to deal with groups. He wanted to deal one-on-one with only one person when it came time to make important decisions. Hal was having great fun, and he obligingly did what Starr said "would be good" for his career.

Chapter Six

Hal Douglas was now way too big to go out as just one more act on the *1967 Rick Starr Cavalcade of Stars*, so the rock impresario organized Hal's own tour of the United States. Hal was the headliner. As supporting acts, Starr signed his friend Dick Clark's stable of Philadelphia regulars, Bobby Rydell, Frankie Avalon, and Fabian. All three were now in the twilight of their hit-making careers. Starr always liked to have a girl group or a girl singer on a tour, too, just for some balance. But, he was also driven by the bottom line.

Because Hal Douglas was now as big as The Beatles, Starr begrudgingly doubled the $1,000 weekly salary he usually paid his headliners. Hal was making $2,000 weekly. That princely sum stunned music business insiders. Even hard-nosed businessman and hitmaker Gene Pitney could only strong-arm Starr for $1,500 per week as a headliner at the peak of his career. Not that Starr HAD to pay Hal that kind of money. The kid from Milwaukee was still swimming in naïveté and really had no idea how much a headliner could be earning on his own tour. But Starr couldn't count on Hal being show biz stupid forever, so he was paving his way into a lucrative tomorrow with Hal Douglas.

Starr had plans beyond the Top 40 for the former BMOC of Messmer High School, so sixty percent of his talent budget on the 1967 tour went to Hal. The Philadelphia boys were well off but still enjoyed working, so they accepted the $500 per week Starr allotted each of them. Trying to keep his talent budget under $5,000 weekly meant he only had another $500 per week to buy a girl singer or girl group. So, he decided on struggling one-hit wonder Jessie James.

Chapter Seven

Twenty-two-year-old Jessie James had topped the charts in the fall of 1966 with a gorgeous ballad "Take Me Now." Hal Douglas's "My Only Girl" eventually knocked it out of #1. Her December 1966 follow up, "Love Me Now," was too similar to her first hit, and the kids rejected it. It didn't even make it into the Top 40 before crashing off the charts three weeks later. That disaster put her career in a holding pattern until she and her record company came up with a bubbly little ditty called "Yes! No! Yes!" It was the perfect summer song. It was released in January 1967. But, whether it would be a hit or not was still uncertain.

Jessie James was a former Miss California who had finished as the runner up in the Miss America Pageant in 1964. Not only was she breathtakingly beautiful, she was also a Mensa genius. Her dad was the former governor of California, Jansen James. Her mother was the two-time Academy Award winning A-list movie star Jayna James. Jessie was dating Oscar-winning movie star Danny Harmon, whose parents were both B-list actors and friends of her parents. Jessie could do anything she wanted to do. But, all she wanted to do was be a pop star. She was in show business, right now, not for the money but for the fun and the stardom.

Chapter Eight

The 1967 Rick Starr Cavalcade of Stars toured the country from January through May. Rick Starr emceed every show, and then he had to fly back to Los Angeles every other week to tape two *Starr Power* programs for TV. The schedule both exhausted and invigorated the thiry eight-year-old rock entrepreneur. He really didn't love the entertainers, but he loved the energy at live shows — and he loved the growing fortune he was amassing.

The Hal Douglas Greatest Hits on Earth Tour began in May — immediately after the Cavalcade tour ended — in sunny Florida. Again, Starr emceed every show and made it back to LA on schedule to tape *Starr Power*. He was the iron man of show business.

Jessie James would open every concert with a short fifteen-minute set. The Philadelphia boys, who fashioned themselves as the new "Rat Pack," fawned all over her but were always extraordinarily respectful. That's because Avalon, who had a bit of a movie career and lived in Hollywood, knew Jessie's mom and dad. He warned Fabian and Rydell to play nice. Hal, who believed he was still in love with Mallory, was always the gentleman's gentleman.

Hal would watch her show from the wings and marvel at her talent. "The voice of an angel," he told everybody on the tour and every reporter and DJ he talked to. All the other stars on the tour were very respectful of and friendly to Hal on the tour. Hal was having a ball. He was now a peer of the stars he used to listen to on WOKY Radio in Milwaukee. On the bus, he would entertain the Philadelphia boys with his dead-on impressions of each of them. They all thought he was a hoot.

Chapter Nine

Jessie James became smitten with the teenage Hal Douglas. She liked the way he looked; she liked the way he sang; she liked his personality; she liked his manners. She loved the possibilities in his future. During the long bus rides from city to city, she would engage Hal in conversations about his hopes and dreams. And she shared hers with him. And they loved to sing Everly Brothers songs together.

The Hal Douglas Greatest Hits on Earth Tour zigzagged through the US. During the tour, Hal's second single was finally released. It was the theme song to a new Gary Cooper western, *Sundown Never Came*. The fourteen-year-old daughter of the movie's producer was a huge Hal Douglas fan. She convinced her dad that he should use Hal to sing the theme song from the movie because it would make teenagers aware of the movie. Rick Starr said "yes" to the deal but only after getting the publishing rights, producer credit, and rights to release it on Starr Records.

The movie producer didn't care what deal Starr got as long as he delivered Hal Douglas. He was doing this simply to keep his daughter happy. Hal had been rushed into the studio just one week before his tour was to start. "Sundown Never Came" was a first person narrative about a lawman trying to clean up a corrupt town in the Old West. Written by the rockabilly legend Narvel Felts, it had a clever romantic twist to it. Hal liked the song but didn't really think it would be a hit. It was so different from everything else on the pop charts at the time — and — it was almost five minutes long. Radio stations didn't play five-minute records. He just thought people who went to see the movie would hear it.

But, after the extraordinary success of "My Only Girl" and his relentless touring, "Sundown Never Came" shot to #1 in three weeks. The happiest man on the tour was Rick Starr. His protégé was not going to be just a one-hit wonder. It looked like Hal Douglas was going to be a superstar.

And Rick Starr would get richer.

Hal appreciated the screaming, frenzied female fans, but he never took advantage of his power as a Teen Idol to bed any of the beauties who implored him just to look at them. He was still engaged to Mallory, but he was really becoming spellbound by Jessie James.

Chapter Ten

The tour eventually made a stop in Hal's hometown of Milwaukee, almost exactly one year to the fateful day in 1966 when Hal's Pals filled in for the way-behind-schedule *Rick Starr Cavalcade of Stars Tour*. Since her move to Tulsa, Hal and Mal had exchanged phone calls frequently. First it was on a daily basis, then it fell off to weekly. By sheer coincidence, Mallory and her mother were going to be in Milwaukee for a family reunion at the same time that Hal's tour would hit the city.

They fell into each other's arms as soon as he got off the tour bus. Hal wanted to tell her all about the fun he was having recording and touring and meeting all of the stars he used to (and still did) idolize. Mal wanted him to "just come home, stay home, and marry me." Hal was a bit taken aback. He thought she would embrace his success and be happy for him and his accomplishments. Hal thought Mal was being a bit selfish. After all, he had attained his dream. But, of course, Mal was still pursuing hers.

Hal and Mal had sex after his show in his room at the Schroeder Hotel. The irony wasn't lost on Mal. This was the same place that her prim-and-proper family used to eat breakfast every Saturday morning. But, the sex between the two teen lovers wasn't the same. There was very little sweet conversation. The common bond seemed to be fading away, but the uncomfortable silence remained. He started to think about Jessie James. But, Hal didn't let on to Mal that he now felt different about her.

Chapter Eleven

The tour left Milwaukee and made continuous stops as it headed west to Los Angeles then all the way back east through the Dakotas, Minneapolis, Chicago, Cleveland, and Cincinnati to the East Coast. The conversations on the bus between Hal and Jessie got longer and more and more personal. He became her biggest fan. He would even surprise the audience by sitting with them to watch her sing and lead the cheers. Jessie was deeply touched by that. She knew it was Hal's way of saying, "When you're on stage you are the star. I am just another fan in the audience."

He was now one of the biggest stars in the world, but Hal was too naïve to realize that by humbling himself and sitting in the audience for all the world to see, he was telling the world that Jessie James was worthy of their attention. As a result, all of his fans were now becoming Jessie James fans, too, and her record "Yes! No! Yes!" had soared up the charts. Hal didn't realize that he had single-handedly saved Jessie's career.

The tour kept them out of the recording studio for a long time, and both of their labels wanted to release one more record before the tour ended. Top 40 radio ate up music very quickly, so hits were usually on the charts only for a month or two.

One of the songs that Hal had recorded in August 1966 was "On The Street Where You Live" from the Broadway show *My Fair Lady*. Rick Starr wasn't happy about it for two reasons. First, and foremost, he didn't have the publishing on it, which meant less money for him. Second, it was a Broadway song, and he didn't think it would work for a budding Teen Idol. But, he gave in because Hal had been so sincerely insistent that it was his mother's favorite song and, as he told Starr repeatedly, "It would make my mom very happy."

In the rush to get a new Hal Douglas single out, Mary Pat MacGregor, the vice president of Starr Records, without consulting Starr, spent an additional $500 to add strings to the recording and sent "On The Street Where You Live" to over one thousand radio stations. DJs fell in love with it immediately because it was so different from all the British records that were still dominating the charts, and it was such a change of pace and different sound from Hal's first two hits. It looked like it would be #1 by Thanksgiving 1967. Rick Starr was chagrined but exultant. "Put me in the freezer, and call me a Popsicle," is all he could say. He and Hal were on quite a roll.

And Rick Starr was getting richer.

Jessie James' low budget, independent record company, Sunshine Records, hadn't bothered having her record a bunch of songs to have in the hopper for future release. It was a small company and operated pretty much day to day. Tuesday was the future on Monday at Sunshine. The Sunshine bank account usually held a $200 balance — until Jessie James came along.

Don Jon Ross was the owner of Sunshine Records. Every day of his life he flew by the seat of his pants. He was a forever-jolly, always-cursing, cigar-smoking, three hundred-pound bundle of fun. His two favorite sayings when someone irritated him were, "Suck my ass!" and "You're making my ass tired!" He was also known for punctuating sentences with a loud, "Plus tax!" for no good reason except that he thought it was funny.

Chapter Twelve

Orphaned when he was three years old, Don Jon Ross survived by doing what he wanted to do and doing things people said he shouldn't or couldn't do. As the owner of Sunshine Records he wasn't rich, but he wasn't bowing to anyone either. The success of Jessie James stunned him.

He signed her to his label because he wanted to try to avail himself of all of her Hollywood show biz contacts — and — he wanted to bang her. She signed with Sunshine Records because no other label took a beauty-queen-who-wanted-to-be-a-singer very seriously. "A mutual admiration society" is how Don Jon described the deal.

Don Jon also suggested to Jessie that he become her manager. "Then," he explained, "when America comes knocking at your door, it's one-stop shopping for them. One phone call. We'll write, produce, and record your songs, and we'll make all the deals for concerts, TV, and movies. I'm your guy, Jessie. No one else is all that interested."

Jessie was hurt by the last comment. She tried in her most well-mannered way to show Don Jon her dismay, but her temper was starting to get the better of her. "No one else might be interested in me as a recording artist, I'll give you that," she said calmly, "but, I think with one phone call from my mother I could be in any movie or TV show I wanted. You know my mother, Don Jon, two-time Oscar winner Jayna James?"

Her temper was now winning, and she started to berate Ross. "Oh wait, you don't actually know her. You've just read about her in those fan magazines you read while pooping on your king-sized toilet. She's the real reason you are signing me to your crapola record company. And, please excuse the use of that misleading term…record company."

Jessie James took Don Jon by surprise. She was gorgeous; she sang like no one he had ever heard before; she was certainly self-assured. He didn't expect the outburst from a former Miss America contestant. But, after her little temper tantrum, she calmed down quickly.

"Look Don Jon," she said in earnest, "if we are going to work together we have to do it out of mutual respect and trust. You and I will make hit records but — and I'm sure this has crossed your mind — we will never make love. That's the bottom line. Deal…or…no deal?"

"Deal," said the deflated and defeated Ross, who really wanted her on his label. "But, you gotta give me time to develop you and work your records with my contacts. Give me two years, Jessie. Deal…or…no deal?"

"What is the financial deal, Don Jon?" asked Jessie.

Ross told Jessie James that the standard recording deal at Sunshine Records was a fifty/fifty split of profits after expenses. He explained to her that there was too much bookkeeping to do it the way other record labels did their deals "with their percentages here and percentages there.

"My sister, Fay Kay, doubles as my accountant," he explained. "We don't like a lot of make-work projects around here. If we make $2 profit on the record, then you'll get $1, and Sunshine Records will get $1. It's that simple. No games."

Growing up in the movie business, Jessie knew all about how expenses could be inflated, padded, or simply created out of whole cloth in order to lower the profits on paper. Lower profits meant smaller amounts of money that had to be split with the artist. She insisted that any expense pertaining to her records or her career that exceeded $250 had to be approved by her.

"When that clause goes into the contract, Don Jon," Jessie said pointedly, "you've got a deal."

Ross pulled out two Sunshine Records contracts. They were only two pages long.

On both, he added the clause that Jessie demanded. As she looked on with a smile, he signed and dated both of them. Jessie did the same. They shook hands.

Jessie said, "Thank you, Don Jon, for this opportunity and your faith in me."

Don Jon responded in a tone that took Jessie by surprise: "Get me some hits, Jessie. Please get me some hits. We need them badly."

Jessie's first record for Sunshine took Don Jon by surprise. "Take Me Now" was a song his sister Fay Kay Ross had written during the throes of a post-high school romance with her best friend. He always told her it was "a cute little song," and he would see what he could do with it. Don Jon really thought it was just a throwaway, something to bury on an album. He decided to have J-Squared (as he now liked to call Jessie James) record it just to get his sister off his back. Don Jon Ross did everything at Sunshine except play piano and drums. He hired his brother, Jim Tim Ross, to do that.

Jessie James nailed the record in one take: two minutes and thirty four seconds of sheer musical magic. Don Jon and Jim Tim could not believe what they had witnessed. They both stood and applauded when she was done. Don Jon had tears in his eyes. After he congratulated her over and over again, Don Jon then unruffled himself and calmly asked, with tongue-in-cheek, "J-Squared, do you think you have anything left to record the flip side?"

"California Fun" was a song Don Jon had written while sitting at a tiki bar on the Venice, California, beach. It was a lame moon-June two-minute record that Jessie also knocked off in one take. Don Jon overdubbed rhythm and bass guitar lines to both songs, and the session was over in less than forty five minutes.

Don Jon had a friend at LA's biggest Top 40 station, Boss Radio KHJ. Overnight DJ Kenny Rhodes and Don Jon were cousins. Don Jon let Kenny use his Sunshine studio anytime he needed it. In return, Kenny would take selected Sunshine Records to his program and music directors at KHJ and have them listen to them as a personal favor. Two of those records actually got onto KHJ as "Boss Hitbound" records and sold a couple thousand copies in Los Angeles and were then picked up at other stations along the West Coast. Still, most of Sunshine's releases were only heard on small backwater radio stations. Nonetheless, Don Jon made enough money to be comfortable.

Kenny Rhodes was flabbergasted when he heard "Take Me Now." Two days later the record was a "Boss Hitbound" on Boss Radio KHJ. It was being played every hour on the hour.

Kenny Rhodes talked it up big: "This one is gonna go and grow way up there where the air is rare. The number one spot on the number one station. The station of the stars and the star of the stations. Here's Jessie James and 'Take Me Now.'" Soon, the rest of the country embraced it, and Jessie James had the #1 record in America.

While "Take Me Now" was racing up the charts, Don Jon realized he needed a follow up. Fay Kay scribbled out "Love Me Now" in an hour. Don Jon wrote the flip side, "More California Fun" in fifteen minutes. Jessie James reluctantly recorded both songs, again in one take. She expressed her discontent.

Don Jon growled, "J-Squared, you're making my ass tired! I got you one hit already. You're welcome. Trust me, OK?" He was smiling.

At the time, Don Jon didn't realize that his "I got you one hit already" dismissal of his star was a statement that looked backward and forward at the same time. "Love Me Now" was, in record business jargon, a stiff. No radio station wanted to play it.

Don Jon thought Jessie's run was over. It looked like she was going to be another one-hit wonder. He became depressed and lost his energy for the record business.

A few months later, Don Jon's brother Jim Tim asked if he could try his hand at writing a song for Jessie, whom he had a crush on. First Don Jon said "yes." Then he changed his mind and said "no." But, when Jim Tim hummed the melody of the song that he wanted to write, Don Jon jumped up and said "yes."

The melody was reminiscent of Lesley Gore's bouncy "It's My Party." Jim Tim decided to call it "Yes! No! Yes!" because of the way his brother, Don Jon, had reacted to his request to write a song for Jessie James. Don Jon helped Jim Tim with the lyrics. They were both very, very pleased with the outcome. Don Jon was getting re-energized. He wrote the flip side, "Let's Have Some More California Fun," in fifteen minutes.

Jessie James loved the effervescence of "Yes! No! Yes!" This song took two takes to record because she thought it needed another verse. The Ross brothers cranked the additional verse out in twenty minutes. She sang it with even more zest the second time. She loved the song. To her credit, she refused to record "Let's Have Some More California Fun." It ended up being an instrumental on the flip side because Don Jon wasn't going to fight with her. He needed a hit record. Now.

"Thank you, my little J-Squared," he said happily. "You did a great job on 'Yes! No! Yes!' But, you still really make my ass tired!" He was hurt that she wouldn't record his other song. He was also still hurt that she had called his record company "crapola" and that she had preemptively rejected any potential amorous advances from him. He hadn't come to terms with any of that yet.

A short time later Don Jon got a call from Rick Starr. Starr wanted Jessie on the Hal Douglas tour. Don Jon agreed to the measly $500 per week for his artist because he relished her singing his song in front of thousands and thousands of screaming teenagers on the tour. Don Jon hung up the phone, sat back, and smiled. "Pretty soon they can all suck my ass," he muttered to himself with a sly smile.

The *Hal Douglas Greatest Hits on Earth Tour* was a box office smash. Jessie James' "Yes! No! Yes!" was becoming a monster hit. Rick Starr called Don Jon, wanting to buy the rights to the record — and — to buy Sunshine Records. Don Jon said, "Maybe. Let's talk when you're back in LA."

Chapter Thirteen

The tour was into its final leg heading towards New York and a huge show at Madison Square Garden. "Yes! No! Yes!" was starting to slide down the charts. Don Jon was panicked because he needed another hit record for Jessie, and she was nowhere near a recording studio. He had an idea, an idea that wouldn't cost him a dime and would most likely score another hit for the all-of-a-sudden red-hot Jessie James.

At this point, his motivation was not about Jessie and her career. He had cynically dreamed up a move to make Jessie and Sunshine more valuable to Rick Starr, Mr. Deep Pockets.

Don Jon re-released "Love Me Now." As the original follow up to "Take Me Now," it had gone nowhere a year ago. Few stations had played it, and very few teenagers had ever heard it. Don Jon, anticipating a big follow up hit for his new star at that point, pressed 10,000 copies of the record. Now he was stuck with about 9,900 unsold copies of "Love Me Now" in his warehouse.

This time, on the heels of the success of "Yes! No! Yes!" and the Hal Douglas tour, "Love Me Now" raced up the charts neck-and-neck with Hal's "On The Street Where You Live." Hal hit #1. Jessie went to #2. The songs stayed in those spots for four weeks. Hal and Jessie were King and Queen of the Top 40 as the tour rolled into New York for its finale.

The final show of the tour was also the biggest show of the tour. Friday night, December 8, 1967, at Madison Square Garden in New York City. It was sold out — all seventeen thousand seats. The Madison Square Garden show was not just a concert for Hal; it was also a showcase for him. Rick Starr wanted to make him the next Frankie Avalon.

He really wanted to make Hal Douglas a movie star, so he invited a dozen major movie producers to the show as his guests. He brought them — and their wives and/or girlfriends — in from Hollywood and gave them the red carpet treatment. Hal didn't know anything about who was in the audience. He just put on his usual entertaining show. And, of course, he sat in the audience to watch Jessie's show. Meanwhile, Starr spent over $15,000 hoping to take his new star to the next level.

It worked. The Hollywood contingent saw "star" written all over Hal. What they really liked was how Hal had no ego nor did he know how to play the star. He did everything Rick Starr told him to do. A perfect situation for guys in a hurry to make big money. Whoever signed him would only have to deal with Starr. Deals could be made in one phone call with no demands from the star. The next day, Rick Starr was presiding over a near fanatical bidding war for Hal's services.

And Rick Starr was now thinking about getting even richer.

Chapter Fourteen

At the end of the tour, Hal, who had been on the road the whole year, decided to buy a car and drive himself home. He could have flown home, but it was winter, and he didn't want to be the next Buddy Holly. Rick Starr would take care of business and tell him what to do next.

So, the day after the Madison Square Garden show, while Rick Starr was wheeling and dealing a movie contract for him, Hal went out and bought an Omaha-orange 1967 Ford Mustang from a dealer in Brooklyn. Rick Starr's friend owned the dealership. Hal fell in love with the car at first sight. Starr made sure his budding superstar/cash cow didn't get taken for a ride. After a good night's sleep, Hal was going to start his trip home. He promised Starr he would call him every day to let him know where he was.

Jessie James was going to fly back to Los Angeles. She wanted to get home for Christmas, and Don Jon Ross wanted her in the studio to get an album out right away to cash in on the success of her three big hits. She was set to fly out of New York on Sunday afternoon.

Hal and Jessie said their formal goodbyes at a party that Starr threw for the tour performers after the Garden Show. At the party, Starr surprised all the stars of the tour by giving them a "Christmas bonus" because of the great box office business the tour had done. They each got $500 in cash from Starr. Even Hal — who was now as big as Elvis — got $500. Again, Hal didn't get it. Ninety percent of the fans had come to see him. There was no parity in the drawing power of the stars. But, Hal was just thrilled that his beloved Mr. Starr was "nice enough" to give him a bonus.

The tour was housed at The Algonquin Hotel near Times Square. Starr got a deal on the rooms from an old friend who was a partner in the famed hotel. After the show, Hal and Jessie decided to walk back to the hotel so they could spend a little more time together. The night was cold but not frigid. The chance to be alone together, the cheeriness of Christmas, and the kinetic energy of New York City made the walk very pleasurable for the two pop stars. They walked and talked and talked and walked. They were falling in love, but neither wanted to admit it because of their romantic commitments at home.

Their first kiss was shared hurriedly in the dark about fifty feet from the entrance to the hotel. It was warm and sweet and short. Fumbling for words, Hal awkwardly and quietly said, "Things were too hectic for me to get you a Christmas present, Jessie. That kiss is all that I have to give you, but it comes from my heart. Merry Christmas." Not knowing if that was an opening or a closing, Jessie simply said, "You're a great friend, Hal. I've learned a lot from you. Keep yourself warm and safe and dry 'til we meet again."

Their night ended there and then. Their future also started there and then.

Chapter Fifteen

What happened in Newark, New Jersey, two nights after the huge Friday night Madison Square Garden show in New York, would change Hal Douglas's personal life forever. The snow had started just after six o'clock on Sunday morning. Hal didn't wake up until three o'clock that afternoon. After a quick lunch at the hotel restaurant, he threw his suitcases into his new Mustang and headed west. He was used to driving in the snows of Milwaukee, but it was all different in the gridlock and strangeness of New York City. A wrong turn caused by poor visibility from the snow, a bit of inattentiveness on his part as he was thinking of Jessie James, and honking horns from the speeding New Yorkers sent him north to Palisades Park, New Jersey, instead of west to Newark. When he saw the city sign he started singing the song made famous by Freddy "Boom Boom" Cannon.

Then he realized he was hopelessly lost.

A helpful young gas station attendant recognized Hal as soon as the young pop star entered the station looking for help. Billy Ritt got Hal course-corrected and gave him directions through New Jersey and all the way to Pennsylvania. Hal signed some autographs for Billy and agreed to talk to his wife, Carly, on the phone. Hal even gave Billy his phone number in Milwaukee and told him to call him if he ever got there. Then he was out the door on his way to Newark, then west to Milwaukee. But now it was 6:30 p.m., snowing harder, and getting very dark.

Jessie James had hailed a cab in the snowstorm and headed to LaGuardia for her

Sunday night flight to Los Angeles. It was scheduled to leave at 3:30 p.m. She got to the airport only to find out the flight was delayed. So, she sat down and tried to think of anything but Hal Douglas. She had tossed and turned all night, thinking about what was happening between them. She was conflicted but not worried.

Her relationship — back in Hollywood — with Danny Harmon was more for show than anything. Not surprisingly, she found him to be very self-centered, but he was very kind to her. The thought of spending her life as Mrs. Danny Harmon had never entered her mind. She was just having fun and enjoying the relationship for what it was: the best restaurants; the best Hollywood parties; a lot of show business connections; and fun sex. She was startled out of her reverie by the announcement that the airport was closing and all flights were cancelled due to the weather. One of the gate attendants, an avid rock 'n' roll fan, recognized her as she was standing in line, trying to get help. He walked up to her and politely asked, "Miss James, I'm a big, big fan. May I be of service to you?"

Within thirty minutes, Jessie James was in a cab heading to Don's Starry Starry Night Motel, a small motel and restaurant complex outside of Newark, New Jersey, favored by truck drivers. The gate attendant's father owned the motel and gave Jessie the one room that was always held open — just in case. She would try to get out of New York on Monday, but because of the storm, there were no other hotels or motels near LaGuardia with any vacancies. Jessie checked in and was heading to Don's Coffee Café for a hamburger and a Coke. But first, she stopped to use a pay phone to call her parents to tell them about the delay.

Around 7:30 p.m., Hal was getting tired and stressed from driving in the snow on strange roads with fearless New York and New Jersey drivers whizzing all around him. On the outskirts of Newark, he saw a bright and welcoming neon light towering over Don's Starry Starry Night Motel and Don's Coffee Café. He decided he'd better stop to wait out the storm and get some rest for the night. And that is when he saw her!

As he pulled his orange Mustang into the parking lot, he got the shock of his life. Standing by the pay phone was Jessie James. But, it couldn't be her! She was flying to Los Angeles. What would she be doing in this out-of-the-way roadside motel? He was too excited to gather his thoughts. He was too excited to compose a cool pick up line. He grabbed the first parking place he saw, jumped out of the car, and ran up behind her and, hoping to catch her off guard, mumbled in his best Elvis voice, "Ah, excuse me, Ma'am, do you know where I could get something to eat?"

Jessie James whipped around more out of fright than curiosity. Only then did she realize who it was. "Hal? Hal Douglas? Did God send you to me?" She instantly hugged him but was afraid to kiss him. She wasn't afraid to kiss HIM. She was AFRAID to kiss him. In her heart of hearts, she knew the difference. The hug lasted for close to a minute. Neither wanted to break it off because neither knew what to say or do next.

Jessie reluctantly broke the connection then said, "Let's go to the café. I'm hungry. How about you?" Because of the snowstorm, Don's Coffee Café was empty. The truckers either were already in bed or stuck somewhere else. Hal and Jessie sat in a corner booth near the jukebox. After they ordered their food, Hal decided they should go see if their records were in the jukebox.

They were: all three of his hits and all three of hers. Hal dropped a couple of quarters in the jukebox and selected the songs. Jessie's sensuous ballad "Take Me Now" came on, and Hal asked Jessie to dance. The song was tailor-made for the night. It was about two friends who become lovers in a magic moment of passion. Hal realized what a wonderful year it had been with Jessie by his side. At that moment Hal realized what a special woman Jessie was. He held her tightly as they gracefully slow-danced in the corner of the café.

The next record up was Hal's international smash "My Only Girl." He didn't want to let Jessie go. He couldn't let her go. Their bodies melted together. The suddenness of the kiss — only their second — surprised him more than her. He was unsuspecting of the depth and fervor of his passion for Jessie. She was anticipating it and welcomed it. He moved away from her, but only slightly. As he caressed her hair and cheeks, which were now covered in tears of joy, Hal said in a whisper that came as a thunderclap to her ears, "Jessie, I will never let you out of my life again. I don't want to live without you." And he started to sing along with himself on the jukebox, "…*always together, forever and ever. You are my only girl…* "

As the jukebox played, the young couple stayed lost in each other's arms. Then, the semi-surly waitress interrupted them. "Hey, Romeo and Juliet, your hamburgers and Cokes are on the table!"

Hal did not understand what was happening to him, but he liked it. As the snow was falling on the ground, he was falling in love. He was crashing into love! He decided then and there what he wanted to do. Oh, it had been in the back of his mind during many of those long talks on the bus during the tour. And it was getting clearer as he admired her from the audience. And it almost paralyzed him the night of their first kiss as they walked back to the Algonquin Hotel after the Madison Square Garden show. But it was the kiss in the shadow of the hotel and Jessie's reaction to it that had really sealed the deal for both his heart and his head. He had known that he liked Jessie, but now he was positive that he loved her.

She was him; he was her. They shared the same hopes, dreams, and talents. They could help each other attain their goals. She fulfilled him now the way Mallory McCoy just couldn't or wouldn't. But, it really didn't matter because he couldn't or wouldn't give Mallory what she wanted and dreamed of either.

Then and there, Hal asked Jessie to marry him. And as the exuberant strains of her bubbly summertime hit "Yes! No! Yes!" rang out of the jukebox, she whispered, "Yes, yes, yes."

He asked her if she would stay with him that night. Enthusiastically, she said, "Yes! I was wondering if this would ever happen."

"I've got a room," Jessie said. "A guy at the airport helped me out. Everything within a fifty-mile radius of the city is booked because of the storm, but his dad owns this place, and he always keeps one room open for emergencies."

Quickly, Hal said, "Jessie, why don't we put the room in my name in case your new best friend at LaGuardia slips up and spills the beans to someone as to where you are. It's just safer this way."

After making the name switch at the front desk, they went back to the room and made love. Hal lost control as he caressed her and kissed her. They continued to make love through the night. Intense, impassioned, and intriguing love. Exhausted, physically and emotionally, Jessie finally fell asleep.

Hal got up to write the sad note that strangely enough made him very, very happy. It took him a long time to write the last five sentences. He wanted to be clear, gentle, succinct, and final. Tears filled his eyes as he sat there with pen in hand.

"So, Mallory, I'm in Newark, New Jersey, just outside of New York City. The tour is finally over. As I write this, I'm only twenty-four hours from Tulsa. Mallory, I truly hate to do this to you. But, I'm in love with Jessie James! No more to say."

Forever your pal,

Hal

Chapter Sixteen

Hal and Jessie woke up at the same time on Monday morning. The much more sexually experienced and ambitious Jessie had spent the night with a man before; this was a first for Hal. He was embarrassed and didn't know what to say. Jessie rolled on top of Hal and said, "I love you. Let's get married today."

Seeing a woman naked in the cold light of day was another first for him. He was dumbstruck. He really wasn't sure he should be looking at Jessie's tantalizing naked body without the cover of darkness. Hal didn't know what to say or where to look. "I have to call Mr. Starr," was his awkward response.

"'I love you, too,' would have been better," Jessie said with a laugh. "By the way, it's OK to look at me when I'm naked." Then, breaking into song, she told Hal he could have more than "just one look."

"I love that song," said Hal. "Which version do you like better, the one by Doris Troy or The Hollies?"

"Hal," she said somewhat indignantly, "a former Miss California and Miss America runner-up is sitting naked on top of you, and all you can think of is Doris Troy and The Hollies? Do you see these breasts? They should be in your mouth, not a question about Doris Troy and The Hollies. This relationship might be in trouble already."

Still not knowing what to say to her, Hal blurted out again, "I HAVE to call Mr. Starr. I have to let him know where I am. I promised him. I don't want him to be worried."

"OK, but the rest of the day you belong to me," Jessie said as she brushed her breasts against his face and unstraddled his body. "Also, Hal, I wouldn't mention to Mr. Starr that you spent the night with me and that we are planning on getting married."

"Don't you think he would be happy for us?" Hal asked. Then it was his turn to break into song. "Don't you think Mr. Starr would like to see us *happy together?*"

"Cute, Hal. Very cute," she said with a sigh and a pained look on her angelic face. "Trivia question: whose record knocked The Turtles out of #1 this year?" she asked.

"I remember it well," Hal said with a smirk. "It was that little thing you recorded 'Yes! No! Yes!' And do you remember what record knocked you out of #1?"

"I remember it well," she said, returning the smirk. "That little cowboy thing of yours, 'Sundown Never Came.' You were #1, I was #10. You were on top, and I was underneath you. The same thing happened with 'On The Street Where You Live' and 'Love Me Now.' You went to #1, and I was underneath you at #2, apparently the way you like it best."

The double entendre was too much for Hal. This upfront sexual behavior and talk was all new to him. He rather liked it, but he wasn't sure how to handle it. For a fleeting moment, he did wonder how Gene Pitney would have handled it. He got up, wrapped a blanket around himself, and went to the phone to call Rick Starr.

"Hal, do NOT tell Rick about us," she warned him sternly. This got his attention.

"Why not?" he asked a bit coyly.

"Little teeny bopper girls don't cream their jeans over MARRIED teen idols," she said sarcastically. "They all believe they have a chance to go out on a dream date with you because they entered a contest in *16 Magazine*. They all think you're singing 'My Only Girl' just to them. They don't want to know that there is someone special in your life. They want you to look at them from the stage. They want to believe they have a chance to become Mrs. Hal Douglas. Do you think Elvis Presley's career is going to be the same since he got married?"

Hal really didn't know what "cream their jeans" meant, and he was embarrassed to ask. He really wanted Jessie to think of him as a sophisticated international pop star — just like Gene Pitney. He really didn't realize that his female fans were looking for anything except a good show from him. He was the Babe Ruth of naïveté, but, he did get the gist of her argument.

"Alright, mum's the word," he promised as he dialed The Algonquin Hotel to talk to Starr.

The front desk put the call through, and the phone was picked up in one ring: "Hi, this is Rick Starr."

"Good morning, Mr. Starr, it's Hal…checking in."

"Damn, I was worried about you in this snowstorm, Hal. Where are you?"

"I didn't get very far," Hal explained. "Because of the blizzard I only got as far as Newark, New Jersey. I'm at a place called Don's Starry Starry Night Motel." Then he started to add, "I'm with…" but caught himself in midsentence. "I'm with…a lot of other people stranded by the storm. We haven't heard any weather reports, have you?

"It's a bad one," Starr said matter-of-factly. "The airports are going to be closed again today, so I'm stuck here. I don't want you driving anywhere today, Hal. OK? Don't go anywhere; don't do anything. Also, I've got someone who wants to talk to you. Hang in there. I'll call you back."

"OK, Mr. Starr. Whatever you say."

He hung up the phone and turned to talk to Jessie, but she wasn't in the bed. He heard the shower running in the bathroom and went in to talk to her.

"Mr. Starr says we can't get married," Hal said.

"HAL," she screamed. A wet washcloth came flying out of the shower at him, and she asked between clenched teeth, "What did I just get done telling you?"

But Hal was laughing. The game was on. He was really starting to enjoy the give-and-take banter that Jessie introduced him to. "What?" he asked as he stared at her now wet, naked body standing in the tub with the shower door open.

"By the way," he added with a sly grin, still wrapped in a blanket, "Looking at you like this, I think you should title your next album *Big Hits and Big Tits.*" They stared at each other without exchanging words for what seemed like an eternity. Then, she shook her head in disbelief as to what had finally come out of his squeaky-clean Milwaukee mouth. Hal shook his head, too. But his was out of shock for what had just come out of his squeaky-clean Milwaukee mouth.

"Oh, Jessie, I'm sorry. I cannot believe I said something that crude."

"Oh, Hal," she replied demurely, "I am so glad you noticed my tits and could muster up something crude to say about them. It was very cute. You are now learning the fine art of pillow talk. I give you an 'A' for your first class."

She walked over to him as slowly as she could, letting him take in every inch of her wet, naked body. Then she kissed him.

"*Eso beso*," he sang out. "You know I can sound just like Paul Anka if I want to. His voice is very easy to imitate, and he doesn't have much range."

"SHUT UP!" Jessie cried. Then there was a momentary silence, and she said, "Wait, no, don't shut up. Why the hell did you tell Rick about our getting married? I told you it could ruin your career. He's probably good and mad now, isn't he?"

"I didn't tell him we were getting married," Hal said, defending himself. "I didn't even tell him that you were here with me."

"Hal, three minutes ago you told me that Rick said we couldn't get married."

"Well, sorta, kinda, in a way," he replied. Hal was enjoying this. He realized he really liked this back-and-forth stuff. It was something he never had with Mallory.

"Hal, if you ever want to see, touch, or sexually sample this fabulous California body again you better start making sense."

Hal broke into song one more time: "*Try to see it my way. Do I have to keep on talking 'til I can't go on? We can work it out, we can work it out.*"

"HAL!"

"Alright, Jessie. I'm just having some *fun, fun, fun* with you," he sang. "Mr. Starr just told me not to go anywhere or do anything. So, that means we can't get married, right?"

"If you got one, you are one," she told him with a big laugh.

"If I got what…I am what?" he asked.

"A dick," she said perfunctorily. "You're a dick."

Then, almost as an afterthought, she said, "By the way, Hal, the song game is stupid."

The phone rang. Hal picked it up expecting to hear Starr's voice.

"Hi, Hal. This is Gene Pitney."

Chapter Seventeen

Hal was speechless. He held the phone against his ear and stared into space. He didn't know what to say. While he wasn't talking out loud, he was talking to himself in his head. "Gene Pitney? Gene Pitney is talking to me? Gene Pitney called me? What do I say to Gene Pitney? What do I say so I don't sound stupid to Gene Pitney? How does Gene Pitney know where I am? What do I say…"

The caller again spoke and interrupted Hal's thoughts, "Hal…Hal Douglas? This is Gene Pitney. You got a minute?"

Breaking the silence, Jessie asked Hal, "Who is it? Why aren't you talking? Is something wrong?"

At this point, not even Jessie James, with her gorgeous and ripe naked body standing in front of him asking questions could break the spell. Hal Douglas was flummoxed. His idol Gene Pitney wanted to talk to him on the phone. Hal could barely get the words out. "Mr. Pitney? Mr. Gene Pitney? You want to talk to me?"

"Yeah. Is this a bad time?" Pitney asked, hearing the female voice in the background.

Hal was now pacing nervously around the motel room. "Mr. Pitney, I don't know what to say. This is such an honor. You're my hero; you're my idol."

Jessie's eyes grew wide.

"Thanks, Hal. I appreciate that. But, look, it sounds like you might be busy with your lady, so I can call back."

As he started to compose himself, Hal's in-his-head voice started to ask more questions. "What does Gene Pitney want to talk to me about? What if he doesn't call back? What if he loses my number? What if he's mad at me for something? What if he didn't like my sounding like him on 'My Only Girl'?"

"Hal, whaddya need? An hour or two with her? Should I call you back then?"

"No, please don't hang up, Mr. Pitney," Hal pleaded. "I want to talk with you. I'm just a little shocked. I never expected to get a call from THE Gene Pitney. This is a real honor. But, how did you know I was here?"

"Got the number from Rick Starr," Pitney answered.

"Well, this is going to sound stupid because I don't think there is anything I can really do for you…you know…I mean…I don't think there is anything you need from me…but…what can I do for you, Mr. Pitney?"

"Hal, I'm doing fifty dates in the UK next year, and I want you on the show as my support act. How much are you getting from Rick?"

Hal was always embarrassed by how much money he was making for doing something that he loved and that he didn't consider work. He was even more embarrassed that he made as much money in one month as his dad did in one year. "Mr. Starr is paying me $2,000 a week," Hal said, but hurriedly added, "I share it with my parents and my family."

"I can't pay you that, Hal," said Pitney, a little taken aback by that number. At the peak of his chart hits, Starr only paid him $1,500 weekly as the headliner. "Smaller country, smaller shows, lower ticket prices. But, I want you on the show. Can we do a deal?"

Pitney, who had fast become a brilliant businessman when he started having hit records, ran his own career. He had no agent, only an accountant. He had no idea about Hal's complete lack of business acumen. He did, however, know that Rick Starr represented Hal, but the cunning Pitney wanted to work around that. Pitney had read enough fan magazine articles to know that Hal idolized him, and he was ready to work that to his advantage. He didn't want to take advantage of Hal;

he simply wanted to work around the savvy Starr. Through his friend Bobby Vee, Pitney had learned that Starr and Hal had some sort of agreement but no written contract. Yet.

Pitney wanted Hal on the tour to ensure good ticket sales. After amassing three gigantic hit records in the UK in 1966, Pitney had only scored one hit in 1967. He was concerned that his popularity might be waning. Hal was a rising star and appealed to the same type of audience that Pitney did — young females. In Pitney's words, getting Hal on the tour would be a "winner."

Again, Hal was speechless. He stopped pacing and leaned against a wall, trying to collect his thoughts. He had never negotiated money before. Rick Starr did that for him. He didn't even know what was on his schedule or what he was committed to do in 1968. Rick Starr took care of that for him. While those thoughts raced through his mind, they were quickly overtaken by a scarier thought — working with Gene Pitney.

"Mr. Pitney, I really don't know what to say."

"Say, yes, you'll do it, and I'll make it worth your while," Pitney said.

"Of course I want to do it," Hal said. "You're the greatest singer in pop music. You're my idol. I'd give anything to work with you. But, I really think I have to check with Mr. Starr."

Pitney saw his opening. "Listen to me, Hal. I know Rick discovered you and gave you your big break. I know you're making a lot of money working for him. I know you're having fun. You're hot right now. You're the biggest star in America, and you're starting to become big around the world."

"I don't think I'm as big a star as you are," Hal interrupted.

"Thanks, Hal, but that's not the point," said Pitney, a little miffed at being interrupted.

"The point is, I've been there, I've done that. To quote my friend Dion, 'here's my story, it's sad but true.' I had a great run between 1962 and 1965 in the States. But, I've only had one mid-chart hit this year, and now I can't get arrested."

"'Backstage' was such a great record," Hal interrupted. "It should have been #1."

Pitney continued his lesson in career planning for the neophyte star. "Do you think Rick Starr has asked me to be on *Starr Power* in the last two years? The answer is no, Hal. I'm not making hits like I used to. In Rick Starr's eyes, I'm a has been. Rick Starr is watching out for Rick Starr. To be fair, I'm watching out for Gene Pitney. You should be watching out for Hal Douglas. You've got to take control of your own business, your own career, Hal. Otherwise you'll end up broke and busted out on the rock pile with countless other used-to-be-stars."

"Wow," is all that Hal could muster at this point.

"Remember Jasper Pacetti?" Pitney asked.

"Sure do," said Hal. "He had that great song 'Don't Tell Me No.' I loved that song."

"Top 10 1963," said Pitney. "Heard of him since? A DJ friend of mine knows his parents, Catherine and Tony. Jasper is now running their bakery and working local dinner clubs for $20 a week — when he can get a singing gig. His sister Lena makes more money as a Catholic elementary school teacher than he does. What about Morgen Linn? Remember her?"

"Mr. Pitney, I live and breathe music. I know all the hits, and I know all the words to all the hits. Morgen Linn had a #1 record in 1961 with 'Your Love Breaks My Heart.'"

"Well, Hal," Pitney said with half a grin on his face, "after she couldn't get another hit, she took the money she earned from that record and went to a community college in her hometown. She's now a secretary in an insurance agency.

"They're both one-hit wonders, Hal. And, FYI, they were both managed by Rick Starr. Just like you are. He's not in the career development business, Hal. He's in it for the money, just like the rest of us. And, when you don't make money for him, you're history. You might want to think about running your own career like I do."

"But I have a contract with Mr. Starr."

"No, you don't, Hal," Pitney said quickly. "I think you have a verbal agreement. Have you signed a contract, or has anyone on your behalf signed a contract with Rick?

"Not yet," explained Hal. "Mr. Starr said I could sign it next time I was in LA."

"Have you talked with an attorney, Hal? Has anyone given you financial advice?"

"No," said Hal in a dejected tone of voice as Pitney's exhortations started to sink in.

"Hal, I run my own tours, produce and print my own tour books, and make my own business decisions," Pitney said. "You don't have to do that if you don't want to. The easy way out is to let someone else do it like Jasper Pacetti and Morgen Linn did. Where are they now? Come out on the UK tour with me, and I'll show you how to do it. I guarantee you that I'll be working in this business for another thirty or forty years. You stick with Rick Starr, and you'll be pumping gas back in Milwaukee by 1969."

"Mr. Pitney? Can I call you right back?"

"Better yet, Hal," answered Pitney. "I live in Somers, Connecticut. That's about 150 miles from Newark. After the snowstorm ends and the roads clear up, why don't you drive up here, and we'll talk."

"I'd like that a lot," said Hal, more than overjoyed about the chance to finally meet his idol — and go to his house.

"Hal, one more thing: until you and I talk, don't say anything about any of this to Rick. If he asks, which he will, just tell him I wanted to say 'Hi' and pitch you a song that I wrote. OK?"

"Mr. Pitney, I would be honored if you would write a song for me."

"Do you write songs, Hal?" Pitney asked.

"I haven't yet, but I would like to try."

"We'll write one together when you come to Connecticut. Then I'll show you how much money there is to be made in publishing. By the way, why not bring your lady with you. What's her name?"

Hal froze. Write a song with Gene Pitney, the man who wrote "Hello, Mary Lou," "Rubber Ball," and "He's A Rebel"? This can't be happening, he thought.

Jessie had gone back into the bathroom to dry her hair about halfway through the phone conversation. The hairdryer was making a lot of noise.

"She's just a friend, Mr. Pitney," said Hal, not wanting to reveal Jessie's identity since both of them were still technically involved with other people.

"And your friend's name is…" Pitney prodded.

"Jessie," said Hal in a semi-whisper.

"Jessie as in Jessie James, the singer?" asked Pitney.

"Yes, Jessie as in Jessie James, the singer," Hal responded quietly.

"You're whispering, Hal," said Pitney with a chuckle. "Is everything OK there?"

"Mr. Pitney, I can't lie to you. It IS actually Jessie James, the singer."

Now it was Pitney's turn to be speechless — but just for a few seconds. "First, congratulations on your taste in ladies, Hal. I've seen her picture in the fan mags. She's drop-dead gorgeous. She reminds me of an English lady I know very well, Dusty Springfield. Second, might you stop calling me Mr. Pitney? Most people call me Gene."

"Mr. Pitney, my parents taught me to not call adults by their first names."

Pitney interrupted, "Hal, I'm only twenty-seven years old. I could be your older brother."

Hal laughed. "You know, that's exactly what Mr. Royal said to me."

"Who said that to you?" asked Pitney.

"Billy Joe Royal," said Hal. "I did *The 1966 Rick Starr Cavalcade of Stars* with him. He is a very nice man; he's also a big fan of yours."

"Hal, the first time I heard 'Down In The Boondocks' on the radio I thought I had gotten drunk one night and forgotten that I had recorded it," Pitney said with a laugh. "Same with that Los Bravos record, 'Black Is Black.'"

"Mr. Pitney, I will call you Gene if you promise not to tell anyone that Jessie James is with me right now."

"Deal," said Pitney. "But, you gotta promise to bring her along. My wife, Lynne, is a huge fan of hers."

"She would kill me if I didn't bring her," said Hal. Then, with a laugh he added, "She would LOVE to meet you. Right now, I'm the biggest pop star she knows. How sad is that?"

"Here's my number. Call me when you leave New Jersey."

Hal thought for a moment, then, with some degree of difficulty said, "Thanks, Gene. See you in a few days."

He hung up the phone and turned around. Jessie James, still naked, but now dry and glistening with glitter, was lying on the bed. "You're going to see Gene Pitney in a couple of days?" she asked incredulously. "What's going on, Hal?"

"He invited me up to his house somewhere in Connecticut, about 150 miles from here," Hal said calmly. But then his speech became rapid: "He wants me to go out on his UK tour next year, and he wants to write a song for me, and he wants to write a song with me, and he wants to teach me the business side of this business."

Jessie interrupted him. "Power that jet engine down right now, Hal. Gene Pitney, your idol, your hero, just had THAT conversation with you?"

"Yup."

"Well, now that calls for a celebration," Jessie said as she pulled the blanket away from Hal's body. She started to sing one of the verses from her hit song "Take Me Now." *"Now is the time, this is the place, capture my heart, look at my face…take me now…"*

"Jessie, Gene wants me to leave Mr. Starr," Hal added.

"We can talk show business later," Jessie said as she pulled him on to the bed and started to caress him.

"Oh, and one more thing," said Hal as they were tangled in each other's arms, "he wants me to bring you to Connecticut to meet him and his wife."

Chapter Eighteen

Tuesday morning came, and the big snowstorm left. Hal, now dressed in his favorite navy blue tracksuit, opened the door to see what New Jersey looked like buried under sixteen inches of snow. Jessie was still in bed, naked, as Hal was getting accustomed to, watching Hugh Downs and Barbara Walters on *Today*.

Jessie was getting bored and restless in the dreary cage that was Room 19 of the now drifted-in motel. "Do you think we're getting out of here today?" she asked, not taking her eyes off the TV. "Doesn't really matter, but I have to start making calls to let people know where I am and what's going on."

"You might want to hold off on that," Hal said. Then, he added, "Did you forget? It's only 4 a.m. in Los Angeles right now. I don't think any of your friends are up."

Jessie glared at him. "Keep up that smartass talk, and I may forget how to get your little friend up."

As sexually naïve as Hal was — or sometimes pretended to be — he caught the meaning of Jessie's biting comment. He was momentarily stunned. It was really the first cross words she had ever uttered to him.

"What was that all about?" he asked in a guarded fashion. He just now sensed she was tense, and he wanted to proceed very carefully. He and Mallory had had some minor spats during their years together, but Mallory was a pretty amenable person, and her ruffled feathers were always easily unruffled. This was new ground for him and Jessie.

"I don't think any of YOUR friends are up," she parroted back to him snidely. "Was that necessary, Hal? I didn't appreciate the implication that my friends and my parents are lazy sad sacks because they aren't up at four in the morning just because you're up."

"Jessie, Jessie, that's not what I meant," Hal pleaded. "I was just reminding you of the three-hour time difference between the East Coast and the West Coast."

"It didn't sound that way," she snapped.

Hal was more than a little taken aback by how sensitive Jessie was this morning. Determined to always make her happy, he offered an apology. "I'm sorry. I didn't mean to upset you. It's the last thing I would ever do."

Jessie relented. "I'm sorry I snapped at you, Hal. It's two weeks until Christmas, and I haven't done any shopping because of the tour. My parents want me back home. When I get back to California, I have to break it off with Danny. Don Jon wants me back in the studio to cut some songs for a new single and an album, but he didn't have any songs when I talked to him last week. We've been snowed in somewhere in East Bumble, New Jersey, for two days, and now you want to go to Connecticut to see Gene Pitney. I'm a little edgy."

Hal wanted to say most of that was none of his fault, but he figured that might go over about as well as a hair in a tuna casserole. "Do you want to fly home, and I'll go see Gene by myself?"

"No," she said quickly. "I'm just feeling pressured. I don't know how Danny is going to take it, and I really don't know what I'm gonna do for a new record. And, being holed up in here is getting a bit stifling"

"I've got an idea, Jessie," Hal said as a big grin spread across his boyish face. "I'm going to need a new record, too. Why don't we do a duet? And, why don't we write it ourselves? And, why don't we get Gene Pitney to produce it for us?"

"Hal Douglas," she said with a smile in her voice, "aren't you the cutest little genius I have ever slept with? I love it. Let's go get some breakfast, work on our next #1 smash, then come back, make some phone calls, and then get out of here."

Hal and Jessie, in the same corner booth they had been in on Sunday night at Don's

Coffee Café, picked away at their hash browns and bacon as they kicked around song ideas. They agreed it had to be a ballad; they agreed it should be a love song and not a song of lost love; they just couldn't agree on a style.

Jessie wanted a fluffy, romantic song that could be played at weddings. Hal favored an up-tempo song about two people finding their soul mates and falling in love. Jessie was sipping her orange juice when the idea came to her.

"It can be both," she said excitedly. "It can be our story, Hal. And, it can be told in a way that anyone can relate to it and use it to tell their own story."

"Jessie James," he said with big smile in his voice. "Aren't you the cutest little genius I have ever slept with?"

They both laughed.

One hour later "A Lifetime of Love" was written. Hal had a melody running through his head that he thought was perfect, but he wanted to bounce it off Gene, along with the idea of Pitney producing the record.

Hal couldn't believe that songwriting was so much fun. He was excited about this new aspect of his career and wished he had started sooner. But he realized it was Jessie who had inspired him and was his inspiration; he couldn't have started sooner.

Jessie broke his reverie. "I've got another idea, Hal. Let's get Gene to sing on the record, too — maybe harmony with you."

An incredulous Hal looked at her and asked, "Do you really think he would do that? Has anything like that ever happened before? Can it be done?"

"C'mon, Hal. Think big. Let's make music history. Plus, it would be a great way to promote that UK tour Gene wants you to do with him. And it would sell a lot of records during the tour. Whaddya think?"

Back in the room, Hal called first dibs on the phone. "I need to call Mr. Starr and tell him where I'm going."

"Careful," said Jessie. "Didn't you tell me last night that Gene wants you to leave Rick?"

"I won't mention that. I'll just tell him that Gene wants to pitch me a song. That is the truth."

"Shouldn't you call your parents, too, Hal?" she asked. "Aren't they worried about you?

"That's a 'yes' and a 'yes.' I'll do that, too."

"While you're doing that, I'll take a shower," Jessie said as she started to undress. "Then I can make my phone calls — you know, IF my friends are up by then." They laughed.

"Jessie, you are the most naked woman I have ever met in my life," Hal said with fake incredulity. "And even though that doesn't make sense outside of Milwaukee, you know what I mean!"

The early morning phone call with Rick Starr went well. Starr started his business day in California at 5 a.m. every single day, even on weekends. He was OK with Gene Pitney pitching Hal a song. He told Hal it was a touch of genius. It virtually assured another hit record for Hal. But Starr insisted that if the Pitney song was released as a single the flip side had to be a song that Starr had the publishing on. The writer and publisher of the flip side of a hit record earned the same amount of money as the writer and producer of the hit. Hal didn't tell him about the duet he and Jessie had written and planned on recording under Gene Pitney's tutelage.

Hal then called Gene Pitney and told him that he and Jessie would be heading to Connecticut shortly. Gene gave him very detailed directions to his house.

There was an awkward pause before Hal said, "Gene, Jessie and I have written a song together, and we were wondering if you might be interested in producing the record for us. And, maybe, sing on it, too?"

"I'd love it," Pitney said. Then, always the businessman, he asked, "Are you signed to a publisher?"

"I don't really know what that means, Gene. Maybe you can help us out."

That's all the opening Pitney needed. "When you get here I'll listen to the song, and if we can agree on a deal then I can sign you to one of my publishing companies. I'll explain that whole aspect of the business to you, Hal."

"I'd appreciate that, Gene. I want to learn everything I can about this business. I'm learning every day. Jessie and I want to record it as a duet. We both need a new record, and we figured this would work for both of us."

"Hal, we've got a lot to talk about, and you've got a lot to learn," Pitney said in a nice, fatherly tone. "The problem we have is that you and Jessie are on different labels. We're going to have to get the two labels to come to some agreement on a deal. I know that you're on Rick's label. Who does Jessie record for?"

"She's on a small label called Sunshine Records," Hal said. "Don Jon Ross is the owner. He's also her personal manager."

"Don't know him," Pitney piped in, "but he won't be the problem. Rick Starr will be the problem. He'll want to put it out on his label, he'll want to be involved in the publishing, and he'll want to…he'll just want to control the whole thing. Don Jon Ross will feel like he got caught up in the Kansas tornado with Dorothy and Toto after dealing with Rick Starr."

"Can you help us, Gene? This is what we really want to do."

"We'll talk about that, too, when you get up here. We can work it out."

"Thanks, Gene. I'm going to call my parents then hop in the shower. Jessie and I will be on our way in about an hour."

Hal hung up the phone and turned around to find Jessie, naked, packing her bags. "The phone's all yours, Naked Lady. You know, I think I have seen you naked more in the last two days than my dad has seen my mom naked since they got married in 1944."

"Most guys would call that lucky," Jessie purred. "Speaking of lucky…"

"Jessie! You have to call your parents, you have to finish packing, I have to take a shower, and I have to pack. And we have to deliver our hit song to Gene Pitney. He said he would love to produce it."

Jessie shrugged and stuck her tongue out at Hal. "You don't know what you're missing, Hal. It's early, and I'm rested and ready."

Hal then explained the problem wasn't that he didn't want to have sex with her; the problem was with the duet they wanted to do and their record labels.

"That's what you're thinking about instead of little, old, naked me?" she asked. She paused only slightly and then said, "Oh, I never thought of that. What did Gene say?"

"He said it could be worked out, but Mr. Starr would be a problem."

"Don Jon Ross will be a bigger problem," she said in exasperation. "He'll think he has you, me, and Rick Starr over a barrel, and he will make us sweat before he agrees to anything. But, if there is money in it, eventually he'll agree to something. I just hope he doesn't ruin it for us."

"Let's just get out of here now, and we'll talk about it in the car," said Hal. He didn't like confrontation, and he wasn't savvy enough in the music business to really know what to do or how to maneuver people into doing what he wanted them to do. Hal still hadn't grasped how big a star he was and how he could throw his weight around if he wanted to. He really didn't want to; he just wanted to be nice, make records, and sing to people. Hal was beginning to realize that he loved the "show" part of show business, but he really had a distaste for the "business" part of it. He would have to talk to Gene Pitney about that, too.

Jessie knew her parents were still early risers, so she quickly checked in at home. After the brief phone call, she and Hal checked out at the front desk, thanked the owner, Don, for giving them shelter from the storm, and headed out the door when Jessie stopped in her tracks.

A left over Sunday newspaper was scattered on a small table next to a well-worn chair in what passed for the lobby of the motel. The headline screamed out of the Entertainment section of the *Star-Ledger*: "TONY WINSTON TO SIGN WITH SUNSHINE RECORDS."

Jessie dropped Hal's hand and grabbed the paper. She read the story quickly. Hal read it over her shoulder.

"Good for him," he said. "It's been a tough year for the guy."

"Screw him," Jessie said. "I hate that man."

Hal was just getting to know all the ins and outs of Jessie's personal life. She talked enthusiastically about her mom and dad and her friends, but Hal had never heard a cross word come out of her mouth about anyone except Don Jon Ross. She hadn't liked the fact that Ross tried to hit on her, but she was over it.

"What's that all about, Jessie?" he asked in astonishment. "How do you even know a guy like Tony Winston? Did you work with him and something went wrong?"

"No, Hal, I didn't work with him," she said in a very sarcastic tone. "And, yes, Hal, something went terribly, terribly wrong."

Chapter Nineteen

Tony Winston and the Churchill Sisters were one of the most popular singing groups in America as the 1950s were fading into history. The name was a stage name. They were really Tony Ranzunno and his three sisters Mary, Marie, and Maria from Kenosha, Wisconsin. They were one of the biggest pop groups of the late '50s and early '60s. They appeared on *Teddy Griffin's Talent Jamboree* and were the winners on the final show of the CBS-TV series' final season on January 1, 1957. They beat Rozzie & Rosie, a duo that was being hailed as the female Everly Brothers.

Before they even appeared on the show, Griffin emphatically told the Ranzunnos not to use their Italian family name because many Americans were still unhappy that Italy had been a Nazi partner during World War II. "The Little Leprechaun," as Griffin was affectionately known to his millions of fans, was the most important and influential radio-TV broadcaster of his day. (Throughout the radio-TV industry, however, he was known as "The Little Hitler" for his dictatorial manner in dealing with talent, sponsors, and radio and TV executives.)

He originally wanted the group to call themselves Tony Chesterfield and the Cigarette Sisters. He thought it tripped off the tongue nicely; plus Chesterfield Cigarettes was one of his biggest sponsors.

After a staff member brought up the fact that other sponsors might be irritated with that show of favoritism to both one specific sponsor and one specific act, Griffin relented and suggested something British in style. "My dad was English," said Griffin.

"It's a nice little country. A lot of American boys spent time over there during the war. Pick something British-sounding."

Nobody who wanted a career in show business said "No" to Teddy Griffin. He was THE most powerful man on radio and TV. So, five years before the British Invasion started with The Beatles in late 1963, Tony Ranzunno and his sisters came up with Tony Winston and the Churchill Sisters. Griffin loved it. (Ironically, he hated Hitler and the Germans because of the war, and if he knew that he was called "The Little Hitler" behind his back, a lot of people would pay the ultimate career price.)

He decided that the new name for the group might help the sales of Winston Cigarettes, a new R.J. Reynolds cigarette that had been introduced a few years earlier, and promote his own career. "If Chesterfield is worried, then they'll have to sponsor a brand new TV show for me," he reportedly said, off-the-record, to a *LIFE* magazine reporter.

Following the group's very popular win on the Griffin show, Master Records quickly signed them to a recording contract. Tony Winston and the Churchill Sisters quickly became America's favorite recording group. They scored a total of fifteen Top 10 records between 1958 and 1961 — six of which went to #1.

But, as quickly as they rocketed to stardom, they fell back to Earth. In 1962 they could only manage three chart records, and those barely got into the Top 40. In 1963 the group scored a big goose egg. Not one of their four releases hit the charts. The latter part of that year saw the start of the British Invasion and a sea change in musical tastes. Master Records did not renew their recording contract.

Tony and his sisters had made a lot of money from their hits and their touring. Tony, who had a strong business sense, guarded every penny of it. He made sure that not a dime was wasted. Tony also had oversight on some very wise investments in real estate for himself and his sisters.

Tony was desperate to stay in show business. He loved it and couldn't see himself doing anything else. Plus, there was his ego. He was a star. He was a huge star. What was he going to do…become a travel agent? So, using their modest fortune, the Ranzunno siblings planned to open a nightclub in their hometown of Kenosha. Tony figured they could perform there until they decided to call it quits. He could also book pop acts into the club, many of whom were his friends who were working the big clubs in Chicago and Milwaukee.

In early 1964, Tony got a surprise call from legendary movie producer Jonathan Cushman. Cushman was looking for someone to record the theme song to his upcoming movie *London Lady Falling Down*. The song had to have a 1950s feel to it.

"You'd be perfect for it," Cushman told Tony over scratchy phone lines. Cushman was in London finishing the movie. "I heard one of your songs on the BBC the other day so I tracked you down. Will you do it?"

"Look, Mr. Cushman, me and the girls would love to do it, but we don't have a record deal anymore. Master Records let us go."

"Screw them," said Cushman. "MGM is putting the movie out. I'll get you a deal on that little record label of theirs. MGM's got money coming out of their ying-yang. Do this for me, and I'll make sure they take care of you."

Tony was speechless for a moment. He tried to get his mind around what was taking place on this phone call. It looked like Tony Winston and the Churchill Sisters would soon be back on the charts and back in big time show business.

"We're honored to do it, Mr. Cushman. Tell me where to go and who to see."

The recording session was set. Tony and his sisters flew out to Hollywood in March 1964. Jonathan Cushman had gotten them a one-record deal for $5,000 from MGM. The Ranzunnos were more than thrilled.

The *London Lady Falling Down* movie theme was written by Sam "The Bam" Rockingham who had written a string of pop hits for a few British pop stars in the 1950s. They needed a song for the flip side. Tony wanted to do a Frank Sinatra song, but his sisters had written a song, "Nothing To Cry About," just for the occasion. It was an old-fashioned tearjerker song of lost love. The sisters prevailed. The session was over in three hours. Instinctively, Tony knew they had a hit on their hands with the movie theme.

London Lady Falling Down, starring Cushman's wife, the newest British bombshell Jenny Cobb, came out in July. It was a summer movie blockbuster about a long-distance love affair between a fading American pop star, played by Steve McQueen, and the young and beautiful London socialite he falls for on his British nightclub tour. Its theme song, "London Lady Falling Down," rocketed up the charts to #2 — kept out of the #1 spot by The Beatles "A Hard Day's Night."

Tony Winston and the Churchill Sisters were back! Ed Sullivan called; Rick Starr called; Dick Clark called. Everybody wanted them on their TV shows. Nightclub dates were rolling in from Chicago, New York, San Francisco, everywhere. The Kenosha nightclub idea would have to be put on hold because America was calling again.

MGM Records was stunned by the success of "London Lady Falling Down." The natural thing to do was to capitalize on it and get a follow-up single out. The label was hot with big hits from the latest British stars such as Herman's Hermits and The Animals. Its executives were caught up in the British Invasion and didn't really know what to do with a four-part harmony group from the 1950s.

So, in order to get another record out in a timely fashion, MGM offered Tony and his sisters $25,000 to return to LA and record an album — for immediate release — and two Christmas songs to get the label through the rest of the year.

This time, Tony got his way, and the group recorded Frank Sinatra's "I've Got You Under My Skin" as the next single. The arrangement and production of the song placed Tony so far upfront on the vocals that it sounded as if his sisters were just background singers on the record. That didn't sit well with Mary, Marie, and Maria, but they let it go because of the time crunch. The flip side was another tune written by the Ranzunno sisters, who were quickly becoming budding songwriters.

But, the second act of the group's success didn't last long. Tragedy beset the Ranzunno family in December 1964. As the sisters were heading into downtown Chicago in a limousine to perform at Mr. Kelly's, the famous nightclub on Rush Street, they were killed in a car accident. Their limo was struck by a snowplow. The police reported that the limo might have skidded out of control through a red light before being hit by the plow.

Tony Ranzunno was not in the limo with them. He had gone to Chicago earlier in the day to rehearse the band and have lunch with Art Roberts, one of the star DJs at WLS Radio. Tony was always working the radio guys.

Tony was crushed by the loss of his beloved sisters, as well as the loss of his second shot at fame and fortune. But, he was contractually committed to Mr. Kelly's for two weeks of shows — Christmas shows at that — and the nightclub's management needed the business. All the shows were already sold out. They did agree to push the shows back a week so Tony could grieve and bury his sisters, but they wanted their fourteen shows.

During the days before the funeral, Tony was looking at old photos of himself and his sisters, and he came across one that included the female duo Rozzie & Rosie from *Teddy Griffin's Talent Jamboree*. As he stared at it, an idea came to him: he would hire the duo to work with him on these shows. Maybe, just maybe, he thought, the girls could show their gratitude for the work in a special way.

Chapter Twenty

A long silence ensued as Jessie stared out the window of the motel lobby, barely blinking her eyes. Then she blurted out "Tony Winston is my ex-husband." And then she sobbed.

Now it was Hal's turn to be silent. He was stunned. He had known Jessie for almost a year. A marriage to Tony Winston had never come up in any of the long conversations on the tour bus or in any of the pillow talk in their recent days of intimacy.

For the first time since he had known her, Hal was getting angry with Jessie. He detached himself from her physically at that moment. He actually gave her a gentle shove away from him.

While he was stunned that he was just learning she had been married, that fact was actually taking a back seat to the fact that she hadn't bothered to tell him about it. He could excuse her for not telling him about her previous boyfriends and/or lovers because a woman who looked like Jessie would surely have had a lot of suitors. But an ex-husband!

He tried not to give her past love life much thought as their relationship was just starting to blossom, but a part of him always did wonder about it. How many ex-boyfriends were there? How many had she slept with? How did he compare?

He also had tried hard not to analyze how she could throw over her fiancé Danny Harmon so quickly, and maybe callously, for him.

But an ex-husband?

"Talk to me, Hal," she said quietly.

Hal maintained a calm and poised demeanor on the outside. But, on the inside, he was rattled. What else didn't he know about Jessie? What other secrets might she be hiding from him? What other surprises did she have up her sleeve?

He remained quiet. Now he was staring at her. "No, you talk to me, Jessie. I'm all ears."

"I know it's a shock to you, Hal, but I can explain. I made a foolish, spur-of-the-moment decision that turned into a big mistake. Tony and I were only married for six months. And, we only actually lived together for one of those months. I regretted marrying him within a week."

Feelings of empathy started to sneak up on Hal. He wanted to be mad at Jessie, but his anger was faltering. He wanted to ask questions — a lot of them. He really wanted to know why she had kept her marriage to Tony Winston a secret from him. That's what he was mad about.

"Why didn't you tell me before?" he blurted out in a semi-angry tone.

"I am embarrassed by the whole thing," she said meekly. "I embarrassed myself; I embarrassed my parents. I just wanted to forget about the whole thing. I hoped it would go away quietly.

"I was rebounding from a relationship that had gone sour when I met Tony at an Oscar party at my parents' house," she explained. "Like everyone else at the party, I knew about the accident that had killed his sisters. I had read the Army Archerd interview in Variety about how it had crushed him and his family. And, like everyone else at the party, I knew he had become despondent and had tried to commit suicide just after Christmas, even though the Christmas songs that he and his sisters had recorded had sold a million copies and topped the charts.

"But, his surprise win at the Oscars for Best Song for 'London Lady Falling Down' seemed to put some spirit back into him. He was handsome and funny, and he was flirting with me. Tony was a little older and far more suave and sophisticated than any other man who had ever come on to me. I was impressed."

"So you married him just like that?" Hal asked incredulously, remembering how long it had taken his relationship with her to blossom.

"Hal, let me finish," she said with some minor exasperation. "I know people think that women who look like me have the world on a string and have guys calling them all the time, but that's not the case. I think men are afraid to talk to me, call me up, or ask me out. You'll have to explain that to me. I've been pretty lonely for much of my life.

"That's why I'm with Danny Harmon. I don't love him; I don't really want to marry him. I like him. He's cute; he's fun; and, he's good to me. But, in Danny's life, Danny is number one. I've always been number two, and I will always be number two. But, the bottom line is he asked me out and then asked me out again. Boom. To me, that was a good enough relationship.

"But then, after I met you, Hal, I realized that 'no, that wasn't good enough.' You made me number one in your life. I never had that before. It was a whole new world for me to be number one. I was never number one with either of my parents. Mom has her movie career, and Dad has his political life."

"Tony Winston," Hal said emphatically as he interrupted her story. "Why did you marry Tony Winston?"

"Tony came on to me at the Oscar party," she said, "but in a very gentlemanly way. We danced a little bit, and we talked a lot. He made me laugh. He made my parents laugh, especially my mom. He paid a lot of attention to her, almost fawning. But, a lot of people do, so I didn't take much notice. At one point, my godfather, Bob Hope, came over to say 'Hi,' and Tony even made him laugh. I thought to myself, 'Wow! He made Bob Hope laugh. That's pretty special.'"

"Bob Hope is your godfather?" Hal asked in astonishment.

"He and my mom did a few movies together, and he and my dad are long-time golf buddies," Jessie said with a smile. "Impressed, aren't you?"

That did make Hal smile. Jessie James was an impressive woman even though he was still very irritated with her.

"Jessie, how did you become Mrs. Tony Winston?"

"He asked me out on a date, Hal," she said, more than a little miffed that Hal was hectoring her now. "He paid attention to me, Hal. He made me feel like I was number one, Hal. We dated every night for two straight weeks. I couldn't get enough of him, and he couldn't get enough of me.

"On a beautiful, warm night in April, just as the sun was retreating over the Pacific Ocean, Tony asked me to marry him. I was swept away by the emotion of the moment and the beauty of the setting. I said 'Yes.'

"We were married two weeks later on the beach in Malibu. It was all such a fairytale, Hal. I was floating on a cloud. I couldn't believe it was happening to me. I was so happy; I felt so loved."

Hal interrupted again, trying to advance the story more quickly. "But you said you were only married for six months and you only lived with him for one of those months. What happened?"

"The son of a bitch tried to screw my mom," she yelled back at him. "There, Hal. There's the end of the fairytale. Is that what you've been waiting for? The son of a bitch tried to screw my mom. He used me to get close to my mom. She's the woman he was really interested in."

"Geez, Jessie, sorry," Hal said as he flinched a little bit in reaction to her ire. "How would I know that?"

"I'm sorry," said Jessie. "It makes me furious every time I think about it, Hal. He set it up so painstakingly. Tony didn't have any club dates set until the summer. We only lived about a half hour from my parents' home, so we'd go over to the house during the day for lunch and to swim in the heated pool. It was just my mom, Tony, and me. Dad would be down in Sacramento Monday through Thursday. He loved being Governor James; he loved his job and lived and breathed it day in and day out. Even though it took him away from my mother, neither one of them complained.

"I did notice that Tony would stare a lot at my mom in her bikini, but, to tell you the truth, so did I. She still has a stunning body. She'd wear a white bikini on her bronzed body, and you couldn't help but look at her. One afternoon Tony said that he had come down with one of his severe migraine headaches and asked me to go back home to get his prescription pills. I thought that it was a little strange that we just didn't go home so he could lie down in our darkened bedroom, but I wanted to be as nice to him as he was to me. So, I went.

"When I got back, the police were there, and Tony was in handcuffs."

"What the hell?" said Hal.

"My mom had fallen asleep on a deck chair and was awakened by a fully erect naked man straddling her and taking her bikini top off."

"Tony?" asked Hal.

"Tony," said Jessie with disgust.

"My mom leaped up, pushed him off her and into the pool, and then ran across the street to the neighbor's house and called the police. The Beverly Hills cops arrived in less than two minutes. Since I had the car, Tony had no good escape plan. The cops took him to jail, and I moved out of our house back into my parents' house that evening. We were divorced five months later."

"Why did that never make the papers or the TV news?" Hal asked.

"It's Hollywood, Hal," she explained. "When reputations and careers are at stake, deals are made. Under the threat of being blackballed in the entertainment community, Tony was forced to give me an uncontested divorce, give me $100,000 in settlement money, and leave California and never step foot in the state again. My parents know everybody in show business, and they could have — and still could — ruin Tony's career. They didn't want to do that because nothing really happened, so they looked at the settlement money as his punishment. It nearly wiped him out financially.

"Now you know how I embarrassed myself and my parents and why I wanted to forget the whole thing. I wanted to make believe it never happened. I'm so, so sorry it came up like this. But when I saw in the newspaper that Tony was signed to my record label I was frightened.

"I'm scared, Hal. I don't know what to do. I couldn't bear seeing him again. I don't know where he is. He's not supposed to be in California, but that's where my record label is located. I don't know what's going on, Hal. I need help."

Chattering back and forth as they headed for the parking lot, Jessie was getting agitated. She was upset that Hal wasn't as upset about this turn of events as she thought he should be and that he wasn't coming up with a suitable enough solution.

"Jessie," Hal said firmly, "your dad was the governor of California. Your mom is an Oscar-winning actress. They arranged the deal that led to Tony's quick departure from California. Don't you think one call to them would be the quick fix?"

Hal and Jessie threw their bags in the trunk of his Omaha-orange Mustang. "Hal, I'm tired of counting on my mom and dad to get me out of a fix, and I don't think either one of them wants to re-visit Tony Winston. Plus, there is Don Jon Ross. He probably thinks that Tony will help Sunshine Records. I don't want to do anything to ruin that deal. Don Jon stayed with me when I needed label support. I can't hurt him."

"OK, let's do this," Hal said as he started up the car. "Let's get on the road to Connecticut and come up with some options. I'd also like to ask Gene his advice. I read in *Billboard* that Musicor Records was developed for and built around him. I bet he has some pretty good insight into artist-label relationships."

The roads were clear, but there were the occasional slippery spots. Hal was not an aggressive driver, and Jessie was thankful for that. Hal drove at about fifty five miles per hour and always stayed to the right. Anyone who didn't like how fast — or slow — he was going could go around him.

Afternoon crept up on the love-struck couple as they drove and talked about Jessie's dilemma. Jessie was the prisoner of her emotions and argued from that point of view. Hal liked to stick to the facts.

"Jessie, how do you even know IF Tony is in California?" Hal asked. "He could be in New York or Chicago or anywhere right now."

"How do you know he's not?" she answered quickly.

"I don't," said Hal, "but before I would make any life- or career-altering decisions I would find out. Don't you think that's a better plan than getting your knickers in a knot over speculation?"

Discussing the options with Hal had not lessened Jessie's agitation with him or the Sunshine Records situation. She was growing more irritated by the minute. He wasn't taking her seriously, and he didn't realize the gravity of the situation for her.

Finally, she lost her patience and yelled, "HAL! Pull the car over. NOW!"

He did. Immediately.

"Hal, he tried to rape my mom. Do you get it? I hate him. Do you get it? I don't want to be in the same state he's in much less on the same record label. Do you get it?" She was sobbing now.

A few, long seconds passed in quiet as Jessie looked out the window and wept. Then, Hal took her hand in his and said very, very firmly, "I get it, Jessie." He stroked her California-blonde hair and repeated, "I get it Jessie. I will take care of you. I will take care of this."

"Thank you, Hal," she whimpered. "That's all I wanted to hear."

Hal didn't have a solution, but he was going to pray to God in Heaven that one popped into his head during the rest of the journey to Connecticut. Or, better yet, that Gene Pitney would have one.

Chapter Twenty One

Five hours later, the Mustang pulled into Gene Pitney's circular driveway. It was 2:30 p.m., but Jessie was sound asleep. Hal was nervous. He was about to meet his idol. He wanted to make a good first impression so he had practiced some things to say to Gene while Jessie slept during the last hour of the trip. Still, he was sure he would trip all over himself anyways. He also wanted to make a good impression on Mrs. Pitney, so he had stopped at a flower shop in the middle of Gene's hometown, Somers, Connecticut, and bought a bouquet of roses for her.

Pitney bounded out of the house to meet his guests. Jessie was slowly waking up and in her disoriented grogginess couldn't quite figure out where she was and what was going on.

"Hi, Hal, I'm Gene," the wiry international superstar said as he grabbed Hal's hand. "Glad you and Jessie made it OK. How were the roads?"

As soon as she heard Pitney introduce himself to Hal, she snapped back to reality. Jessie never had to worry about how she looked because God had blessed her with a face that always looked fabulous and a body that always wore clothes well.

She quickly popped a Sen-Sen into her mouth, then started to open her door, but the gentlemanly Pitney beat her to it. "And you are the beautiful Jessie James." He kissed her on her cheek and gave her a quick hug. "And you smell good, too," he added with a quick smile.

"Come on in, and get out of the cold," Pitney said. "Let me help you with your bags, Hal. Can you stay a day or two?"

"We don't want to impose," Hal said, without really meaning it. His idol Gene Pitney just invited him to stay at his house for a few days. His head was spinning. He wanted to move in and talk to Gene twenty-four hours a day.

"Not an imposition," Gene responded. "It's a big house with plenty of room. Lynne loves company, and she loves to cook."

Hal and Gene got the bags from the Mustang's trunk and started to head for the house. Hal stopped quickly, turned back to the car, and retrieved the bouquet of roses he had bought.

Chapter Twenty Two

The Pitney "mansion," as Hal and Jessie kept referring to it on the trip up from New Jersey, wasn't a mansion at all. They had had visions of a lavish, mouth-watering Hollywood-type mansion like the ones they saw in fan magazines. From the outside, Pitney's home was a non-descript, two-story, Dutch Colonial house set in a former apple orchard on a very hard-to-find road. It was a very nice house, but it wasn't a mansion. It reminded Hal a bit of the house that Mallory McCoy lived in back in Milwaukee. Was it possible that Mallory's house was as nice as that of an international superstar? How could that be? Wasn't Gene Pitney a multi-millionaire? Shouldn't he live in a humongous house…the biggest in town? Now, in addition to being nervous about meeting his idol, he was forced to wonder why Gene Pitney didn't live in a mega-house. And, he had to pee.

There was a formal front door entrance, but that was not the way that Pitney led them into the house. There was a second, less-obvious entrance adjacent to the attached garage. It led into a small anteroom between the garage and the house. "This is where we leave the winter coats and boots," Gene said as he helped Jessie out of her fire engine red, form-fitting, low-waisted wool coat.

"This isn't from Sears," he laughed as he hung it up on a wall-mounted rack.

"Dicker and Dicker of Beverly Hills," Jessie said with a little laugh. "Just like on *Hollywood Squares.*"

"I would expect nothing less from someone whose mother has won an Academy

Award," Gene said. He liked Jessie — a lot — already.

Hal never wore winter coats. Hated them. Too bulky for his taste. He wore a lightweight yellow jacket that he had bought at a Penneys store during the last tour. He handed it to Gene and whispered in his ear, "Excuse me, but I have to use the bathroom."

Gene poked his head out of the anteroom into a long hallway that led to the kitchen. "Lynne," he shouted, "Hal Douglas is here, and he has to go pee!"

Pitney then turned back to Hal and asked, "You just have to pee, right? Nothing else?" Pitney was playing with him. Hal was mortified.

Lynne Pitney, a thin, gorgeous redhead, came down the hallway to meet her guests. Hal stuck out his hand to greet her, but she ignored it, giving him a warm hug instead. "Hi, Hal, it is so nice to meet you. Love your records, especially 'On The Street Where You Live.' Don't mind Gene, he's just having fun with you. By the way, Gene did a nice version of that song, too. Did you know that?"

Hal was well aware of Gene's version, and he wanted to compliment him on it, but Lynne didn't give him time to answer as she quickly turned to Jessie and gave her the same warm hug. "Hi, Jessie. I'm glad you're here. Love your records, too. Gene can't wait to talk to you two about this duet you want to record. He's been yapping about it since he talked with Hal on the phone. Come on in and get settled."

Lynne led them through the hallway and into the kitchen. "We'll have lunch after you get unpacked and settled in your room upstairs. It's the first room to the right at the top of the stairs. And, Hal, there is a bathroom to the left."

Hal was very grateful that there was another bathroom upstairs. He didn't like using downstairs bathrooms in houses because he had an inordinate fear that people would listen to him going pee.

Ten minutes later Hal and Jessie returned to a very warm kitchen where Lynne Pitney was scouring the refrigerator for a bottle of wine. The Pitneys' new son, Todd, born in August, was asleep in a mini crib near the kitchen table. Hal and Jessie oohed and aahed over him as he slept peacefully. After a quick lunch of sandwiches, potato chips, and wine — Coca-Cola for Hal — the three singers were eager to talk business.

"Gene, before we talk about the UK tour and the duet that Jessie and I wrote, we really need your advice on another situation," said Hal.

"Yeah, sure, what's up?" Gene asked curiously.

"I'll give you the *Reader's Digest* version of the situation," Hal said. "Some of this you might already know and some may be new to you."

Hal spelled out — in a very truncated fashion — Jessie and Tony Winston's situation to Gene.

"Does Sunshine Records have an office or studios in New York?" Gene asked.

"No, just the little hole-in-the-wall place in LA," Jessie said.

"Well, that's good and that's bad," said Gene. "From what you tell me, Tony better not show his face in California. So Don Jon Ross will HAVE to record him somewhere else. Most likely in New York, but they could also do it in Chicago. Depends on where Tony's living now and what's convenient for him. Does Don Jon know anything about your marriage to Tony and the incident with your mother?"

"If he does it's only by way of gossip," Jessie replied. "I never told him."

"I just found out about it this morning," Hal piped in.

Jessie shot him a dirty look. Gene felt the tension growing between the two stars. He didn't know how to diffuse it so he just kept the conversation moving forward.

"Let's go down into my office, have a look around, and make a plan."

Chapter Twenty Three

Pitney had his office in his fully finished basement. The view through the sliding patio doors was of the new in-ground swimming pool he had installed over the summer. The walls were decorated with his many gold records as well as magazine covers and photos of himself with other stars. In the corner of the room behind his massive desk was a row of filing cabinets.

Gene Pitney saved almost everything related to his career in those filing cabinets: receipts, contracts, letters, and so on. Oddly, he didn't have a collection of his own records anywhere in the house. His mother, Anne, took care of his fan club as well as collecting and cataloguing his records and his press clippings. She sent hand-written answers to any fan who sent a letter or a note to Gene.

Jessie and Hal walked around the office gazing at all the artifacts on the wall that chronicled Pitney's worldwide success as a recording artist. Hal was especially impressed by the gold records from England, Australia, New Zealand, Japan, Canada, and Italy. He stopped and stared at Gene's UK Gold Records for "Twenty Four Hours From Tulsa," "That Girl Belongs To Yesterday," "I'm Gonna Be Strong," "I Must Be Seeing Things," "Looking Through The Eyes of Love," "Princess In Rags," "Backstage (I'm Lonely)," "Nobody Needs Your Love," and "Just One Smile" all grouped together in one corner of the office

"What's that like?" Hal asked in wonder. "What's that like to grow up in a small, small town in Connecticut and then one day be famous all over the world and tour all over the world? I mean, do people know who you are when you walk down the street in London?"

"Well," Gene started to answer then broke into a small laugh, "I can't walk down most streets in London. That's the price of fame, Hal. As much as I'd like to be a tourist in London, I can't. Well, I can, but it's hard. The first time I went over to England to do TV to promote 'Twenty Four Hours From Tulsa' my press agent took me to the Tower of London. I was stopped every five minutes for autographs and pictures. We were both shocked. Pretty soon people were just following us around. And, not just Brits. Tourists from other countries, too.

"And, you know what else, Hal? I've never been able to go on the Tube. Do you know what the Tube is?

Hal shook his head side to side. He was enthralled listening to his idol talk about his career in such a casual way.

"The Tube is the London subway," Gene explained. "It's what most people use to get around the city. It's a London icon, but I can't go on it because I'd get mobbed. So, it takes some of the 'thrill' away from being famous in London.

"On the other hand, sometimes I get recognized in the oddest places, and it's OK. During my last tour of the UK, I decided to go for a walk around my hotel in London — The Westbury. It's pretty close to all the shopping on Oxford Street so I can blend in pretty well with the crowds. I was out maybe a half-hour, and three different cabbies rolled up to me and said, 'Hey Gene, loved the show last night, need a lift?' That's one of the nice things about being famous in London."

Hal wanted the conversation to go on forever. He had a million questions for Gene about his career, about England, and about the record business. But, he caught a glimpse of Jessie out of the corner of his eye, and she was glaring at him.

Hal walked over and whispered, "What's wrong, Jessie?"

She whispered back at him, "Look, Hal, do want to be President of the Gene Pitney Fan Club, or do you want to get down to business?"

Gene could still sense the tension and the awkwardness of the conversation between Hal and Jessie, and he pretended to sort through the piles of mail on his desk.

Hal was taken aback at the way she snapped at him. "C'mon Jessie, I may never get this chance again. Can't I have five minutes with the man who is the biggest influence on my life and career?"

"Well I need to talk with him before I call Don Jon," she said in a little softer tone. She now realized how much this moment meant to Hal. She also recognized that she wasn't irritated with Hal at all. It was the Tony Winston situation that was eating away at her, and she wanted to resolve it sooner rather than later.

"Gene," Hal said, "Jessie says that I'm driving her crazy with my starry-eyed fan club member questions, so I must be driving you nuts, too."

"Not at all," said Gene. "I'm flattered that you're that interested in me and my career."

Little did Pitney know how very interested Hal Douglas was in his career; little did Pitney know that the young Hal Douglas had assembled dozens of scrapbooks of Gene Pitney clippings from American, English, and Italian fan magazines and newspapers; little did Pitney know that this new teen idol used to buy his Musicor albums to see what he was wearing on the cover and then try to buy the same clothes and shoes at the stores in Milwaukee; little did Pitney know how much Hal Douglas obsessed over him; little did Pitney know that Hal always wondered "What would Gene Pitney do or say?" in a given situation.

Pitney was ready to go in whatever direction the young stars wanted to go: answer more of Hal's questions, help Jessie resolve her Tony Winston problem, or talk about the duet that he was going to produce for them. He was eager to discuss the latter because that was what he was most interested in, but he would let them lead the way.

Hal said, "We can wait to call Don Jon. That gives us time to discuss what Jessie is going to say to him."

Pitney was not one to mince words when it came to business. He was a shrewd businessman who knew how to make money, but he also knew how to manage a career. Those were two distinct art forms.

"Look, Jessie," Gene said, "you're a major star right now. You've got power. This is a situation where you have to use it. How long are you signed to Sunshine Records?"

"It was just a two-year deal," she answered. "It's almost done."

"The big labels will be coming after you pretty soon if they haven't already started in with offers," Pitney explained. "If Don Jon Ross wants to keep you and you want to stay there, he's gonna have to listen to you. Right now, you're his meal ticket."

"But, I owe him, Gene," Jessie said. "He signed me when no one else would take a beauty-queen-who-wanted-to-be-a-singer seriously. He stuck with me when my second record flopped. I owe him."

"And he owes you, too," Pitney shot back. "You don't have to screw him over, but you do have to make your position perfectly clear and then don't take 'no' for an answer."

"I can do that because I will not be in the same room, the same city, or the same state as Tony Winston. Period."

Jessie was quiet for a moment as she looked out at Pitney's tarp-covered swimming pool. It reminded her of the pool in her parents' yard back in California, and she was lost in thought as she mentally reminisced about her life growing up there.

She broke the silence with a momentous question. "How far do you think I can push Don Jon, Gene? Can I tell him it's either Tony or me? My insides are screaming right now at the thought of ever running into him — even accidentally. I won't do that. I won't take that chance. I might kill the son of a bitch. I want to give Don Jon an either or proposal. I think I can pull it off. Do you?"

Pitney was impressed that Jessie had gotten her head around the situation so fast and realized — maybe not one hundred percent yet — that she was in the driver's seat at Sunshine Records.

Hal was taking it all in and was only somewhat bewildered. He knew Jessie was smart. After all, she belonged to Mensa. He knew she was a good businesswoman. When push came to shove, she had pushed Don Jon Ross into a very limited record contract with her. But, up until this point, he had not seen her be even borderline ruthless. Her suggestion to Gene certainly was that.

Gene started in, "If that's what you want to do…" but a now very emotional Jessie James interrupted him.

"It's what I have to do," she said, staring out the sliding doors of Gene's office as the early evening darkness of winter was moving in. "Otherwise, I will kill the son of a bitch."

Then she turned and looked at both Hal and Gene, and, with a hearty laugh, added "And if I do that the two of you will be touring England next year while I'm touring the California penal system."

"Look," Gene said after sharing a good laugh with Hal and Jessie, "I'm sure I can come up with a business plan for Don Jon and Sunshine Records that will get Tony Winston out of the picture — alive. I just need a little time. Does that work for you two?"

Hal was quiet because he was so amazed at what he just witnessed and how quickly his idol, Gene Pitney, had become a part of both his professional and personal lives. Subtly, he looked at his watch. He had been at Pitney's house less than two hours, and his life was changing quickly and dramatically. He couldn't believe what was happening to him.

Jessie, noticing Hal's slight discomfort, piped up, again with a laugh, "Gene, if you can make it work where I don't have to kill that sleazeball son of a bitch Winston, I'm in!"

"Great," said Pitney, "I'll make it work. And, Hal. I'll come up with a plan to deal with Rick Starr, too. It doesn't appear that he has screwed you yet, but that time is coming. I guarandamntee it. Now let's move on to this duet that you two lovebirds wrote. Tell me about it."

Hal told Gene the story of "A Lifetime of Love" then asked if he and Jessie could sing it for him.

"Can't wait," said Pitney. "The piano is over there. I read up on you."

At the piano, Hal started in first, singing the melody that had been stuck in his head for some time.

This love so real
This love so true
It's a lifetime of love
That I offer you

Jessie's turn.

You came to me
Out of the blue
It's a lifetime of love
I need from you

The stars' voices joined on the chorus.

If you walk with me
Down this aisle
A lifetime of love
Is what I'll…I'll

I'll promise you

So, promise me
End my fear
A lifetime of love
Is oh so near.

Hal sang his second verse.

I give you my hand
You own my heart
From this day on
We will never part.

Jessie, now with tears in her eyes, trembled as she sang her second verse.

Hal, you are the one
The love of my lifetime
And a lifetime of love
Shall be yours and mine.

Hal took Jessie's hand in his as they sang the chorus a second time. They ended the song with a tender kiss.

Gene let the moment linger then said, "Love it! Nice twist in the chorus with that stutter step line. You know, the song reminds me a lot of 'Only Love Can Break A Heart' in its beautiful simplicity.

"I'd love to produce it. I hear a lot of strings and piano. What would you think about using a Black gospel group to back you up? I think it would be spine-tingling on that chorus. One other thing. I think it needs a third verse."

"We're open to anything, Gene," said Hal. "Jessie and I can write the third verse when we get home. We also talked about having you sing on the record. Jessie said it would be a great way to promote the UK tour, and the UK tour would be a great way to make it a hit."

"Now THAT'S a brilliant idea, Jessie," said Gene. His respect for her business sense was growing by leaps and bounds. She was beautiful; she had the voice of an angel; and she had brilliant business acumen.

Gene knew instinctively that "A Lifetime of Love" was, at best, only a good song. For it to be a hit he would have to produce a great record. The production on it would be the key. He also knew it could re-launch his own recording career and make his upcoming UK tour the biggest of his career.

"We've got to get it done fast," pointed out Gene. "But, it's got to be done right. I'll make some calls. Would you two be insulted if I asked a friend of mine to write the third verse? He's in New York and could get it done fast. He's brilliant. Ever heard of Al Kooper?"

"He wrote 'I Must Be Seeing Things,'" said Hal. "What a great song. But I thought some of those album tracks he wrote for you were great, too. We'd be honored to have Al Kooper as a co-writer on the song."

Kooper had also co-written "This Diamond Ring" for Gary Lewis & The Playboys. Pitney knew that Kooper could punch up the song with a strong third verse, but he also had an ulterior motive. Loyal to his friends, Pitney knew that Kooper hadn't had a hit for a while and could use the money. Al Kooper knew how to craft a great two-and-a-half-minute pop classic. Pitney could also lean on him for production advice.

"When you two get home, just enjoy Christmas and New Year's," said Pitney, trying to close the deal quickly. "I'll get us studio time in New York in January."

"What about Don Jon Ross and Sunshine Records?" asked Jessie. "What about Tony Winston? When can we get that resolved?"

"And, while we're on the subject," Hal interjected, "what are we gonna do about Rick Starr?"

"Over the holidays I'll put together a game plan to deal with all of them and a business deal for the three of us to agree on," said Gene. "But it is crucially important that we keep Don Jon and Rick in the dark. If you can, steer clear of them until I talk to them. "How about if I call you between Christmas and New Year's Day, and we'll discuss it? Also, Hal, you need an accountant. My guy in New York is the best. I recommend him. Here's his card. Promise me you'll call him as soon as you get back to Milwaukee."

"I can't thank you enough for all of your help and advice, Gene. I promise I will call him before Christmas. I've got some things I need taken care of pronto."

Chapter Twenty Four

Gene Pitney was an international star and a shrewd businessman who knew the inner workings of the record business. He was already a multi-millionaire, but he was always looking to grow his career and bank account. Pitney still loved to perform, but he also liked to call the shots. His skills at both were profoundly abundant and abundantly profound.

And, he just loved the idea of working with two of the biggest teen idols in the world. For him, it would be a new twist on an old idea. In 1965, simply as a marketing ploy by his label, Musicor Records, he had recorded a few albums with country stars George Jones and Melba Montgomery who were also on the label at the time. Those odd collaborations produced a few minor country hits, but most of his teen fans never knew he had recorded those albums.

He was convinced that the collaboration with Hal and Jessie could put him right back on top of the charts — and keep their careers going at full throttle. It would also establish him as a producer of hit records, and that would open up a lot of doors for him in the music industry.

Gene Pitney wanted to have creative control over everything he did. It wasn't that he didn't trust other people; he just trusted himself and his ears more. Like a man he had worked with early in his career, Phil Spector, Pitney had a great ear for what songs could become hits, and he knew what it took in the studio — from the artist, the musicians, the arranger, and the producer — to make a hit record.

He always wanted to be in complete control over every aspect of his career. He acted as his own manager, promoted his own tours, wrote and designed his own tour books, and decided what interviews he would and wouldn't do. Producing hit records for himself and other artists was part of his career game plan, but he wanted to do that his way, too. He didn't want to work for a record label; he wanted to be an independent producer.

To get the Hal Douglas-Jessie James duet done — on his terms — he had to solve three problems: Rick Starr, Don Jon Ross, and Tony Winston. Pitney thrived on the challenge. He had great business instincts, and he was now champing at the bit to put this deal together in a way that showed the music industry he was more than just a former teen idol singer.

Don Jon Ross and Tony Winston would be a package deal, he figured. Winston needed Ross to rekindle his career; Ross needed Jessie James to keep his small record company afloat. Make a deal with Ross, make Ross deal with Winston, and — BIN-GO! — problem solved.

Pitney had an idea. He felt that his time as a hit maker for Musicor Records was about to run out. The musical landscape was changing fast, and pop star balladeers were becoming passé. Heavy metal rock was the next big thing.

Even though he was still a huge star and a major concert attraction, there were no major record companies beating down his door to pick up his soon-to-lapse Musicor contract. And, he wasn't interested in staying with the Musicor label when his deal was done. He felt the label was becoming a dinosaur because of the people running it. Not so affectionately, Pitney called them "Wingtip Wonders." He felt the music world had raced past them. Artistically they were still stuck in the pre-Beatles era, so Gene would offer his star power to Don Jon Ross and Sunshine Records.

It would be a win-win for him and Ross: Pitney would have a place to land after his Musicor deal ended, and his situation at Sunshine Records would replicate his situation at Musicor. He would be a BIG star on a SMALL label. The label would have to cater to him, and he liked that because, again, it left him in charge of his career and his own fate. Ross would get a major star for his label to bolster his roster, which was currently comprised solely of Jessie James. Ross would have to agree to Pitney's terms, otherwise Pitney would threaten to hold up the duet until after Jessie's contract with Ross ended in a few months.

Pitney decided it was better to cut Ross in on the deal than alienate him. Controlling the deal, Pitney would let Ross release the duet on Sunshine Records but only in the United States. How could Don Jon Ross turn down a guaranteed million seller? He couldn't, and Pitney knew he wouldn't. It would make Sunshine Records a major player in the music business, and it would make Don Jon Ross rich.

But, to get the record for Sunshine, Pitney would insist that Ross sell Tony Winston's contract to Rick Starr and Starr Records, no ifs, ands, or buts about it. That's how he would fix it for Jessie.

Rick Starr would be easy. While Starr could easily be manipulated out of the deal because he had no written contract with Hal, Pitney understood that it was more important to get Starr's blessing and cooperation. Pitney would cut Starr in on the deal but on his own terms.

He would give Starr the publishing on the flip side song, which Pitney had decided he would write himself to earn even more money and keep the project under his control. Since the songwriter and publisher on the flip side of a hit earned the same money as the songwriter and publisher of the hit, this would keep Starr happy.

Starr was a very powerful force in pop music, and Pitney wanted and needed him on his side. At the same time, Starr would be neutralized because, by trying to take advantage of Hal and not having a signed contract, he ended up with no real bargaining power with a shrewd guy like Pitney.

Pitney had Starr over a barrel, but he wasn't going to play it that way. His plan was to become Rick Starr's new best friend. If he had to, he would create a fictional scenario where Hal was wising up to show business and was ready to leave Starr completely. Pitney would then ride in to his "friend's" rescue and convince the rebellious teen idol to stay with Starr. Then, Starr would think that he owed Pitney BIG.

Pitney was also going to force Starr to buy Tony Winston's contract from Sunshine Records. Starr would also be strictly forbidden from ever putting Tony Winston on any performance venue — concert, TV show, movie, stage show, radio performance, or interview — with Jessie James — anywhere in the world. And, if it ever came to pass via a third party, Starr would see to it that that didn't happen either.

Additionally, Starr would have to contract Pitney to both write songs and produce records for Winston. Gene wanted to always know what Winston was up to, and he figured that would be the easiest and most convenient way to do that. He was confident his plan would solve the Rick Starr problem, and it was a win-win-win-win for himself, for Starr, for Ross, and for Hal and Jessie.

And, just to make sure that the powerful Starr was kept happy, Pitney would let Starr Records release the Hal Douglas-Jessie James record in England and any other country in the world they mutually agreed on.

Pitney wanted to make sure it was a sound plan with no holes in it, so he called his friend, Johnny Tillotson. Tillotson was another recording artist who was also a good businessman, but Pitney had a secondary agenda. He wanted to pay Johnny Tillotson back for likely saving his life on a Rick Starr tour a few years back. Again, Pitney was loyal to a fault to his friends.

Chapter Twenty Five

Gene Pitney was the headliner on *The 1964 Rick Starr Cavalcade of Stars Tour* when it rolled into Huntsville, Alabama, on an unusually crisp August night. The Supremes were second on the bill, followed by Lou Christie, Johnny Tillotson, The Ronettes, Paul and Paula, The KupKakes, Gene Chandler, Randy and The Rainbows, and The Reflections. The band that accompanied all the artists on the show was a four-piece group from Brooklyn called The Mob. Rick Starr hired them as the band and as bodyguards for his stars. They were great musicians who could all read music, and they all allegedly dabbled in organized crime as enforcers for a Brooklyn gambling organization.

The tour bus rolled into the parking lot behind the theater in Huntsville at 4:30 p.m., and the show began at 7 p.m. Since Pitney was the headliner, he'd go on last to close the show, which meant he now had almost four hours to kill. He and the gorgeous Billie Danbury of The KupKakes had struck up a friendship during the long tour. For him it was strictly platonic, but the bright and engaging Danbury did fascinate him. Danbury, on the other hand, had a major crush on Pitney and his matinee idol good looks. They decided to get out of the building, get some fresh air, take a walk, and enjoy the nice weather.

A short distance from the theater, which was located on a state highway in an outlying part of the city, a group of six rough-looking teenage boys — all white — accosted the two stars. The teens had no idea who Pitney and Danbury were. They only knew he was white and she was Black, and they weren't going to stand for that.

They started to bait Pitney and Danbury with vitriolic racial slurs.

"Where you from, Boy?" the apparent leader of the teenagers screamed at Pitney as the group circled him and Danbury.

"Connecticut," Pitney said slowly as he was trying to size up the situation to determine how much trouble he and Billie might be in. "Rockville, Connecticut."

"So, you like nigger girls in Rockville, Connecticut," another one of the boys yelled.

"I like my friend, Miss Danbury, a lot, and I would appreciate it if you would watch your mouth," said Pitney as he watched the teenagers' faces to see if he could calculate how serious they were about causing trouble.

Pitney was five-foot-nine and weighed all of 145 pounds. Not a daunting figure. He was hoping he could talk his way out of this and whispered to Danbury, "Don't say a word."

The leader of the group pushed the now-frightened Danbury and said, "There are a lot of nigger boys down in the ghetto. Why don't you go down there where you belong. Me and my boys here are called the Huntsville Hunters. We hunt niggers, and we know how to take care of nigger-lovers like Mr. Connecticut here."

Pitney remained calm and said, "Don't touch her again."

The teens' leader screamed at Pitney, "I ain't gonna touch that nigger girl again. There ain't enough soap in Huntsville to get me clean if I touched her nigger ass again."

Just then, Pitney saw someone coming down the street at a rapid pace. It was Johnny Tillotson. A radio DJ had shown up to do a scheduled interview with Pitney, but Pitney had forgotten about it. Tillotson had seen Pitney and Danbury leave the building, so he went looking for them.

Tillotson saw and heard part of the ugly situation, sized it up quickly, did a one eighty, and left. Pitney was shocked and disappointed — and now scared. Why would his friend abandon him in this dangerous situation? He didn't have time for a pity party, though. He and Billie were in big trouble, and he had to defend her while trying to get both of them out safely.

Another of the teenagers approached Danbury. He was the smallest — and ugliest — of the group. "You know, Boys," he said with a little grin on his face as he stared right at her, "nigger girl here is kinda pretty. You know, for a nigger! You know what else boys? I ain't never seen a real girl naked before. I seen 'em in my daddy's Playboy but never a real one. I think maybe I'd like to see some real naked nigger tits today."

Pitney was starting to panic. The situation was quickly escalating beyond anything he could control. He decided that whatever was going to happen would only happen after he put up a fight to defend himself and Danbury.

Suddenly, behind him came a voice Pitney recognized: "Is there a problem here, Gene?"

It was Johnny Tillotson, and two members of The Mob accompanied him. Tillotson knew that Tony Trileggi and Frankie DeFazio were both hotheads who carried guns. He also knew that The Mob had become very close with The KupKakes during the tour. They were very protective of all the stars on the tour, but The KupKakes got special attention because they, like The Mob, were from Brooklyn. The Mob boys were made-to-order for this situation.

The Huntsville Hunters, not seeing the guns, were ready for a fight and turned their attention to the three newcomers. They froze, though, when Trileggi and DeFazio pulled their guns and pointed them.

As DeFazio kept the six teenagers frozen in place with his gun, Trileggi walked over to Pitney and Danbury. He put his arm around Danbury very tenderly and asked, "Are you alright?"

"I'm OK. We're both OK," she said and then broke down crying.

"Down on the ground," Trileggi screamed at the teens while waving his gun in the air.

"Don't hurt them," Pitney said. "They're just punk kids."

"Punk kids that were ready to beat you and Billie to within an inch of your lives because she's Black and you're white," said Trileggi. "They might even have killed you." Then he lowered his voice and said, "Let us handle this, Gene. Please take Miss Danbury back to the theater. Take Johnny with you. None of you want to be witnesses to what's going to happen."

In a panic, Pitney pulled Tony Trileggi aside and asked, "What's gonna happen here that I don't want to witness, Tony? I think they're pissing their pants right now. Isn't that enough?"

"They're gonna pay a price," Trileggi answered, "but they will live to see tomorrow. You've got my word on it, Gene."

After the three stars left, DeFazio grabbed one of the teens off the ground, stood him up, put his gun in his face, and said, "We don't like the way you treated our friends. They are guests in your beautiful city, and you worthless pieces of protoplasm rough them up. Not nice."

"Oh, good word, Frankie," said Trileggi. "Protoplasm. Very good word. I don't think these little prickdicks know what it means."

"Speaking of good words," DeFazio said with a laugh, "I love how you used prickdick in a sentence like that. Would you call that a compound word?"

"I'm not really sure if it's a compound word," answered Trileggi. "I don't think it would be hyphernated or anything. So I think it's just a onepound word."

He looked at the teenager standing up and asked his name.

"Bobby Lee," the scared boy said with a tremor in his voice.

"How old are you, Bobby Lee?" Trileggi asked.

"Eighteen. I'll be nineteen next week."

"Well, Bobby Lee, at that age you should know better. My friend Frankie and me wanna talk to you and your scumbag friends, but we don't have a lot of time. So, we just wanna talk to you about one word. Which one of you called our lady friend a 'nigger'?"

Bobby Lee stood mute.

Trileggi slapped Bobby Lee's face and said, "Maybe you didn't hear me." Then, like the wind, he put his gun next to Bobby Lee's ear and fired it into the air. "Did you hear THAT, Prickdick?"

Bobby Lee held his hand to his ear, trying to massage the pain away, and he started to cry.

Trileggi then ordered the other five up off the ground. "Here's what's gonna happen, Prickdicks," he started to explain. "You picked the wrong people to screw with, and now you have to make amends.

"But, we're not gonna hurt you," said Trileggi. "We're not gonna hurt them are we, Frankie?"

"No we ain't. They're gonna hurt themselves," said DeFazio "That's how we do it in Brooklyn."

Trileggi was wiping his fingerprints off his gun with his hanky. "Give my friend Frankie your driver's licenses. We want to know who you are and where you live."

Trileggi then lined the frightened teenagers up in a straight line, all facing in the same direction. "Now, here's how we play our little game," he said. "I'm gonna give Bobby Lee my gun, and he's gonna shoot the next person in line. Where you wanna shoot him, Bobby Lee?"

"I don't want to shoot my friends," Bobby said through the tears streaming down his cheeks. "We're sorry. Can we just go?"

"Ain't buying it, Bobby Lee," said Trileggi. "Didn't your daddy ever teach you not to bullshit a bullshitter? You're just sorry you got caught, ain't ya? Where do you wanna shoot him, Bobby Lee? You better pick a place on his body, or I will."

Bobby just stood there, shaking and crying.

"Not so tough now are you, Bobby Lee?" said DeFazio. "I suggest you shoot him in the foot. It only hurts for a little while. Maybe he'll limp the rest of his life; maybe he won't."

With DeFazio's gun to his crotch, Bobby Lee shot the next teenager in line in the foot. He was then ordered to give the gun to that teenager who had to shoot the next kid in the line in the foot.

After a lot of tears, a lot of screaming, and a lot of blood, the game was over. The six Huntsville Hunters were all writhing on the ground, whimpering.

"Okee-dokee," said Trileggi. "That was fun. It looks like our work here is done. We gotta go now. Remember you little prickdicks, we know who you are and where you live. And, we got the gun with all of your fingerprints on it. So, we really don't care how you explain this mess to your mamas and daddies. From now on, Boys, be nice to everybody. Just a free tip from us."

Trileggi and DeFazio walked away and didn't look back. They had settled the debt for Gene Pitney and Billie Danbury.

Chapter Twenty Six

"Johnny, I'm ready to take a major step in my career, and I want to make sure that I've got all the bases covered," Pitney said over the phone.

After hearing Pitney's plan for Hal and Jessie and how he was going to maneuver through and around Don Jon Ross, Rick Starr, and Tony Winston, Tillotson laughed and said, "Poetry in motion, my friend. It sounds like a Colonel Tom Parker plan."

Pitney knew that Tillotson could write hit records. Big hit records. He had written "Dreamy Eyes" and "It Keeps Right On A-Hurtin," two of the biggest hits in pop music history in the pre-Beatles era.

Pitney then spelled out his plan to cut his friend in. "Johnny, I want you to write a song that Hal and Jessie can record for the flip side," Pitney said. "Let me tweak it a bit so I can get co-writer status. It will be worth a fortune. This will be as big or bigger than any Elvis or Beatles record ever was. Deal?"

"Exactly how the Colonel did it for Elvis," Johnny said with a laugh. "Deal. When do you need it?"

"Right after Christmas," Gene told him. "But, Johnny, do not, I repeat, do not write me a hit. 'A Lifetime of Love' is the 'A' side, and I don't want DJs flipping it over and playing the 'B' side. One more thing, Johnny. We've got to set up a publishing company with a third party to share the wealth to get this deal done. OK?"

"No worries," said Tillotson, using a phrase he had picked up on one of his British tours. "I've got a bunch of songs that I wrote for my next album. There's one that I wrote in about ten minutes called 'The Tide Is Turning.' I just couldn't get it worked out the way I really wanted it. It's not an embarrassment, but it's not a hit either."

"I'll take it," said Pitney. "Get it to me fast."

"I'll send a demo tape of it Air Mail Special Delivery tomorrow," said Tillotson. "And, thank you, my friend. I owe you."

"No you don't Johnny. It's my thank you for Huntsville, 1964," said Gene, and he hung up.

Chapter Twenty Seven

The trip home for Christmas should have been enjoyable for both Hal and Jessie. Jessie loved the sunshine and warmth of California; Hal loved the comfortable familiarity of Milwaukee. Being with their families and friends and reveling in their great success while planning what promised to be an exciting future would make most people very happy. But, Hal and Jessie each had some not-so-fun activities to tend to as well as celebrating Christmas with their families.

Jessie had to dump her movie star boyfriend Danny Harmon and keep her record label owner Don Jon Ross at arm's length until Gene Pitney could deal with him.

Hal wanted to somehow visit Mallory, explain everything to her, and not fall back in love with her. She still held a very special place in a corner of his heart. First loves are always hard to let go of. And, he needed to dodge Rick Starr — Rick Starr, who made him a pop star/teen idol and now wanted to make him a movie star.

After storing Hal's Mustang in his heated garage, Pitney dropped the two stars off at Bradley International Airport in Hartford about two hours before their departures because he knew they wanted to talk before their long holiday separation. He promised to call them right after Christmas with details on how he was going to put all the pieces of their career puzzles together.

"Hal, do you think this will all work out?" Jessie asked as they ate pizza and drank Cokes at the airport. "Are we doing the right thing, you know, sort of turning our backs on the people who gave us our breaks?"

Hal stroked her long blonde hair and assured her that Gene Pitney was the person to listen to. "I believe what he said about Jasper Pacetti and Morgen Linn. Rick Starr dropped them like hot potatoes after they didn't score a second hit right away. Now they have no careers.

"This is what I want to do for the rest of my life," said Hal, "and I really like the idea of taking some control over my career. I know I'm still very wet behind the ears, but I'm ready to learn. Jessie, I want to be a partner in my career; I want to be in on the decisions; I want to write some of the songs; I want to do it all."

"Well, look at me sitting at the airport with Gene Pitney, Jr.," she laughed. "I don't disagree with any of that Hal. But, are we rushing into it? Should we take direction from Rick and Don Jon a little bit longer? Should we slow down a little bit and just worry about getting a few more hits under our belts? That's all I'm asking."

"Jessie, I adore you; you know that," said Hal. "So, I am willing to listen to what you have to say. But, I think what Gene is saying is compelling, don't you?

"Look at the crap that Don Jon is putting on the flip side of your records. Don't you care about that? Wouldn't you like to, maybe, write some of your own flip sides? I know it's not all about the money, Jessie, but we do need to be pragmatic, don't we?"

"Now, Hal Douglas, when did you become such a tough music critic, and where did you learn a word like 'pragmatic'?" she asked.

"I am a high school graduate," he said with a chuckle. "I did learn some of those big words in little old Milwaukee. Probably not as many as a Mensa genius like you learned out there in Hollywood, but I didn't need as many. We are very simple folks in Wisconsin."

He snickered at his little joke, then continued, "And I actually listened to the flip side of your records, Jessie. They are songs that a fifth grader could have written. And, I don't know this for a fact, but my guess is that you refused to record 'Let's Have Some More California Fun' because it was so bad, and that's why it became just an instrumental on the flip side of 'Yes! No! Yes!' Am I right or wrong?"

After an uncomfortable length of silence, Jessie ignored his question but asked, "Would you mind if I talked to my mom and dad about this, Hal? Just to get a second and third opinion. They both have great insight into business dealings as well as personal and professional relationships. They'll have a perspective that we don't because they aren't invested in it the way we are, and they don't know the players like we do."

Hal was a little miffed that Jessie hadn't answered his very legitimate question. He thought he had made an excellent point, and he wanted that recognized as well. With Gene Pitney's guidance, Hal was starting to figure things out about the record business, and he wanted to show Jessie that he could think things through and come up with valid and cogent points.

He knew he couldn't stop her from the discussion with her parents, and he didn't want to get into a fight with her. They were going to be apart for two weeks, and he didn't want bad feelings simmering during the lengthy separation.

"Maybe I could visit you and your parents in Los Angeles after Christmas," Hal said. "This might be the perfect time for them to get to know me and vice versa. Maybe we could tell them about our plans to get married."

Alarm bells were going off in Jessie's head. She loved Hal, or at least she thought she loved Hal. She wanted to love Hal, but did she really want to marry him and say good-bye to all the many other great guys who could be/would be potential suitors some day?

What about Danny Harmon? No, she didn't love him, and she firmly believed that he would cheat on her if they ever got married. But then that left the door open for her to play the field, too, while enjoying the semblance of security that a marriage like that would offer.

Danny had already won an Oscar, and, in 1967, in terms of status, that was light years ahead of having a #1 record on the pop charts. Movie stars were the major leaguers of show business; pop stars were in the minor leagues. Appearances and status were everything where Jessie came from.

Would her parents approve? Yes, Hal was a star, but in a whole different world than Jansen and Jayna James lived in. And, he was from Milwaukee, Wisconsin. The glitterati in Hollywood believed that the unwashed masses still cooked over campfires surrounded by their covered wagons in Wisconsin. They hadn't asked — jokingly — if there were indoor toilets in Milwaukee, but Jessie knew they wanted to.

Jessie had to stall Hal. She didn't want to say "No" outright because she wanted him to believe that theirs was the "everlasting love" they had talked about while stranded at Don's Starry Starry Night Motel in New Jersey. Even though she was having some doubts about their romance, she wanted a professional relationship with Hal. Her woman's intuition was telling her that the duet she was going to record with Hal would blast their careers into the same league as The Beatles, The Rolling Stones, and The Beach Boys. Superstars among superstars.

"Hal," she said after what seemed like an eternity of silence, "I'm nervous about breaking off my relationship with Danny. I have no idea how he's going to react, and, to be honest, I have no idea how my parents will react either."

More than a little hurt by that comment, Hal asked, somewhat defensively, "Do you want to break it off with Danny? Are you committed to our relationship? What the hell is going on, Jessie?"

Now Jessie's temper was starting to get the best of her. They were in a public place, so she had to keep her voice down so as not to cause an embarrassing scene. But, she was getting irritated with Hal.

"Look, Hal," she said, gritting her teeth more than she had intended. She took a sip of her Coke to give her time to settle down and choose her words carefully. She didn't want to tell Hal that she was having second thoughts about everything, so she decided to make Hal feel like he wasn't giving any of it enough thought.

"These are life-changing things we are talking about here," she said in a stern matter-of-fact way. "This isn't about buying a pretty pink dress or a pretty black dress. OK? What happens in the next few weeks changes my life, our lives, forever.

"We're in the big leagues, Hal. This isn't Hal's Pals playing someone else's hits in a school gymnasium in Milwaukee for five dollars and free Cokes. We are on the verge of becoming two of the biggest pop stars in the world. Do you get that? We are on the verge of dumping the two people who were instrumental in getting us to this point. Do you get that? And, we are on the verge of making a huge change in our personal lives that will affect a lot of people. Do you get that?"

Hal slammed his glass of soda down on the table a little harder than he meant to. Coke sprayed out of it like Old Faithful exploding. No one in the small airport restaurant noticed it, so Hal's embarrassment was simply his regret for letting his temper get the best of him.

"Yeah, I get it, Jessie," he said tersely. "I get all of it, and I'm OK with all of it. I'm OK with all of it right now. I don't have to run home to my mommy and daddy to ask them what I should do."

As soon as he said it he regretted it. He loved Jessie beyond belief. He wanted her by his side for the rest of his life — personally and professionally. He needed Jessie for her wisdom, for her intuition, and for her life skills. Hal truly realized that he was really just a small-town boy in the big-time world of show business, and he needed Jessie to help him navigate those oftentimes-troubled waters. And, he knew that thinking things through was not his long suit.

Jessie did not want to be in this fight with Hal just before their holiday split. They were at an impasse, and she wanted to end the conversation before Hal accidentally swerved into the truth of the matter.

Knowing how to get his goat, she put the conversation to rest by getting up from the table, staring coldly at Hal, and saying, in a quavering voice, "Would Gene Pitney talk to me like that?"

Then she walked away.

Chapter Twenty Eight

Hal was more than stunned at Jessie's behavior. He was now angry, but a big part of him also felt very, very guilty. Of course, he was not mature enough in personal relationships to know that she had played him into that guilt trip.

He wanted her to feel the same way he did. He wanted her to tell him that he was making good choices and that everything would be alright. Instead, he felt like he had disappointed Jessie. He felt like he had let her down. He didn't feel, at this moment, that he was her hero. And that is what he wanted most in the relationship: he wanted to take care of Jessie for the rest of her life, but he also wanted her to look up to him as a man who was bright, witty, sensitive, thoughtful, caring, and talented. He wanted to be her hero.

Right now, he was feeling like yesterday's hero.

Hal really wanted Jessie to agree with him one hundred percent on everything, but he also wanted to resolve the lovers' quarrel before they went to their respective homes for the holidays.

Even though it had "International" in its title, the airport wasn't that big. Hal wandered around for only a few minutes before he found Jessie sitting at her gate, staring into space. He walked up behind her, and, in the best pre-pubescent voice he could muster, he said, "Excuse me, Miss James, can I have your autograph?"

Without turning around, she rifled through her purse for a pen. Jessie always signed every autograph for every fan. The screechy little voice behind her quickly said, "Oh, Miss James, I have my own pen. You can use it."

When she turned around to sign the autograph for what sounded like an eleven-year-old boy with potentially horrifying acne, what she was met with instead was Hal Douglas, pop superstar, holding eighteen yellow roses.

"I love you, Jessie James, and I'll do whatever you want me to do," said Hal.

"Good," she said quickly with a hint of a smile. "Go get me red roses, you nincompoop. Yellow roses represent a platonic relationship."

"C'mon, Jessie, it's late," he explained. "This is the only color they had. I got you eighteen yellow roses in a beautiful bouquet because I think you're worth more than just a dozen."

Flashing a smile as bright as the full moon, Jessie winked at Hal and said, "Now, that's exactly what Gene Pitney would say." She hugged him and whispered in his ear, "But Gene Pitney would have bought red roses."

They both laughed. It made Hal feel very good, but she didn't say "I love you," and Hal didn't even notice.

Chapter Twenty Nine

Hal's plane was scheduled to depart about an hour after Jessie's, so he waited with her at her gate. Both had to make connections at O'Hare in Chicago, but they would be at different terminals, so this was the last time they would see each other until after Christmas.

As they sat there holding hands, Hal suddenly blurted out, "Hey, Jessie, how 'bout Christmas in Connecticut?"

"C'mon Hal," she said in a frustrated manner. "We've already worked this all out. You're going to Milwaukee, and I'm going to LA."

"No, no, I mean when we come back here to work with Gene," he explained to her. "Neither one of us has had time to do any Christmas shopping for each other, so I thought we could have OUR Christmas when we come back to Connecticut. How 'bout it?"

"You're a sweetheart, Hal," she said as she leaned in to kiss him, "and I am going to miss you so much."

"United Flight 97 to Chicago is now boarding," came the announcement over the loudspeaker.

Jessie jumped up, pulled Hal up with her, and gave him another warm, tender kiss and a big hug. "I will call you in Milwaukee, Hal Douglas. You'd better be there."

One more kiss and she darted off to the boarding gate.

Again, she didn't say "I love you." But, this time, Hal noticed it.

Chapter Thirty

Hal was sleeping soundly in his old bed in his parents' lower-middle class home in Milwaukee when his mom woke him up.

"Honey, Rick Starr is on the phone. I told him you got in late last night and you were still sleeping, but he said it was important."

There was only one phone in the Douglas' aging, two-story home on Oakland Avenue on Milwaukee's aging East Side. Hal had offered to buy his parents a new home anywhere they wanted, but they insisted that they were comfortable where they were.

That one lone phone was in the dining room — downstairs. Hal got up, put on his favorite green and gold Green Bay Packers sweatshirt and a pair of running shorts, and trudged downstairs.

The well-worn house felt like it was sixty degrees. He shivered a bit as he called out to his mother who was now in the kitchen tending to a new pot of coffee. "Mom, what's the chance we could turn the heat up to, oh, let's say, human survival level?"

"Harold, it's warm here in the kitchen," she said. "I've got the oven on and all the doors are closed. Your brothers and sisters are all at school, and Dad is at work. We don't need to heat the whole house."

His mother was the only person in the world who ever called him by his given name, Harold, and Hal knew that she only did it when she was irritated with him.

Hal grabbed the phone off the dining room buffet and said, "Good morning, Mr. Starr."

"Hal," Rick yelled excitedly into the phone, "you are now officially a millionaire."

Hal Douglas knew he was rich from his record and concert ticket sales, but he didn't believe he was a millionaire. Still a little groggy from his long flight from Connecticut the night before, Hal asked Starr what he meant.

"Well, that little Madison Square Garden showcase concert paid off," Starr said.

"That little Polack, Sam Stepniewski, from Family Films, made us an offer for six films for $6 million dollars. You're gonna be a movie star!"

Hal was trying to pull himself together mentally so as not to say the wrong thing to Starr. He needed to buy time because he wanted to talk to Gene. What he really wanted was Pitney — or anyone at this point — to just tell him what to do. Yes, he wanted to be involved in his career, but he was still too wet behind the ears to be making critical career decisions. But he wanted someone he could trust. After his discussions with Pitney about how Starr used and then discarded people left and right, Hal knew he didn't want Starr to be in charge of his career. And he didn't like Starr's use of the term "Polack." Hal wondered what Starr might be calling him behind his back.

"That's very exciting, Mr. Starr," said Hal. "Is everybody sure I can be a movie star?"

That put Starr on the defensive a bit and gave Hal more time to think as Starr answered his question. "Look, Hal, they're not gonna try to make you into the next Dustin Hoffman or Warren Beatty, OK? Family Films makes fluff movies aimed at teenagers. They do stuff like *Young Love, First Love*. Remember that?"

"Well, Mr. Starr, I don't go to a lot of movies, so I can't say that I'm familiar with that one," Hal said.

"Doesn't matter," said Starr, now sounding a bit impatient with his budding movie star. "They're gonna write some teenage-angst stuff, and you're gonna star in it. You'll get to kiss some pretty starlets in bikinis and then sing some songs. We're gonna cash the checks and live happily — and richly — ever after. Got it? I need you in LA to sign this deal. Now."

Now it was Hal's turn to get a little peevish. "Mr. Starr, I was on the road for you for a whole year. I came home to be with my family for Christmas. If they want me to sign a contract and pay me $6 million dollars to star in their movies, why can't they come here to Milwaukee?"

Rick Starr wasn't used to his stars talking back to him. Of course, most of his stars were one-hit or two-hit wonders. None of them had ever come close to the level of stardom that Hal had already achieved. Starr knew instinctively that Hal Douglas was destined for superstardom. Hal was a cash cow, and Starr did not want him wandering off the farm.

Now Starr had to balance his greed with his ego. He did not like to be manipulated or pushed around. He felt Hal was getting a little pushy, but he wanted to continue to get a piece of the action of Hal's career now and forever.

"OK, Hal. We'll do it your way," Starr said very tensely over the phone "but you're making my job harder, and that's gonna cost you money."

There was silence on Hal's end.

Starr waited but got no response to his last statement. He wondered if he had gone too far. Starr felt that Hal Douglas was still very naïve about show business — bordering on stupid. He never said it, but he also felt that Hal was pretty much an unsophisticated hayseed from Wisconsin.

Starr didn't know that Hal had been having career discussions with Gene Pitney. He didn't know that Hal was quickly learning the ropes and was very interested in taking more control over his career. If Starr had known all that, he probably wouldn't have lost his temper and said what he said next.

"Don't make me play hardball with you, Hal!" Now Starr was shouting. "Just remember it was me who got you away from your stupid loser Pals and made you an international star; remember it was me who found 'My Only Girl' for you to record; remember it was me who put that Madison Square Garden showcase together for you at my expense. I'm calling the shots, and you'll do what I tell you to do."

Very politely, Hal responded, "Mr. Starr, I owe you a lot. Everyone knows that."

Up to this point Hal had felt more than a little guilty about talking to Gene Pitney about dropping Rick Starr and running his own career with Pitney's guidance. Not anymore.

"Mr. Starr, you're upset right now, and I'm not thinking clearly because of my long flight last night. Let's not say anything else we don't mean. I promise I will call you after the holidays. I hope you have a blessed and safe Christmas. Thank you for everything you have done for my family and me. Bye, bye."

Hal was very upset as he hung up the phone. Rick Starr had threatened him about money, maligned his former band mates from Hal's Pals, and pretty much indicated that Hal had no say in his career at all. All of it was very insulting, Hal thought. He was now convinced that Gene Pitney was right: it was time to take control of his career.

Just then, his mother walked in the room with a steaming cup of coffee and asked, "What did that nice Mr. Starr want to tell you that was so important?"

Hal never lied to his mother, but he had to measure what he said to her now. "He wants me to do some movies, Mom," Hal said truthfully. "But I'm not sure they are the kind of movies I want to do. And, I don't even know if I can act."

"Oh, my. He doesn't want you to do dirty movies does he, Hal?" she exclaimed.

"No, Mom, he wants me to do movies like Elvis does."

"Well, your father and I saw that *Viva Las Vegas* movie," she said. "You know Dad has always wanted to go to Las Vegas. We thought that was a fun movie. Elvis seems like such a nice boy. Have you met him yet? Maybe you could ask him about those movies."

"I told Mr. Starr that I will talk to him after Christmas. I'm here to spend the holidays with you guys. I don't want to talk business. And, no, Mom, I haven't met Elvis. But, when I do, I'll get an autographed picture for you."

"That's very sweet of you, Hal," said his mother as she gave him a hug. "Get one for Dad, too. I think you should do some of those movies like Elvis."

"And I think you should turn the heat up," said Hal with a smile as he hugged his beloved mother.

"Go back to bed *Harold* and put an extra blanket on. That saves money."

"As long as I'm up, I have to make one more call to New York," Hal said. "I'll pay for the long distance charges, Mom."

"Oh, Hal, you worry too much about our finances," his mother said. "Dad and I are doing just fine. We don't need a lot, you know."

She kissed him on the cheek and went back into her warm and cozy, oven-heated kitchen, closing the door tightly behind her.

Hal went back upstairs and found the business card of the New York accountant who handled Gene Pitney's money. Returning to the still-chilly dining room, he dialed the phone number of Dick Naber, CPA.

Chapter Thirty One

Jessie James always slept naked. This morning she woke up at nine o'clock with all of the blankets on the floor — and yet — she was warm. She was back home at her parents' Beverly Hills mansion. It was already sunny and sixty degrees outside — and — seventy four degrees inside.

Her mother, two-time Oscar winner Jayna James, had low blood pressure and was always cold. So, day in and day out, twelve months a year, the James' home was kept at seventy four degrees. Jessie, too, liked to be warm. She really hated cold weather, and in her teenage years vowed never to live anywhere that had cold, snowy winters. No matter what.

Jessie couldn't believe how happy she was to be back in California, back in Beverly Hills, back in her parents' home, and back in her own bedroom. And back in warm weather.

She had fallen asleep the night before while listening to Sam Riddle, her favorite Boss Jock, on KHJ Radio. She woke up to Robert W. Morgan, the morning guy, playing "Next Plane To London" by The Rose Garden. She thought that was funny since she might be on an airplane to London with Hal Douglas and Gene Pitney in the very near future.

Her bedroom window faced east, and it was right over the good-sized swimming pool in the James' well-manicured backyard. Her bedroom and the pool were the first to greet the California sunshine every morning.

In spite of the music on the radio, Jessie could hear conversation drifting up from the pool through her open window. She could hear her mother talking on the phone, and she heard her own name crop up in the conversation.

"I don't know what Jessie's plans are," Jayna James said to her friend Bonnie Harmon, the mother of Jessie's fiancé Danny Harmon, on the other end of the phone line. "She mentioned the possibility of going on a British tour with Hal and some singer named Gene Pitney next year. You know I don't listen to that kind of music, but Jessie said he's a huge star and a great singer. Other than that, I don't know anything."

Then there was silence. Jessie couldn't hear Bonnie's end of the conversation.

Then she heard her mother again. "Oh, those plans. Her plans with Danny. I don't know that either. I presume they're still engaged, but you wouldn't know it by those pictures I saw in Photoplay last week. Danny looked pretty cozy with that adorable little starlet, what's her name, Allison Faith or something like that?"

Silence again. Jessie, still naked, walked over to the window to look.

"Oh, Bonnie, I know it's all about publicity, but he needs to be a little more discreet about who he's sleeping with when Jessie is on the road," Jayna said as she sat, fully-clothed, on a custom-made, heated chaise lounge.

"I know that Jessie is no angel, but she's not tramping around with every boy singer known to modern man. But, even if she is, she's not letting photographers take big, beautiful color pictures of her tongue in their mouths. That's all I'm saying, Honey."

The conversation didn't surprise Jessie. She knew that Danny Harmon would never be faithful to her or anyone. He was one of the hottest young movie stars in Hollywood before he won an Academy Award for his starring role in the WWII movie *Gunning For Hitler*. After he picked up that Oscar, he was the king of the hill in Hollywood. Any movie was his; any woman was his. And everyone in Hollywood knew that Danny Harmon was very picky about his movies but not about his women.

As her mother was ending the phone conversation, Jessie turned away from the window and went to her closet. She didn't want her mother to know she had been listening in. She put on a T-shirt, underpants, and shorts and headed down to join her mother at the pool for breakfast. She wanted to open a conversation with her mother about Danny and Hal — and the rest of her life.

Jessie was ecstatic to be back home with her parents, especially her mother, and she bounded onto the patio that surrounded the pool and almost jumped into her mother's arms.

"I LOVE you, Mom, and I LOVE California," Jessie said with unbridled joy. "This is all so perfect. The sunshine, the light breeze, the beautiful flowers and palm trees. Why would anyone want to live anywhere else?"

"I love you, too, Jessie," replied her still-gorgeous movie star mother. "And your father and I are very glad you're back home — even for a short while. Other people live in other places because that's where they were born," she added with a laugh. "Don't tell them about this paradise. They'll all want to move here, and then our freeways and supermarkets will be even more crowded than they are now."

Jessie looked over all the fruit on the platter on the table that was set for two. She put a handful of grapes on her plate, poured some coffee, and casually asked, "Where's Dad?"

Jessie's dad, Jansen James, the retired governor of California, now worked as a high-paid political consultant. "Governor Reagan is in Los Angeles this week, and he's asked your father to accompany him on all of his meetings," her mother said. "Ronnie is still learning the ropes, and he asked Dad to stay close to him. I think Dad is bringing Ronnie and Nancy here tonight for dinner. Can you join us?"

Jessie thought this would be a good opportunity to broach the subject of Danny Harmon with her mother. "Only if I can invite Danny over," she said coyly, not letting on that she had overheard her mother's phone conversation with Danny's mom.

Jayna James put her coffee cup onto her saucer, looked at Jessie, and said, "We'd love to have Danny come over, Honey. I think Ronnie and Nancy would love to meet him."

Jessie was a little disappointed, thinking that her mother hadn't taken the bait. Then Jayna added with a goodly amount of motherly concern in her voice, "What exactly is going on with you and Danny?"

"Oh, Mom, I've got to talk to you about that," Jessie said with more than a hint of relief in her voice. "You've got to help me figure this all out."

In rapid-fire speech, Jessie explained her personal and professional relationship with Hal Douglas and Gene Pitney, how she felt about Danny Harmon, and what she now needed to do with her business relationship with Don Jon Ross because of Tony Winston.

"So, you've slept with Hal? Is that what I heard?" her mother asked very non-judgmentally.

"Yes," said Jessie with no hint of embarrassment. "We plan on getting married. But Mom, I think I walked into that in the heat of the moment. I'm not sure I want to marry anybody right now. I know I don't want to marry Danny, even though it would be good for my social life in Hollywood. I don't think I really want to marry Hal, right now either, even though I do think I love him, and I know it would be good for my career. And I feel a little guilty about Don Jon Ross and how he's going to be manipulated, but he's going to get rich, so that mitigates a lot of my guilt."

Jayna James smiled at her beautiful daughter and, with a sly grin on her face, said, "Honey, this sounds like one of those wacky 1930s B-movies. It would have made a great script for Clark Gable and Claudette Colbert as a follow up to *It Happened One Night*, wouldn't it?"

"Mom, that's not helpful," said Jessie. "Insightful, but not helpful."

Paraphrasing one of the lines from *It Happened One Night*, Jayna took her daughter's hand and said, "Jessie, I think you're smart enough to know that you're just a headline to Danny. To him, this engagement is just a PR stunt. I don't think he wants to marry you any more than you want to marry him. He wants to screw every Hollywood star and starlet that he can while he's on top." Pausing and raising her eyebrows at Jessie, she continues, "He would be relieved if you broke it off."

A smile took over Jessie's face. Beaming she said, "OK, Mom, one down, two to go. What about Hal and Don Jon?"

"Let's talk to Dad about Don Jon," said Jayna. "But if he is going to get as rich as you and this Gene Pitney say he is from this little love song, I don't think that's a problem either. Dad will pick up the phone, and before you can say 'Yes! No! Yes!,' Don Jon will do what he is told to do with that pig Tony Winston."

"You're two-for-two, Mom," Jessie blurted out, "but, I think dealing with Hal is going to be the hardest component of this whole situation. What would you do if you were me?"

"I'd ask for a re-write on the script," her mother said with a hearty laugh. "Failing that, I could have my agent, Howie Brown, talk to Hal about how a marriage at this point could kill your careers. You know, the girls will get mad at Hal for not marrying them and then won't buy his records and won't go to his shows to punish him. Howie can spell out all the inherent dangers for performers dealing with their teenage fans. It happens in Hollywood every day; that's why young movie idols are always single."

"That's what I said, too, but hearing it from Howie would certainly drive the point home. I think that's the trifecta, Mom," said Jessie, now feeling much more in control of her life. "That's a load off my shoulders. Now I can really relax and enjoy being home."

There was a lingering moment of silence between mother and daughter. Both were stunningly beautiful women and major stars in their own fields, and they both knew it. They both had the whole world at their feet. Nonetheless, they both embraced the small things in their lives and felt blessed to have each other.

"Mom, I cannot tell you how much I love being home with you and Dad," Jessie said with tears starting to form in her eyes. "I have all the success that I ever wanted, but this makes me the happiest. Being here, with you and Dad, in California, in this house. I LOVE you so much." And the dam burst.

Overcome by her daughter's soul-baring emotions, Jayna said, "You light up our world when you're here, Jessie. As your dad has told you since you could comprehend it, 'For you…the world.' We hope you know how true that is."

Jayna James looked wistfully at her gorgeous daughter, now on top of the pop music world, and spoke quietly to her. "When I sit out here in the morning, I drift into my memories of your growing up right here on this patio and in this pool. Dad teaching you how to swim; my hosting your outdoor sleepovers with your girlfriends; the cookouts and parties with our family and friends where you would hold your talent contests and shows. Most of it unfolded right here on this patio in this backyard.

"Those Oscar nights were great, Jessie, but I look at them as events that I had to be at. Everything that happened here I wanted to be at. It's a double-edged sword for us, Jessie, this life of yours. While Dad and I were thrilled to watch you grow up and mature right here, at the same time we realized that you were slipping through our fingers. We were just preparing you for the rest of the world to enjoy and embrace. We are so proud of what you have accomplished."

Trying to lighten the emotional moment, Jessie said, "That sounds like a great song title, Mom. I should write 'Slipping Through Our Fingers' before someone else does. And, I gotta tell you, I was very proud that you knew my song 'Yes! No! Yes!'"

Jayna once again took her daughter's hand in hers and said, "Jessie, I know every word to every song you've recorded. And, you know what else? Dad and I have danced quite often to Hal's record 'On The Street Where You Live,' right here on this patio. It was the lead-in to our very own outdoor sleepover — if you know what I mean — more than once. It's a pretty romantic record."

"Mother, I'm shocked," Jessie said, starting to giggle. "You and Dad have had sex out here on the patio?"

Jayna was laughing now, too, as she responded, "Yes, my dear, both in and out of the pool. You should try it if you haven't already."

"Hm-m-m," said Jessie. "That could be great breakup sex with Danny tonight. How fast can you get Governor and Mrs. Reagan out of here after dinner?"

The laughter of the two stunning stars rang through the morning air.

Chapter Thirty Two

Don Jon Ross was talking on the phone to his soon-to-be newest star, Tony Winston. Ross had concocted a deal with Winston — off the top of his head — two weeks prior. Ross offered Winston, who was at the nadir of his career, a two-year deal that required him to record four albums: two albums of songs that Ross chose, one album of World War II classics, and a Christmas album. The deal was significantly tilted in Don Jon's favor: a flat per-album fee paid to Winston with some catches. Only half of the yet unspecified fee would be paid in upfront money. There would be a 50/50 split on the back end money between Winston and Sunshine Records after expenses, expenses that Don Jon Ross could control and create to his advantage. Those were not spelled out in the deal offered to Winston over the phone. Tony Winston was not as shrewd as Don Jon's other star, Jessie James, who had demanded — and received — approval of any expenses over $250 as part of her deal.

In the wake of the huge success of his major recording artist Jessie James, Ross was looking to expand his Sunshine Records label. He figured he could pick up Tony Winston "for a song," as he said to his brother, Jim Tim, and his sister, Fay Kay. If Winston agreed to this deal, Don Jon was right.

Not counting the Christmas songs, Tony Winston's last pop hit — before tragedy struck him and his career — was in 1964. That's when he and his three sisters — known as the Churchill Sisters — topped the charts with "London Lady Falling Down," the theme song from the film of the same name. The song had won an

Oscar and re-launched the faltering career of the family act. They had scored a run of major hits in the late 1950s and early 1960s, coming off a win on the popular Teddy Griffin Talent Jamboree TV show in 1957.

But, in December 1964, his sisters were killed in a tragic car accident in Chicago. Tony's comeback died when his sisters died. A suicide attempt and a failed marriage to Jessie James had left Tony a personal and professional wreck.

A Chicago DJ friend of Tony's, Jimmy P. Stagg, had befriended Don Jon Ross when Stagg worked at KYA Radio in San Francisco. Stagg had heard through the radio grapevine that Ross was looking to sign new recording artists. He knew that Winston was down on his luck — and himself.

Stagg called his old friend Ross and "convinced" him to call Tony Winston. Ross really didn't have to be convinced. As soon as Stagg told him that the former star was available and "down on his luck — and himself," Ross knew this was a very exploitable situation for himself. He was on the phone with Winston five minutes after he hung up with Stagg.

"So, do we have a deal, Tony?" Ross asked a third time.

"Yes, I want to do this, Don Jon," said the sadly desperate Winston softly and calmly. "But, I'd like to meet you in person. I'd like to talk with you face-to-face."

"Great," said Ross. "Fly out to LA as soon as you can. Bring me your airline ticket, and I'll cover the cost," Ross said.

"That's very generous of you, Don Jon," said Tony. "Actually, I was hoping we could meet in Las Vegas. I'm going out there to see some friends and figured we could kill two birds with one stone."

Winston was fibbing a bit. After his attempted rape of Jayna James a few years back, he had agreed to a legal deal with Jansen and Jayna James never to step foot in California again under the threat of being blackballed from show business. The Las Vegas trip was just a cover story, though he did have friends he could visit there.

"I'll be heading out in December," Winston added. "Any chance we could meet there, Don Jon?"

"That's great, Tony," said Ross with a big smile in his voice. "I'll be there. I can't wait to meet Sunshine Records' next superstar. And, Tony, let me pick up the tab for your whole trip. I like to treat my stars like stars."

Don Jon Ross would use those receipts to charge to Tony Winston's expenses against the profits on his four albums. He was also going to get a free trip to Las Vegas, courtesy of Tony Winston's deal. After all, meeting up with his newest star, discussing a recording contract, and signing the deal all were legitimate business expenses.

Don Jon would also live like a king while in Las Vegas. No expense would be spared. He was going to enjoy himself, and there would be plenty more expenses to come, many of which Tony Winston would never expect.

Don Jon Ross hung up the phone with Tony Winston and immediately called the music editor at the LA Times, telling him of the impending deal with Sunshine Records' next star.

Chapter Thirty Three

Two days before Christmas, Don Jon Ross called Jessie James at her parents' home in Beverly Hills. He needed to get his star into the studio to record a new bunch of songs. Jessie James was red hot, and Ross wanted to keep new songs available for her insatiable teenage fans.

Jayna James answered the phone, which shocked Ross. "Good morning, this is the James' residence," said the Oscar-winning actress in her very recognizable voice. After a moment of silence, Ross explained to her that he was taken aback because he was expecting a maid or a butler.

"You've been watching too many Hollywood movies, Mr. Ross," she laughed loudly. "We're very self-sufficient here. Governor James and I even do our own laundry and grocery shopping."

"I am a huge fan of yours, Mrs. James, and it would be an honor to meet you some time," Don Jon said with a bit of trepidation. He didn't want Jayna James to think — even for a second — that the reason he signed Jessie to his label was to get to her mother.

"Thank you, Mr. Ross," she replied. "That's very flattering. I do hope we can meet some time. Governor James and I are so very appreciative of everything you've done for Jessie. That record she made with you, 'Take Me Now,' was gorgeous. Did you want to speak with her?"

"Yes, please," Ross answered. "Sorry to call so close to Christmas. It's just a little business Jessie and I need to take care of."

Jessie was preparing to go on a Christmas shopping expedition with a few of her girlfriends from high school. These were the six girls she grew up with, had the sleepovers with at her house, and stuck with all through school. Two of them were heiresses, two of them were minor TV stars, and two of them had married money. It was pretty equal footing among the seven friends as far as ego and finances went.

She picked up the phone and said, "Hi, Don Jon, you caught me as I was heading out the door to go Christmas shopping."

"J-Squared," he said affectionately, "how's my superstar? The unwashed masses need more Jessie James' hits. We have to get into the studio, Sweetie. How's 'bout after Christmas?"

Jessie needed to buy time. She needed to stall Ross because of the plan that Gene Pitney was hatching to free Hal Douglas from Rick Starr and get Tony Winston off Sunshine Records.

She decided to tell Ross a half-truth. She didn't want to lie to him, but she couldn't let him in on Pitney's plan. "I'm going to need a little more time than that, Don Jon. I'm writing some songs myself, and they're not really ready to record yet."

Ross was willing to cut her some slack because of her efficiency in the recording studio. He knew that Jessie could record twelve songs in two days without breaking a sweat. And, each one of them would be a quality recording. She was that good.

"Here's the deal, Jessie," he explained. "We need to release your next single at the end of January so it's on the charts for Valentine's Day. I've got radio stations calling me already, wondering when the next single is coming out. I like that they're hungry for it, and I can't keep them waiting too long. Radio stations are as fickle as teenagers, Jessie. KHJ will find someone else's record for their next 'Hitbound.'

"I want to take an ad out in *Billboard* and *Cashbox* right after Christmas to promote the next single."

"How are you going to do that?" she asked. "We haven't recorded it yet."

"Oh, I know what it is, Jessie. Jim Tim, Fay Kay, and I wrote it yesterday. You'll love it."

Jessie knew Ross' siblings, Jim Tim and Fay Kay, quite well. Fay Kay had written "Take Me Now" and "Love Me Now," Jessie's first and third hit records respectively. Jim Tim was the composer of her second hit, the now iconic "Yes! No! Yes!"

Ross was trying to keep as much money and Sunshine Records business as he could in his family. He told Jessie the story about what her next Sunshine Records hit was going to be.

On his way into work two days prior, on the radio he heard "Have I The Right?" by The Honeycombs. That reminded him that it was one of his favorite songs of all time. He loved the production on the record, especially the driving, thumping drums. He raced to Sunshine Records because he had decided — then and there — to write an "answer" record to "Have I The Right?"

"We're calling it 'You Have The Right,'" he explained. "I wrote the first verse; Fay Kay got the second; and Jim Tim added the third. Jim Tim couldn't figure out how to get the same drum sound that The Honeycombs had on their record so he called their producer in England. You won't believe it. The band stomped their feet on the wooden stairs that led up to the studio, and the producer added that to the drum track. How fucking cool is that? Jim Tim has figured out how we can do that here."

"That's quite a family dynasty you've built there, Don Jon," she said laughing. "I can't wait to hear the song."

Jessie then took a step that she hadn't really considered until this conversation had started. She wanted a piece of the songwriting action. She knew there was a lot of money to be made as the songwriter on a hit record.

"But, this time, Don Jon, I get the flip side," she said somewhat curtly. "No more of your 'California Fun' crap. I want a song that I write on the flip side. And, I want to put some of my songs on the album, too."

Don Jon was extraordinarily giddy about "You Have The Right." He was convinced that with Jim Tim's precise production and Jessie's gutsy vocals it would be an instant #1. He didn't want to fight with Jessie James. He wanted her to go into the studio with even more fire than usual to record "You Have The Right."

"How many songs have you written?" he asked her.

Again, she didn't want to lie to him, so she told him the truth. "I've written one so far, but I want to do some more. It was fun and easy to do."

"What's your little gem titled?" Ross asked, a bit too condescendingly for Jessie's taste.

"Knock it off, Don Jon," she barked back. "You wouldn't want your little superstar to get sick and not be able to get into the studio, would you?"

Ross knew that he had been put on notice and responded sheepishly, "Sorry, Jessie. I'm just so excited about 'You Have The Right.' I think it could be one of the biggest selling singles of all time. I'm sorry. We'll put your song on the flip side. You'll make a fortune, too. What's it called?"

"Well, Don Jon, it's called 'A Lifetime of Love,' and this song is not going on the flip side of any record," Jessie said matter-of-factly. "It's written as a duet, and it will be the 'A' side of one of my next records. I'll write a different song for the flip side of 'You Have The Right.'

"A duet," he said incredulously. "That's a brilliant idea, Jessie. I've got just the guy to sing it with you. Did you read in the papers that I'm gonna sign Tony Winston to Sunshine Records? We're signing the contract in Las Vegas right after Christmas."

A cold shiver ran down her spine. As much as she wanted to scream at him until his ears were bleeding, she kept her cool. She also didn't want to let the cat out of the bag. "We'll talk about it in January."

"Jessie, I gotta know what's going on so I can buy those ads in the trade magazines," said Don Jon, suddenly deflated. "The ads will get the radio guys off my back. It's a promise to them that a new Jessie James record is coming out. You gotta help me here."

Jessie was silent for a moment as she pondered the situation. Then she said, "Don Jon, get a pen and paper."

He scrambled around on his desk and found a legal pad and a pencil.

"Here's your ad," she said confidently. "Write it down in capital letters."

THE BIGGEST HIT OF JESSIE JAMES' CAREER COMES OUT IN SPRING! YOU'LL BE SURPRISED! THE WHOLE WORLD WILL BE SURPRISED!"

Chapter Thirty Four

Christmas Day 1967 was cold and snowy in Milwaukee, Wisconsin, just the way that Hal Douglas had hoped it would be. He loved the Norman Rockwell Christmases that the Douglas family shared in their drafty, old home. He felt so much comfort around his parents and his siblings. Hal was going to make sure that THIS Christmas would be a Christmas for everyone to remember.

The Douglas family had trooped off to Midnight Mass at Saints Peter and Paul on Christmas Eve. Presents would be opened at nine o'clock Christmas morning around the Christmas tree that was set up in the dining room. Frank Douglas, called "Dad" by all of his kids, would call out names and hand out presents.

Nobody could open a present until everyone had one. Once that criterion was met, all hell broke loose. As presents were opened, Christmas wrapping paper, crumpled into balls, went flying around the dining room like multi-colored snowballs, each sibling picking out another unsuspecting sibling as a target. Only Mom and Dad Douglas had immunity from the wrapping paper wars.

Hal patiently waited — dodging wrapping paper fastballs coming his way — until all the presents under the ten-foot Christmas tree were handed out and opened. A lot of clothes, books, and a couple of bicycles were under the tree for the Douglas kids. As usual, Hal's mother found some WWII books for Hal. Reading about that world conflict was his passion. As the gift-opening excitement was ebbing, Hal handed his parents and each of his siblings an 8x10 manila envelope with a red bow on it.

As they all stared at their envelopes, Hal quietly said, "I'm in the Lou Gehrig club. Today I consider myself the luckiest man on the face of the Earth.

"I am only nineteen years old, and I have everything I've ever dreamed of. I'm a successful singer beyond my wildest dreams; I'm in love with a beautiful woman who is also in love with me; and I am in love with one of the greatest families in the world.

"I hope I've made each of you proud. I hope I can make each of you as happy as you make me. I promise I will never do anything in my career to intentionally hurt or embarrass you.

"From this day forward, Mom and Dad, you will never want for anything — ever. And, to each of my brothers and sisters, from this day forward, please know that I am always in your corner, spiritually, physically, and financially."

In his parents' envelope was a handwritten note from Hal. *Mom and Dad, I thank you for giving me life and for teaching me how to live that life. I promise to always make you proud of me. I know how hard your lives have been and how you tried to shelter us all from your trials and tribulations. I now want to share with you some of the blessings that the Lord has bestowed upon me. I have asked my accountant, Dick Naber, CPA, New York, New York, to arrange to pay off your home mortgage. Additionally, Mr. Naber has set up an appointment for you with Heiser Ford on the day after Christmas. Please go pick out any new car on the lot that you want. Mr. Naber will arrange payment. Finally, Mr. Naber will arrange for a $1 million trust fund to be set up for you at North Shore State Bank in January. It's yours to do with as you wish. Love you to a MILLION bits and pieces, Harold.*

In each of his siblings' envelopes was also a handwritten note. *The Douglas Family is like The Three Musketeers — except there are eight of us! One for all and all for one. Even the bad times were good in this house. The Lord has blessed all of us in different ways. We should continue to share our blessings with each other. I am living my dream. I want to help you live yours. I am arranging for a trust fund of $100,000 to be set up in your name at North Shore State Bank in January. There will be only one string attached to it: all the interest income derived from the trust fund must be given to a charity or charities that you designate with my accountant, Dick Naber, CPA, New York, New York. Otherwise, it is yours to do with as you wish. Use it wisely. Make sure you include Saints Peter and Paul Parish and Messmer High School in your giving! Your loving brother, Hal.*

It was the best Christmas ever at 2574 N. Oakland Avenue. There was not a happier family in the city of Milwaukee that Christmas. Hal was thrilled to use his success to make his whole family safe and secure because he needed very little in life to make him happy. He was very non-materialistic, and he considered the mountain of money coming his way as simply a tool to help others.

Yet, it did not go unnoticed to Hal that the love of his life, Jessie James, didn't call him on Christmas Day.

Chapter Thirty Five

Christmas Day 1967 was sunny and pleasant in Beverly Hills, California, just the way that Jessie James had hoped it would be. She loved the not-so Norman Rockwell Christmases that she shared with her parents. Give her a palm tree and sunshine over a Christmas tree and snow any time. Jessie wanted THIS Christmas to be memorable for her parents.

Jansen and Jayna James had everything that money could buy. They were both successful beyond belief in their chosen professions. They were respected for their talents, their ethics, and their philanthropy. Christmas shopping for them was almost impossible.

But, this year, Jessie had a unique idea. She had bought each of them some little gifts, just to have something wrapped under the tree, but she had hatched a very grandiose plan. She, too, had taken Gene Pitney's counsel and contacted accountant Dick Naber in New York.

Wiser in the worldly matters of high finance than Hal was, Jessie knew a year ago that she needed a financial advisor. Both of her parents had suggested their advisor, Jansen's brother Stewie James, but she had never followed up. Wanting to be independent from her parents on a business level, she, too, opted for Dick Naber, as recommended by Gene Pitney.

She worked quickly to ensure that her Christmas gift to her parents this year would be one that would allow their legacy to live on forever. Both of her parents spent a lot of time and a lot of money helping WWII veterans. Any time either of them was asked to appear at a benefit for the vets, they agreed immediately. Bob Hope, Jessie's godfather, tapped them often for USO benefits.

Jessie had arranged, through Dick Naber, to donate $1 million to the Veterans Administration to build a new Veterans Home in Los Angeles. She asked only that the VA name the new center the *Jansen and Jayna James VA Home for Heroes* and they be given some input into its location.

Jessie had it all planned out. She had arranged for her godfather, Bob Hope, to call her parents on this Christmas morning. As the phone rang, Jayna James walked towards the wall phone in the kitchen, asking out loud of no one in particular, "Who would be calling on Christmas morning?"

She recognized the voice on the other end immediately. "Bob, darling, does Dolores know you're bothering important people on Christmas Day?" she asked with a laugh.

"Hey, Jayna, Merry Christmas to you, too," Hope said in his trademark mile-a-minute speech pattern. "Look, my wife is not the boss of everything. She's just the boss of everything that I say, do, watch, buy, and eat."

"So, to what do we owe the pleasure of a call from Mr. Bob Hope on Christmas Day?" Jayna asked.

"It's about your Christmas present," he said.

Knowing the legendarily tight-fisted Hope never bought any of his friends or employees Christmas presents, Jayna was more than a little confused. "You got us a Christmas present?" she asked trying to hide her shock.

"No, no, no," Hope said. "It's about your Christmas present from Jessie. She wanted me to surprise you with it."

Sitting at the breakfast table in the nook of the kitchen that overlooked the backyard pool and patio, Jessie was smiling. Even though she could only hear her mother's side of the conversation, she knew what Hope was about to tell her, and Jessie couldn't wait to see the reaction.

"Can you get the Governor on an extension phone?" Hope asked. "I want him to hear this, too."

"Jan, it's Bob," Jayna called out to her husband, using the name that she and their close friends and family only used in private. "He wants to talk to us about some sort of Christmas present our daughter got us."

Governor Jansen James walked into the adjoining cavernous great room and picked up the phone. "Bob, you son of a gun. How the hell are you?"

"Jan, I'm great," Hope responded quickly. "Merry Christmas. I'm gonna need you and Jayna for a veterans benefit. It's for wounded vets. Can you pencil it in?"

Jayna James was now very confused but decided not to butt in and ask about the Christmas present surprise from Jessie.

"Give me the date, and I'll check my schedule," Jansen said. "If I have something on it that I can re-schedule you know Jayna and I will be there."

"I don't have the date yet," Hope said. "But, it will be some time next year."

This mildly irked the extraordinarily busy former governor of California, but he decided to play nice. "OK, Bob. Can you tell me where the wounded vets benefit is going to be held?"

"Sure can" Hope snapped back quickly. "At the *Jansen and Jayna James VA Home for Heroes.*"

That stopped Jansen in his verbal tracks. Jayna looked at their daughter, somewhat bewildered.

With a huge smile in his voice, Hope explained Jessie's Christmas gift to her parents and then said, to their shock, "I'm throwing in a million bucks, too. And I'm gonna strong arm Sinatra and Crosby. And I'm gonna get money from Dean Martin, Jerry Lewis, and Johnny Carson, too. We're gonna get that thing built for these guys. Jessie doesn't know that part of it. Let her know, please. Merry Christmas. I gotta go. See ya at the benefit." And the line went dead.

Jessie's parents were thrilled by the gesture — and the thought of all the vets who would benefit from their Christmas gift. They hugged their precious daughter and thanked her profusely. And her father said with a little laugh, "Oh, we almost forgot to tell you. Your godfather is kicking in a million dollars for the project, and he's going to 'fundraise' another $5 million from his rich and famous friends."

It was Jessie's turn to be thrilled by a kind gesture. As she sat in the warmth of the sun beaming into the bright yellow kitchen, her father quietly asked, "Jessie, might I ask, where are you getting a million dollars?"

"Dad," she exclaimed. "Do you know who I am? Do you listen to the radio? Do you know what I do?"

Jansen James, former governor of California and father of one of America's biggest pop stars answered, "In order, yes, no, yes. And that's not irony, Jessica!"

Jessica was her given name, but she disposed of it in fifth grade, favoring the riskier sounding "Jessie James." Her parents rarely called her Jessica. And when they did, it was only to get her attention.

"Jessie, your mother and I are very proud of you," Jansen said in a way only a father could. "I follow every aspect of your career even though I don't get to listen to the radio that much. But when I'm driving around Sacramento or LA and one of your songs comes on, I crank my car windows down and I crank the radio up. I know all the words to all your songs."

"But a million dollars," Jayna said with a question mark in her voice.

"Don't worry Mom," Jessie assured her. "I got a guy...in New York...good with numbers. It's all good to go."

Jessie's parents started calling all of their friends. They were so excited by the gift and so overwhelmed by the generosity of their daughter that they almost forgot to give her the gift that they had for her.

Then Jayna handed Jessie a neatly wrapped package the size of a Kleenex box. "This is for you, Jessie," said Jayna. "We think it will fit you perfectly."

That comment threw Jessie off. She really had no idea what could be in the box as she carefully opened it. Inside was a contract. Their gift to her was her very own TV show. Jansen and Jayna James were going to produce a musical variety show for her in partnership with Ziv Television Programs. Ziv was the syndication company responsible for such huge TV hits as *Sea Hunt*, *Death Valley Days*, *The Adventures of Superman*, and *Mr. Ed*.

Jessie was stunned. She was going to get her own TV show, and she was going to get to sing on her own TV show, and she was going to get to work with her parents on her own TV show.

"I can't believe this," was all she said. She really didn't know how to react because this was nothing she could have ever dreamed of receiving…as a Christmas present…from her parents…or from anyone, for that matter.

"I can't believe this," she repeated. "I'm flabbergasted. A TV show. You gave me a TV show for Christmas. This is too much to comprehend. I'm trying not to cry, but I think I'm going to cry."

Then, the usually sophisticated and reserved James family was jumping around and hugging each other like sugar-charged ten-year-old kids at a birthday party. It was a joyous, profound, and memorable Christmas for them.

The excitement of getting a shot at TV stardom so consumed her that she completely forgot to call Hal until she was falling asleep just after midnight. "I'll call him tomorrow," she murmured to herself as she snuggled under the blankets.

Chapter Thirty Six

Christmas Day 1967 was just another day for Don Jon Ross. He didn't celebrate the holiday. He had no interest in it. Orphaned at the age of three when his parents were killed in a fire, Don Jon never experienced the warmth of a real family Christmas. Their iron-fisted spinster Aunt Mechtilde had raised him and his siblings Fay Kay and Jim Tim. Theirs was a very austere and severe childhood.

Don Jon spent this mild Los Angeles Christmas morning working on a couple of new songs he was writing for both Jessie James and Tony Winston. He did call both of his siblings, but no mention of Christmas was made. The Ross siblings liked each other well enough, but there were no outward signs of anything more than that. There were never any displays of affection, public or private. He simply called wanting to see how their songwriting was coming along. He was expecting them to be very prolific in 1968: he had two stars who needed material.

He assigned Jessie James to Fay Kay and Tony Winston to Jim Tim. Fay Kay was fine with that, and her conversation with her brother was over in less than two minutes.

But, the assignment didn't sit well with his brother. "Look, Don Jon," said Jim Tim. "I love to write these songs, and I'm very happy with the money I'm making, but I'm a little tired of being your marionette. You seem to enjoy making me dance like a little puppet. I want more say in what I write, who I write it for, and what goes on at Sunshine Records."

"You're making my ass tired, Jim Tim" was Don Jon's quick response to his younger brother's challenge to his authority. He continued the mini-lecture. "Look, everything you touch is not genius," he added. "I know what's best for Jessie and for Tony and — for that matter — for you."

But, wanting to keep the peace and keep the songwriting assembly line on pace, Don Jon decided quickly to pacify his brother instead of argue with him. "Jim Tim, I need your help to get these two albums done for Jessie and Tony, and then we can talk about a new business arrangement. I have been thinking of having you involved in some different areas of Sunshine Records as we expand, but we hafta get these albums done now.

"I want and need, really, really need Jessie's new single out for Valentine's Day. Tony's first single can wait until the middle of March. We'll need that month between Valentine's Day and, say, March 15th to promote Jessie's record and get it to #1. Then we can concentrate on Tony. After that, we'll restructure Sunshine Records. Deal?"

"I appreciate the thought you've put into my role at Sunshine Records," Jim Tim said. "I love what I'm doing Don Jon, and I thank you for the opportunity. I just want to do more, OK?"

"We'll take care of that in March," Don Jon said, relieved that he had avoided a near disaster. "I want 'You Have The Right' to be Jessie's next single, but I talked to her on the phone the other day, and she's angling for a song that she wrote to be the next release. She said she's written it as a duet. That's all I know. I'm talking with her more in January.

"So, one way or another, we have Jessie taken care of. But, we have to create a blockbuster for Tony Winston. By the way, I'm heading out to Las Vegas this afternoon to sign the deal with him later this week. You wanna go?"

Jim Tim appreciated the entreaty from his older brother and jumped at the chance to meet Tony Winston. Jim Tim was forever star struck, and Tony Winston was one of his favorite singers of all time. "Are you kidding me? What time are we leaving?"

"How many songs do you have ready for him?" Don Jon asked. "I figured we could go into the studio and cut some quick demos, then head out to Las Vegas."

Jim Tim had turned into a very efficient tunesmith. He could write a dozen songs a day, but usually only two of his daily musical creations ended up being keepers. The refining process to turn those two raw songs into quality songs that would merit the attention of a Jessie James or Tony Winston took a bit longer.

"I have four songs that I'm proud of right now, Don Jon. I've got another six that need some attention. We can demo those four songs pretty quickly today and take 'em with us."

Jim Tim was writing songs that fit Tony Winston's smooth balladeer style and some that would stretch and challenge him a bit. While he hadn't totally ignored Don Jon's suggestions to write some Bobby Vee-type songs for Winston, he still didn't want Don Jon to say "no" to any of the songs he had written because he had worked very hard on them. That's what had set off his short marionette rant. Being a huge Tony Winston fan, the project meant a lot to him.

"You should know up front, Don Jon, that the songs are probably not what you're expecting," Jim Tim said with just a little hesitation in his voice. "But, I promise you, they're all great songs. You're gonna have a problem deciding which one to release as the first single."

"OK, make me proud, Kid. It's ten o'clock now. I'll meet you at the studio at noon. I wanna hear some hits."

The first song that Jim Tim played on the piano that Christmas afternoon for Don Jon was titled "The Devil's Soul Is Black." Don Jon was stunned. "I've never heard anything like it. I love it. That's a #1 record."

"The Devil's Soul Is Black" was a combo platter of doo-wop, rhythm and blues, and pop. Jim Tim told his brother that they should spend any money needed to augment the record with strings and horns. And Jim Tim was adamant that a French horn should be the signature instrument on the record. He also implored his brother to get The Four Tops to sing on it.

"Don't scrimp on this one, Don Jon," he pleaded. "Please...this is my masterpiece."

Don Jon grinned from ear to ear. He hadn't really meant what he said to his brother earlier, about finding an expanded role for him at Sunshine Records. Don Jon was just trying to keep the peace then. Now, he was rethinking that. Jim Tim had already written a few hit records, but Don Jon was thinking there and then that Jim Tim might be a nascent musical genius.

"I'll give you what you want on that one, Jim Tim. What else do we have for Tony?"

Jim Tim surprised his brother with the other three songs, too. One was a waltz titled "I Ask Forgiveness," another was a soaring Gene Pitney-esque ballad, "Never Forever," and the third was the jaunty Bobby Vee-type song "Better Stay Away From Her." In the short time span of fifteen minutes, Don Jon Ross realized his brother had presented him with four of the greatest pop songs he had ever heard. Each one of them could go to #1.

"Good God, Jim Tim, where did all of this come from?" was all he could say. "With these songs we're gonna make Tony Winston three times the star he was before. It's almost a shame that he's getting these songs and not Tom Jones or Engelbert. You know what I mean?"

"Don't kid yourself, Don Jon," Jim Tim shot back, a little miffed at the shot that his brother had taken at one of his favorite singers. "Tony Winston is a very under-rated singer. With the right arrangements and the right producer, Tony will be perceived to be as good as or better than Tom Jones and Engelbert. And, by the way, I'm going to be the arranger and producer on Tony's album."

Christmas Day 1967 proved to be a life-changing day for both Don Jon and Jim Tim Ross. As they finished recording the demos for Tony Winston, Don Jon turned to his brother and said, "With apologies to Humphrey Bogart, Jim Tim, I think this is the beginning of a beautiful friendship."

Chapter Thirty Seven

Christmas Day 1967 was quiet at Rick Starr's palatial mansion in Pacific Palisades. No one was there. The public knew very little about Starr's private life. He paid handsomely for that. His compound of three residences, two garages, two swimming pools, and a tennis court was protected from prying eyes and potential prowlers by cypress trees intermingled with palm trees, thick bushes, and state-of-the-art security apparatus.

Starr employed a private security agency around the clock to protect him and his family. It might have been both overkill and a bit of a moot point because Starr never allowed his family to be with him in public, so no one really knew what they looked like. He was scared to death of being kidnapped and held for ransom like Frank Sinatra, Jr. was in 1963. "I'm more famous than that no-talent ever was," Starr was heard to say many times. He also feared for the safety of his wife and two daughters and — if truth be told — his bank account. He didn't want to pay out his money to ransom anyone.

A few years back, Starr's wife, Kim Klett, was a minor movie star. She was a pixie-ish, energetic blonde starlet who had appeared in many of the Frankie Avalon-Annette Funicello beach movies in the early 1960s. Because of his irrationally heightened fear of kidnapping-for-ransom, after they were married, Starr made her alter her looks — permanently. He paid for plastic surgery that changed her face enough that she couldn't be recognized when compared to her 8x10 publicity glamour shots from her movie days — or her wedding photos.

His money protected his daughters, too. Through a special arrangement with the private school they attended, Starr's two daughters, Brooke and Francesca (she was called Frankie), were enrolled under Starr's mother's maiden name. That "special arrangement" was a $25,000 annual contribution made by Rick Starr to the school. They were chauffeured to and from school in a private car with darkened windows. Since a number of movie and TV stars also sent their children to this private school, Starr's secretive transportation measures for his daughters didn't really get any attention at all.

For Christmas 1967, Rick Starr took his family on a skiing trip to the Very Vermont Ski Resort, a five-star resort in Stowe, Vermont, where there was no fear of being recognized. He was just one more anonymous rich guy treating his family to a holiday getaway. Rick Starr loved a white Christmas. He wanted to give his sun-kissed, California-born kids that Currier and Ives experience. The resort offered a "Christmas Eve Party with Santa Claus" and a "White Christmas Skiing Party" on the slopes with sleighs and real live reindeer. The whole family was going to take skiing lessons. Rick was hoping to make the Vermont trip an annual family tradition.

Like many people in the early days of rock 'n' roll, Starr grew up and got his start on the East Coast. He hailed from the Bronx and attended the same grade school that Dion DiMucci did. He was a few years ahead of the "Runaround Sue" star, but their families knew each other. Rick's real name was Ricardo Francesco Ruffalo. He was in a street gang before he was thirteen. The young Ricardo Ruffalo had moxie, street smarts, charm, and good looks. He was also fearless. No one pushed him around. These were all traits that took him to the zenith of the pop music world during the Golden Age of Rock 'n' Roll.

Rick loved his wife and daughters; he just loved his businesses and his money a little bit more. The Starr family wanted for nothing. Rick gave them everything that they wanted or needed that money could buy. He just couldn't give them the husbandly and fatherly attention they needed and deserved. That kind of attention was only and always devoted to business.

Kim Klett became accustomed to many things after meeting and falling for Rick Starr. At first, she liked how possessive he was of her; then she began to resent it. Eventually she became accustomed to it. The downside was that it was perceived by many of her friends as a troubling and controlling May-September relationship; the upside was it made Rick happy, and that was always good. An angry Rick Starr was a dangerous Rick Starr.

Kim also originally liked how concerned he was about her security — and his own — in the wake of the Sinatra kidnapping. But, she truly resented it when he suggested she get plastic surgery to change her looks. Eventually she accepted it. The downside was that it took away her identity; the upside was that it gave her a whole new sense of freedom.

Kim Starr — ten years younger than her husband — learned to like the superficial relationship after a while. As a matter of fact, she enjoyed the freedom it gave her to do what she wanted, with whom she wanted, whenever she wanted to do it. Nonetheless, she was also a fiercely loyal and doting mom.

In spite of her love of the good life with all of her Beverly Hills housewife friends, her kids always came first. She was always home when they returned from school; she was always home to share supper with them; she was always there to tuck them into bed.

She did resent Rick for not having a close relationship with his daughters. There was no daddy's-little-girl relationship with either one of them. Kim had been and still was her daddy's little girl, and she cherished that relationship with her father. She wished her girls could have known what it was like to be truly adored by their father. As it was, they had to settle for their daddy buying them things and taking them on trips.

The girls were too young to know that what they had was just a superficial relationship with their father. All too soon, Kim thought, they would sense the estrangement and feel a certain emptiness. The trade-off was that they would always have all the creature comforts they wanted, but Kim knew that possessions could never replace relationships. One could get accustomed to pretty dresses and expensive jewelry, but there was never getting accustomed to a lonely heart. The Beatles song always sprang to mind, *money can't buy you love.*

For Kim, her arm's-length marital relationship with Rick Starr was an okay trade-off because she still had her golden relationship with her father. Her daughters would never have that. In addition to making her resentful, that made her sad. She only hoped that she could build a loving relationship with her girls that could inure them to their father's lack of a deep-seated love for them.

Chapter Thirty Eight

Christmas Day 1967 was a melancholy and sad day for Tony Winston.

At the height of their career comeback, his three beloved sisters, Mary, Marie, and Maria, better known as The Churchill Sisters, had been killed in a tragic car accident in Chicago just before Christmas 1964. Since then, Christmas was a sad time of year for the entire Ranzunno family.

Tony was also getting set to travel to Las Vegas to ink his new recording contract with Don Jon Ross from Sunshine Records. The three years since the tragic turn of events had been excruciatingly cruel to him. His career went into a tailspin after his personal life went into nuclear meltdown. Winston's failed marriage to Jessie James, marred by his attempted rape of her movie star mother, led to a second suicide attempt that was less publicized than the first.

He felt, on the one hand, the phone call he received from Don Jon Ross gave him a new lease on life — both personally and professionally. He wanted very badly to be a star again. He loved life at the top of the hill. He would do just about anything to reclaim his stardom. He was desperate for it. But, on the other hand, he was uneasy about Don Jon Ross and the proposed deal.

As a light afternoon snow fell in his hometown of Kenosha, Wisconsin, Tony sat in a well-worn corner bar that was festively decorated for Christmas, talking with the owner, Steve "Shortstop" Alioto. Tony and Alioto first met in kindergarten. After a bit of a tussle over some chocolate milk that Tony claimed "accidentally jumped" out of his mouth onto Alioto's crisp white shirt, the two Italian kids bonded and became inseparable throughout high school. Alioto was a widower and opened the bar every day except his birthday. It was his life.

Tony's show business career took off and took him to undreamed of heights. Alioto's hoped-for baseball career was ended when his knee was ripped apart by the spikes of an opposing minor league player sliding into him at second base. Alioto had been drafted by the Milwaukee Braves and assigned to their Louisville Colonels farm team. The Braves thought he would be their shortstop of the future as Johnny Logan's career was starting to fade. But, that was not to be. After the career-ending injury, Alioto took his signing bonus money and bought a bar in his hometown, where he would always be a star to the infatuated locals.

"Jeez, Tony," said Alioto as his buddy downed another Schlitz. "What could be so bad about signing another big record contract?"

"I don't trust the guy, Shortstop," said Winston, using the name that everybody in Kenosha called his friend. "Not that I have any other options, but there's just something that rubbed me the wrong way when I was yapping with him on the phone. Plus, who the hell has a rhyming name? Don Jon Ross! I just wanna slap the guy. Know what I mean?"

"You're feeling sorry for yourself, Tony," said Alioto. "I know this is a tough time for you what with the girls dying the way they did before Christmas. But you're the one who is in here day after day complaining about all the no-talents on the radio while you're wasting away here in Kenosha. Do you know how many other singers out there would love to sign a big record contract like the one you're getting?

"This Don Jon guy is giving you another chance, Tony. You should be grateful. If I didn't know you the way I do, I would say that you should be kissing his keester. That's what I would tell you if you were just another guy drinking in my bar."

Alioto just stared at Winston for about a minute as the fallen star gazed out the window, not saying a word. Alioto thought that he was pouting, just like he used to do when he didn't get his way in grade school.

Then he said, "Tony, I'm telling ya, I would give almost everything I have in my life to get a second chance to chase my dream. I was gonna be the next Johnny Logan. You know that, right? I was gonna be the next big thing for the Milwaukee Braves.

I was gonna play in the World Series and the All Star Game. Now look at me. I'm an oddity. I'm the guy who *almost* made it. There is no second chance for me. Like him or not, trust him or not, Don Jon Ross is doing you a favor. He's giving you a third chance. You should be humble enough to kiss his fanny but smart enough to keep your eye on him. That's my advice. No charge."

Tony picked up his glass of beer, looked at his long-time friend, then raised the beer and said, "*Chin don*, Shortstop! You're right. I can make this deal work for me. Don Jon Ross is a chump who runs a two-bit record company out in Los Angeles.

"He's no match for me. I've recorded for one of the biggest record companies in the country; I had some of the biggest hits in the history of music; I've been on the biggest TV shows around; the biggest stars in the world like Frank Sinatra and Tony Bennett are my friends. I can beat him at his game — and I don't even know what his game is. Yet."

"There you go," said Alioto. Then, with deep concern in his voice, he told his friend, "Now, go home Tony. No more Schlitz. What time is your flight tomorrow?"

"It's OK, Shortstop," said Winston. "I'm OK. It's an afternoon flight. I'll sleep it off."

As Winston put on his coat to leave, he took out a plain white envelope and handed it to Alioto. "A Christmas present for my oldest and best friend," Winston said. Then he turned and left the bar.

Alioto opened the envelope and found a hand-written note wrapped around a check. The check was for $10,000. The note read: *"Shortstop, I know you've run up some medical bills with your diabetes problems. I'm guessing your insurance isn't all that great. I hope this helps. I don't want to hear a word about it from you. Got it?"* Tony R.

Alioto couldn't believe it. He hadn't told Tony that he was facing bankruptcy and losing the bar because of his medical bills. He was too proud for that. This changed everything. He made the sign of the cross and whispered, "Thank you, Jesus, for a friend like Tony. Please always keep him in your loving arms and tender mercies. Amen."

Chapter Thirty Nine

Christmas Day 1967 was a new experience for Gene Pitney. It was the first Christmas that he was a dad. His son, Todd, born in August, was still sound asleep, as he and Lynne opened the gifts that they had gotten for each other.

He presented his bride with a beautiful 1968 Jaguar — sort of. "To match your gorgeous red hair," he said to her as he showed her a picture of the gleaming red car.

"You sure know how to treat a girl," she said with a soft purr and a knowing smile. "A picture of a car that you cut out of a magazine. Well, Mr. Pitney, I'm here to tell you that it just doesn't get any better than that."

Then they both broke out in gales of laughter.

"It's at the showroom right now," Gene explained. "I custom ordered it, and they are putting on the finishing touches. The dealership will have it delivered from Boston next week."

"Sounds like a pick-up line to me, Mr. Pitney. But, I'll fall for it! Can't wait to drive it!"

The red Jaguar was extraordinarily significant to Lynne because one of her favorite songs recorded by her superstar husband was "The Boss's Daughter." The song was a Top 20 hit in Australia and was the flip side of one of Pitney's medium-sized hits in the UK, "(In The) Cold Light of Day." The song included the line, *she drove me in her own red Jaguar*, with Pitney singing the word "Jaguar" in three syllables as only he could.

Lynne then pulled a large, beautifully wrapped box out from under the tree and presented it to her husband, saying, "For my friend, my husband, my hero."

As Gene slowly inspected the gift-wrapped box and mumbled about it being "too pretty to rip open," Lynne thought about the great lengths she had gone to secure the gift, and she hoped that Gene would be happy with it.

"A case of Harrods Tea," Gene said, somewhat dumbfounded. "Lynne Pitney, how in God's name did you get a case of Harrods Tea all the way from London?"

She knew then and there that her gift was a winner. Gene was not a coffee drinker. He loved his tea, and after every British tour, he constantly raved about the tea from the world-famous Harrods department store on Brompton Road in London. "The best in the free world," he would always say to her.

"How did you do it?" he asked again.

"Well, 'how' is the operative term," she explained. "Actually it's Howes. Arthur Howes. Your tour promoter took care of it."

"You got Arthur to do this for me?" he asked, still incredulous.

Arthur Howes was one of the biggest rock 'n' roll tour promoters in all of England. His clients included most of the biggest stars of the British Invasion, including The Beatles.

"To be honest, Gene," she said with a little laugh, "Arthur did it for ME. I called him up while you were out on tour with The Troggs and told him how much you adored the Harrods tea. I asked him to send me a year's supply so I could maybe keep you at home for a while. Merry Christmas!"

"I'm home now, so why don't we brew some of this up," Gene said. "It will put me in the mood to work on my plans for Hal and Jessie. I've been tinkering with that song they wrote that they want to duet on, and I've been mapping out their business strategies for next year, but I've got some problems to work out."

As the young couple walked into the kitchen to make the tea, Lynne turned into him, gave him a hug, and said, "I like them, Gene. I just wanted to hug little Hal and take care of him. He seems like a sweet boy. Jessie is gorgeous, and she looks like she's really in love with Hal. Do you think it will all work out?"

"Well, that song they wrote, 'A Lifetime of Love,' isn't exactly Burt Bacharach and Hal David material," Gene pointed out very matter-of-factly. The Brill Building team had written four of Gene's biggest and best hits, "Only Love Can Break A Heart," "Twenty-Four Hours From Tulsa," "(The Man Who Shot) Liberty Valance," and "True Love Never Runs Smooth."

"It's a little weak lyrically, but I've got Al Kooper writing a third verse, and he's lining up a Harlem church choir to sing on it, too. Those two components will make it a great record. Then we'll throw some strings and horns on it like Burt does, and it soars to #1, guaranteed. It will be so different from anything else out there — and anything else either one of them has ever done before."

"It seems like you've got that solved," Lynne said. "What problems do you still have?"

"Jessie came up with the idea of my singing on it, too, as a way to cross-promote the upcoming UK tour. I haven't figured out a good way to incorporate me into the record that makes sense. If you can come up with anything, let me know."

Then, with a wink, he added, "I'll cut you in on the profits."

"That's simple," she said as she pulled the whistling teapot off the stove burner. She nodded her head towards the whistling kettle.

"Simple?" he said with astonishment. "I've been trying to construct a third-voice-on-a-duet scenario since they left, and I can't figure it out. And that's hard for me to believe because all of the music magazines and newspapers in England call me a musical genius. A Genius with a capital G!"

Now Lynne was waving the whistling tea pot right in front of him. Gene looked at the whistling pot, then looked at his gorgeous wife staring at him with mockery in her eyes, raised his hands in the air like a lawyer presenting his closing argument to a doubting jury, then mocked himself, "Maybe Gene could whistle on the record."

"That's a good idea, but I have an even better one...a great idea," said Lynne. "All you have to do is sing with the choir. Just be up front so we can pick your voice out."

"That's it!" Gene exclaimed.

"I'd like ten percent of the profits Genius with a capital G," she said, shaking her head. "I can see it at the top of the *Billboard* charts now, 'A Lifetime of Love' by Hal Douglas and Jessie James featuring Gene Pitney and the So-and-So Harlem Choir. I'll take another five percent for that!"

Gene smiled, sipped his beloved Harrods Tea, gave his wife the thumbs up, and said quietly, "This is a good Christmas. A very good Christmas."

Then baby Todd started to cry.

Chapter Forty

In the early morning hours of New Year's Eve 1967, Gene Pitney was sitting in his basement office ruminating about the future and being slightly miffed about the recent past. He had just heard Frankie Laine's 1967 hit "Making Memories" on the radio and was quietly irritated that songs like that were no longer being presented to him.

"Damn it," he whispered. "That should have been my record!"

The sun was setting on Musicor Records, and Gene wasn't ready to ride off into the sunset with the label that had made him a wealthy international recording star, touring attraction, and pop idol. He was on the verge of taking complete control of his career — and perhaps the careers of the two biggest pop stars in the world, Hal Douglas and Jessie James.

The pieces of the puzzle were starting to fall into place. Pitney's long-time friend Johnny Tillotson had sent him a demo of the song that would go on the "B" side of "A Lifetime of Love."

Pitney listened to the tune, "The Tide Is Rising," and thought out loud, "Perfect. As mediocre as they come." He didn't want to run the risk of having DJs turn the record over and start playing the "B" side as they had done with his 1962 smash, "Only Love Can Break A Heart." He was convinced, for no good reason, that "Only Love Can Break A Heart" *would* have gone to #1 on the *Billboard Hot 100* if DJs hadn't split the airplay between the "A" side and "If I Didn't Have A Dime" on the

"B" side. He was just a tad bit more irritated with himself because when the record was first released he was actually urging DJs to play "If I Didn't Have A Dime."

It was really more of a blow to his ego than his bank account because the fact of the matter was that the song that kept his "Only Love Can Break A Heart" out of the #1 spot was The Crystals hit "He's A Rebel," a song Gene had written.

As part of the deal with Tillotson, Pitney was changing a couple of lines of lyrics so he could cash in on co-writing credits. He had thought of just adding his name to the song without actually doing any creative work on it, but he actually liked writing lyrics, so he got a pencil out of his desk drawer and went to work.

Tillotson had written this line:

The tide is rising
The wind is blowing
I'm floating to you
Our love is growing.

Pitney changed it to this:

The tide is rising
A flood from above
God sent you to me
God sent me your love.

Even though Tillotson's lyrics made much more sense, Pitney now felt better about the thousands of dollars he was going to potentially earn by being a co-writer and co-publisher of the song that would be on the flip side of what he believed was going to be one of the largest-selling singles in the history of music.

His next call was to Al Kooper. Kooper was busy with his new group Blood, Sweat & Tears but happily agreed to help Pitney by tweaking "A Lifetime of Love," writing a third verse. Pitney liked Al and always made sure that Kooper got a couple of his songs on Pitney albums in order to keep cash rolling in. However, in this case, Pitney misled Kooper, telling him that he was writing the song to pitch to another artist. Pitney was quietly calling in a marker, but he was also giving Kooper another chance to cash in.

Pitney gave Kooper only the information he absolutely needed and craftily did NOT tell him who the song nor the recording session was really for. Kooper and everyone else would presume the session was for Pitney because it was in Pitney's name and being billed to Pitney.

"Al," Pitney said, "I need a Black gospel choir on this song. I want production advice from you and recording time at Bell Sound in New York. And I need you to keep quiet about what we're up to. Can you do that for me?"

Without hesitation, Kooper replied, "Consider it done. Can you give me a week? I've got some shows with BS&T, and I got a little partyin' I have to do, too. But I'll write you the best third verse you've ever heard. And…thanks again, Gene. Thanks for everything."

With that key piece of the puzzle in place, Pitney immediately picked up his phone and dialed Hal Douglas' phone number in Milwaukee. He knew time was of the essence now. No matter how good Kooper was at keeping a secret, once he started making phone calls to secure a Black gospel choir and recording time for Gene Pitney at the famous Bell Sound Studios in New York, word would leak, and gossip would start. Pitney needed to keep any kind of news — official or unofficial — of this recording session from getting to Don Jon Ross or Rick Starr for as long as he could.

Chapter Forty One

The phone rang in the dining room at 2574 N. Oakland Avenue at nine o'clock on New Year's Eve morning. Hal Douglas' mom answered it the way she always did and the way her entire family was taught to answer it: "Douglas residence, Mrs. Douglas speaking. How may I help you?"

"Good morning, Mrs. Douglas. My name is Gene Pitney. I'm a friend of Hal's. It's very nice to speak with you. How was your Christmas?"

Rita Douglas may have been the fifty-three-year-old-matriarch of a family of eight, and she may have been brought up on Big Band and 1950s music, but she knew who Gene Pitney was. She listened to the radio from the moment she woke up until the moment she crawled exhaustedly back into bed. Her favorite station was WOKY, The Mighty 92, and they played a lot of Gene Pitney records.

"Well, Mr. Pitney," she said calmly, "our Christmas was very good. We are very blessed. Hal got back home, and the entire family was together again. How about you?"

Pitney looked out the sliding doors that led from his office to his now-covered swimming pool and noticed it had started snowing. "Well, Mrs. Douglas," he said, "we had a white Christmas, and now it looks like we're going to have a white New Year's Eve, too. Imagine my excitement!"

"Were you with your family for Christmas?" she asked quickly.

"I was," Gene said.

"Then you, too, had a blessed Christmas, didn't you?" she chided in a serious tone. "And where do you call home, Mr. Pitney?"

"Gene," he said quickly.

"I never heard of that city," Rita Douglas said in all seriousness. "I've heard of Eugene, Oregon, but not a city called Gene. What state is that in?"

"Um-m-m, sorry, Mrs. Douglas," he said with a little chuckle in his voice, "I meant, please call me Gene. I live in Somers, Connecticut."

"That sounds like a very nice city," she said. "Mr. Pitney, might I have a moment of your time?

"Mrs. Douglas you can have all of my time that you need," Gene said, again wanting badly to persuade her to call him Gene but thinking he was not going to get this very proper and polite lady to call him by his first name.

"Mr. Pitney," she began, "I want to thank you for being nice to Hal and helping him out. He's a good boy, a nice boy. He's been a fan of yours since he first heard that 'Liberty Valance' song of yours on the Zenith radio in the kitchen one day."

As the phone conversation continued, a very sleepy Hal Douglas trundled down the stairs into the kitchen to get some breakfast. He was going to fry up some bacon and eggs to make his favorite bacon-and-egg sandwiches and knock them back with a morning Coke.

"And every time that you put out a new record he'd hop on the bus on a Saturday morning and go to Sears up there on North Avenue and use his paper route money to buy the record. It was about an hour trip. He had to catch the #15 bus on Oakland Avenue then transfer to the #21. Hal knows all the bus routes around here."

The dining room phone was only one wall and about ten feet from the kitchen, so Hal couldn't help but overhear some of the conversation. He wondered who his mother would be telling about his riding the #15 and #21 buses. It piqued his interest, so he listened a little closer.

"And then he would come home and play those records on his little Sears Silvertone record player in the playroom. He would play them over and over and over until he knew all the words."

It was becoming quite clear what his mother was talking about, but it was still unclear to Hal who she could possibly be talking to. Maybe an aunt or an uncle. Maybe one of his grandmas. He kept listening.

"And he would go downtown to some special store to get the *Billboard* magazines and some English and Italian magazines and newspapers every week. He could take the #15 all the way downtown and just walk a few blocks to that store."

Much to Hal's chagrin, his mother still hadn't given any great clues as to who she was talking to. He kept listening.

"And, Mr. Pitney, he'd look at those pictures of you…"

All of a sudden, her voice seemed to fade away as Hal came to the shocking realization that his mother was talking to Gene Pitney on the phone.

"…and he would search high and low to find shoes and pants and shirts and sweaters that matched the ones that you wore on the covers of those albums."

Hal didn't know if he should laugh or cry. He was a bit stymied and really didn't know what to do. Should he interrupt? That might be rude. Should he just walk into the room and let his mother see him and maybe she'd hand the phone off to him? That might be too obvious. Should he just continue eavesdropping? While it might be a bit unethical, it did seem like the best plan for him. So he did.

At this point, Rita Douglas had been talking non-stop to Gene Pitney for a good five minutes without the singer getting a word in edgewise.

"And, in one of those teenage magazines he found the address for your Fan Club, and he joined it. Mr. Pitney, you are his hero. I just wanted you to know that, and I wanted you to know that I am so pleased that he picked someone like you and not one of those Rolling Stones boys or someone like that."

Hal was more than surprised to hear all this tumbling out of his mother's mouth and heart. It didn't ever seem to him that she really paid much attention to the minutiae of his life, like what kind of record player he owned and which buses he took and where he went. And it certainly never crossed his mind that his mother was sizing up — and approving — of his role models.

Gene finally broke into her one-sided conversation as politely as he could, "Mrs. Douglas, I don't know what to say. I'm flattered that Hal holds me in such high regard, and I'm very happy that you approve of me, too.

"Hal has asked me to work with him on his new record, and he's asked me to help him with his next career moves. I know if you're OK with everything then Hal will be OK with everything."

"I am OK with it," Mrs. Douglas responded. "Mr. Pitney, do you know anything about money? Can you help Hal manage his money? He's still very young, and I don't want anyone to take advantage of him. You know, I was a big fan of Frank Sinatra, and I know what happened to him. I don't want that to happen to Hal. Can you help?"

"Mrs. Douglas, I've already taken care of that," Gene assured her. "I gave Hal the name of my accountant in New York. The guy's name is Dick Naber. He's the best in the business, and he won't screw — I mean — take advantage of Hal."

"Mr. Pitney, I don't know how much money Hal has, but he gave all of us very expensive Christmas gifts," a very worried Rita Douglas admitted to a man she was gaining more confidence in every minute she spoke with him. "Can he really afford that? Is he really making THAT kind of money? He did mention that Dick Naber to us, too."

"Mrs. Douglas, your son, your very talented son, is one of the biggest stars in this country right now," Pitney said, more than a bit mystified that that fact apparently hadn't sunk in with Rita Douglas.

"He has plenty of money, and I promise you," Pitney said very softly and sincerely, "with me by his side, Mrs. Douglas, he'll become even more famous AND richer than Frank Sinatra ever was. And Dick Naber will see to it that the money will last Hal's lifetime."

"Oh, Mr. Pitney," she said, "I am so relieved. You've made a mother very happy with those words. Would you like to speak with Hal? He just got up."

"That would be great," Pitney said. "I want to tell him my plan."

"By the way, Mr. Pitney," she added quickly before handing the phone to her son, "I like your records a lot, especially that 'Only Love Can Break A Heart' song. That's a very pretty song. You're a very good whistler, too. Here's Hal."

Chapter Forty Two

"Good morning, Gene," Hal said, more than a little chagrined to be privy to the last minute or so of his mother's conversation with his hero and mentor. "Um-m-m, you've met my mom, huh?"

"Now I see where you got all your niceness from, Hal," Pitney said with all sincerity. "She's a sweet woman, and, I'm glad to hear you're taking care of her and your family. She told me about your Christmas gifts."

"Gene," Hal retorted quickly, "my mom and dad have worked so hard all their lives to make something for us that they didn't have growing up. They're from the Depression, you know? They still fry everything in bacon fat because, essentially, it's free.

"From my mom's point of view, throwing away the bacon fat is wasteful. It's just as good as margarine to her. I'm so used to eating my food fried in bacon fat that I can't argue the point with her. Besides, it tastes pretty good to me."

"Just a little advice, Hal," Pitney said matter-of-factly. "Take care of them the way they'll let you. That'll make them happy."

"I want them to have a wonderful life for the rest of their lives," Hal explained. "I want them to relax; I want them to travel; I want them to move into a nicer house. I can afford all that, but they're pretty frugal, and I'm not making a lot of progress."

"Baby steps, Hal, baby steps," Pitney said. "Let 'em get used to the fact that you're wealthy and are gonna get wealthier. Let them accept that first."

"I guess that's what I'll do," Hal said. "How was your Christmas, Gene?"

"White and cold and full of tea," Gene said with a laugh. "Just like my New Year's Eve is gonna be. You got a minute, Hal, to talk some business?"

"Sure do."

"I really need you and Jessie to get back here to Connecticut right after the holidays," Gene began. "I'll explain: I have Al Kooper working on organizing and setting up the 'Lifetime of Love' recording session. He's got a couple of Blood, Sweat & Tears gigs to do, then he'll put it all together, probably in a week to ten days. We've gotta get it done before word leaks out to Don Jon Ross and Rick Starr and they decide to stick their noses into this."

"I can get out of here by Wednesday," Hal said, remembering today was Sunday, and he was going to 10:30 High Mass with his family at Saints Peter and Paul. Hal loved that Mass because whenever he was home he got to sing with the choir.

"Jessie, on the other hand, I'm not sure of. She loves the warmth and sunshine of California, even if the temperature is only in the 60s. I haven't heard from her, but I'll call her and explain how important this is. I know she's looking forward to this and the UK tour, but getting her away from her home, her parents, her friends, and the weather could be tricky. I'll call her today."

"Thanks, Hal," said Gene. "Then call me ASAP."

Chapter Forty Three

Rick and Kim Starr had been killing time doing a little window shopping on New Year's Eve morning in Stowe while their two daughters were taking skiing lessons. As she was patiently waiting for her husband to come out of the hotel he had dashed into so he could make a quick phone call, Kim was pleasantly surprised to see a friend of hers walking across the street.

Actress Michele Miller, who was starring in a new TV series, *The Ninja Nurse*, featuring a caring nurse during the day and cunning crimefighter at night, was also enjoying the crisp Vermont morning. But she wasn't shopping. Miller was simply out for a nice long walk to settle herself down. She had just had a long argument on the phone with the director of her TV show who, she believed, showed her no respect and treated her like a child.

Kim Starr had appeared in one episode of the first TV series that Miller had starred in, *Teen Queen*, and the two actresses had hit it off instantly.

"Michele…Michele Miller!" Kim yelled out to her friend.

Miller, more than a bit taken aback to be recognized in Stowe, Vermont, on New Year's Eve morning, decided that, in the mood she was in, she didn't want to deal with a fan, so she picked up her pace, ignored the person calling her name, and kept walking.

Kim picked up her pace as well and called out again, "Michele…it's Kim Starr. What are you doing here?"

Michele stopped in her tracks, spun around, and ran quickly into Kim's arms and began bawling. "Boy, Kim do I need a friend right about now," she said in between her whimpers. "I just got off the phone with that prick director of mine, and I'm furious."

"What's going on?" Kim asked with sincere interest in her friend's problem.

"They treat me like I'm some sixteen-year-old boneheaded ingénue," the twenty-one-year-old actress said. "They insult me to my face. They're actually starting to make me feel like I can't act and that I don't belong in this business. I hate the show."

The two friends had stopped about a half block away from the hotel where Rick had gone to make his call. As the women were talking, Rick approached them but didn't recognize Michele. He was way too busy to watch a lot of TV, especially the "cheesy shitcoms" as he called most of the half-hour TV comedies of the day.

Kim didn't want this to be awkward for either her husband or her friend, so she chimed right in. "Rick, this is my friend Michele Miller. I did her TV show *Teen Queen* quite a few years back. She has a new show on ABC called *The Ninja Nurse*. Michele, this is my husband, Rick."

"Charmed," he said. "I gotta get back to our resort. Got a problem with my TV show. Will you two ladies be OK?"

"Seems like everyone has a problem with their TV show," Miller said quietly.

Rick didn't quite hear what she said but — always defensive about his *Starr Power* TV show — he thought it might have been a cutting remark.

"What?" he barked.

Sensing impending danger if Rick got upset, Kim said, "I'll tell you later, Dear. We'll be fine. We're gonna get a cup of coffee and catch up with each other. See you back at the resort. Don't forget to get the girls at noon. Love you."

As Starr sauntered to the parking lot and his car, Michele asked, "What was that all about?"

"That was all about a quick temper," Kim explained. "Not his most attractive trait. C'mon, let's go find a cup of coffee."

A few moments later, comfortably ensconced with steaming hot coffee in the newly remodeled Stoweflake Café, the two actresses started spilling out the facts and secrets of both their personal and professional lives to each other. The café was cozy, warm, and small, and conversations were easy to eavesdrop on.

And that's exactly what Gary Ford was doing. He instantly recognized Michele Miller, but it was her friend that he was really taken with. He couldn't take his eyes off her. That's why he kept his sunglasses on, even as he pretended to read the *Stowe Reporter* newspaper. He just wanted to stare at her.

Twenty-six year old Gary Ford was strikingly handsome. And rich. And bored. And horny.

Married and divorced, Ford was the son of a wealthy car dealer in Chicago. He now owned three of his own successful dealerships in the Windy City. He was also a budding politician and lover of beautiful women.

Even though he saw the gigantic diamond on the woman's left hand, he was willing to take the chance that she might take a chance — and maybe take a chance on him. Ford knew he looked good, and he knew women were attracted to him.

"Kim, I am so glad I ran into you," Michele said with a smile on her face.

"Actually, you were running away from me," Starr said with a hearty laugh. And, as she reared her head back with that laugh, she caught sight of Gary Ford two booths away.

The women had chattered away a good forty five minutes when Kim glanced at her watch and said, "I've gotta get back because the girls will be done with their ski lessons soon, and Rick won't have a clue what to do with them." She raised her hand, signaling for the waitress.

As the elderly waitress walked over to the table, she motioned her head towards Ford's booth. "Mr. Beautiful over there picked up your bill."

Michele looked over and, under her breath, said, "Jesus Christ, he's gorgeous, Kim. This might be what I need to take my mind off *The Ninja Nurse*. Whaddya think?"

"I think we both go over there and thank him, and I'll be your wingwoman," Kim said, urging caution. "I'm not gonna leave you here with him because tomorrow I don't want to read about the beautiful, young TV star murdered in Stowe, Vermont, by a handsome vagabond thrill killer."

They approached his booth, and Ford jumped up and kissed their hands as he introduced himself.

Chapter Forty Four

"I'm Kim, and this is my friend Michele," Kim Starr said matter-of-factly as she tried to size up the situation. "We were just on our way out, but we wanted to say 'thank you' for buying us our coffees."

"No need," said Ford, staring at Kim. "It was my honor to buy the two most beautiful ladies in Stowe a hot cup of coffee on a crisp winter morning. Especially one of my favorite TV stars, Michele Miller. As a matter of fact, I was just on my way out, too."

He then pointed out the window to a gorgeous Rolls-Royce Silver Shadow parked across the street from the café. "Can I give you ladies a lift somewhere? I'm staying at The Presidents Residence, which is close to everything in town."

Materialism was not an unknown quantity to either lady. Both were aware that The Presidents Residence was THE best, most expensive, and most exclusive resort in Stowe. It only had twelve rooms, and all were two-thousand-square-foot presidential suites. And beautiful, expensive cars always gave Michele a special thrill. Staring out the window with a huge grin on her face, she asked, "Is that what I think it is?"

"If you think it's a 1965 Rolls-Royce Silver Shadow Mulliner/Park Ward then it is," he quipped with no air of smugness about him.

Ford took this opportunity to brag just a little bit. "You see, Ladies, I own three car dealerships in Chicago. One of them is a Rolls-Royce dealership. This is a very rare and valuable car because 1965 is the first model year for the Silver Shadow. It's the follow up to the Silver Cloud."

"Did you drive it here from Chicago?" Michele asked as her interest in him became even more intense.

"Nah, it's too far to drive. I had it shipped here via train," Ford explained. "Anyone up for a ride in it? I'd love to tell my friends back in Chicago that *The Ninja Nurse* was in my car!"

"I walked into town from my hotel," Miller said quickly as she first ogled Ford then the Rolls-Royce. Looking for an opportunity to find out more about this movie-star-handsome stranger, she said, "I wouldn't mind a ride back. How about you, Kim?"

Starr thought to herself that this wasn't the best idea Michele ever had, but it appeared her frustrated TV-star friend wanted more than just a two-minute conversation with him and was almost drooling to get a ride in his car.

"Well, my husband did sort of abandon me here," Kim said, with emphasis on the word "husband." "He took the car and went back to the hotel to iron out some business problems, so I guess I could use a ride, too. We're staying at the Very Vermont Ski Resort. Where are you, Michele?"

Miller had convinced herself that Mr. Gary Ford would be a fun one-night stand, in the car or in her bed. Now she had to quickly figure out a way to shake Kim.

"Oh, I'm at the Snows of Stowe Resort, about a mile further up the road from you," Michele said. "Gary can drop you off first then take me to my place. Sound like a plan?"

Kim Starr didn't like the plan. Gary Ford didn't like the plan. Only Michele Miller liked the plan. Michele wanted Gary. Gary wanted the woman he knew only as "Kim." Kim wanted nothing to do with this seemingly rich Lothario, for her friend or herself.

For their own completely different reasons, both Starr and Ford were thinking on their feet as fast as they could to thwart Miller's plan. Miller was thinking about how fast she could get Ford into her bed at the Snows of Stowe Resort. Ford was thinking how fast he could get Kim into his bed.

Then Kim piped up: "My husband will probably still be on the phone doing business, and the girls won't be done with their skiing lessons for another hour, so maybe I'll tag along with you to take a look at your hotel, Michele. How's that?"

Kim thought it was a great spur-of-the-moment plan that might just rein in Michele's apparent lust for Ford. Gary liked the plan of Kim tagging along because it gave him more time to figure out how to potentially score with her.

This time, only Michele didn't like the plan. All of a sudden her friend wanted to be her mother or an unappointed safety supervisor.

The thought of a three-way did suddenly and enticingly start rolling through Michele's head. Gary Ford was beautiful. Kim Starr was beautiful. Michele always considered herself cutesy cute but not beautiful. It doesn't get any better than this, she thought to herself.

There was just something about Gary that Kim didn't trust. Now she was glad that her always-wary husband always made her carry a gun in her purse. Just in case.

Chapter Forty Five

"We're gonna step into the ladies room for a minute, Gary," Michele said, touching his arm in a way she thought was a signal of her growing interest in him. "Would you mind warming the car up for us California girls?"

Gary kissed their hands, lingering a bit longer with Kim, and said, "Not too long, Ladies. The Silver Shadow warms up fast. Just like me." And he made his way to the door.

Starr waited for Ford to leave the restaurant before she took verbal umbrage with her friend. "You wanna screw him don't you, Michele?"

"C'mon, Kim," Miller responded quickly. Laughing, she added, "Mother Teresa would want to screw that. He makes Warren Beatty look like a troll. Yes, the Ninja Nurse would like to sample his charms. By the way, 'screw' is such a dirty word, Kim."

As the two friends stepped into the bathroom of the Stoweflake Café, Kim pulled the gun out of her purse.

"Jesus Christ," Michele said, a little too loudly.

"Shhh," said Starr. "You'll have the entire staff in here if you keep that up. Rick wants me to carry this for protection. I think today is a good day to have it with us."

"You've been married too long," Michele said a little too smugly stated. "You've forgotten how it all works out here in the footloose and fancy free world of singles. I don't want to shoot him! I want to screw him! Now put that away; we gotta get going before he comes in here looking for us."

"Michele, please let me go to your hotel with you for just a little bit. It would make me feel better."

"You've got ten minutes when we get there," Michele said. "Then, make like Harry Houdini and disappear. Got it?"

As the two ladies left the restaurant, Gary Ford jumped out of his car to open the doors for them. "Who wants shotgun?" he asked with a laugh.

"I'm the star here," Miller said in a mockingly presumptuous tone of voice. "Kim, my darling, would you be so good as to sit in the back seat?"

As Michele rounded the car, heading for the front passenger door, Ford held open the back door for Kim. He gave her his hand to help her slide into the spacious back seat, then closed the door.

It was only after the door closed that Kim realized there was a piece of paper in her hand.

Ford was now making like a playfully sycophantic chauffer, helping Michele Miller, Hollywood star, into the front seat.

"Miss Miller, is the car warm enough for you?" he asked.

"It's grand, Mr. Ford. Let's not dawdle now. There is IMPORTANT business to take care of at my hotel." When she said that she turned to look at Kim in the back seat. Michele then said, "First we have to give my lovely friend here a quick tour of my hotel, and then we have to give you a not-so-quick tour of…me."

Kim barely heard Michele because she was stunned by what Ford had scribbled on the piece of paper he had slipped into her hand.

"I want YOU, not her! You are stunningly beautiful. Any husband who would abandon YOU to go do business on the phone while on vacation is a self-absorbed fool. I want YOU, not her! I'm at The Presidents Residence. Presidential Suite. I'm here 'til the end of January. Discreetly yours, Gary Ford.

Gary pulled away from the Stoweflake Café, and, as fate would have it, The Rolling Stones' hit "Let's Spend The Night Together" was playing on the radio. As he turned the radio down, he also turned around just a bit to give Kim a wink.

It happened very fast, and Miller didn't catch it. She was way too busy setting the stage for what she hoped would be a night to remember. Her hand was slowly moving over to Ford's leg. It grazed his leg at mid-thigh before landing on his penis.

Even though she was gorgeous and worldly, because of whom she was married to, no one in Hollywood ever flirted with or made a pass at Kim Starr. All of the well-known Hollywood players were afraid of Rick Starr personally and professionally. If they crossed him, he could ruin their careers or find someone else who could. He was not a man to piss off.

Kim was both a little flattered and a little flustered by Gary's note. Flattered because no one — no one — had tried to put a move on her since she married Rick. The note reminded her of her empty marriage. The Mamas and Papas were right, *"… unrequited love's a bore…"*

She was flustered because of Ford's brazen lust AND the fact that she was honestly interested in it. The only lover she had had for the last ten years was Rick Starr, but the thought of cheating on him — even though she was lonely and could really have her choice of many secret lovers in Hollywood — had never crossed her mind… until now.

She piped up from the back seat, "So, Gary, I think my husband — Rick Starr the famous TV star and concert promoter — might love a car like this. Michele, I'd like Gary to give Rick a ride in this car. Can we change plans a little?"

Gary looked at Miller, then he looked at her hand on his penis. Michele looked at him, then she looked at her friend in the back seat. As he was thinking that he was really in the driver's seat, literally and figuratively with these two attractive women, Michele retorted, "Gary can send him a brochure. I really want Gary to give me a *ride* after we drop you off, Honey."

She gave Ford's penis a little squeeze. Now he was trying to figure out how he was going to have sex with a TV star and a Kim Starr. He smiled to himself both for Michele Miller's well-placed hand and the interesting dilemma he found himself in.

Chapter Forty Six

Hal Douglas was irritated. He and his family got back home from 10:30 Mass at Saints Peter and Paul, and he realized — again — that he hadn't heard from Jessie James since before Christmas.

She was supposed to call him, but she hadn't. He had told Gene Pitney, earlier that day, that he would call her. He would keep that promise. He was just trying to figure out what he was going to say to her and how he was going to say it. Was he going to sound mad? Was he going to sound worried? Or, was he going to go with the flow and just sound nice?

Hal was actually a bit more worried than he was mad. What if Jessie and Danny Harmon had gotten together, and she decided Danny was her future? What if she didn't want to leave the warmth of the sun in California ever again? What if she decided that she didn't want Gene Pitney butting into her personal and professional lives? What if her parents were advising her to concentrate on an acting career instead of music? Hal had so many questions swimming around in his head.

With the traditional Douglas family after-Sunday-Mass-hot-baked-ham-from-East-Side-Foods-sandwich in one hand and a glass of milk in the other, Hal pulled up a chair at the dining room table and pulled the phone over. He thought about writing down what his first words to Jessie were going to be because he didn't trust himself to get them right and to not be snarky. He was miffed at Jessie for not calling, but he always found it hard to stay mad at her. He really didn't even want to try.

He slowly dialed her California phone number.

"Good afternoon, this is the James' residence," Jayna James said cheerfully.

Hal hadn't planned for this. He had never even seen Jessie's parents in person, much less ever talked with them. After a longer-than-comfortable pause, Hal blurted out awkwardly, "Oh, hi, is this Jessie's mom?"

"I proudly answer 'Yes' to that question," Jayna said with a smile in her voice. "And who might this be?"

"Oh, hi, Mrs. James. This is Hal Douglas. I'm a friend of Jessie's."

"Hal Douglas!" she exclaimed. "I've been waiting for this moment."

Hal didn't know if that was good or bad, if he was in trouble or in luck, if he should laugh or give her a chagrined "uh-oh."

So he simply — and wisely — threw the ball back in her court. "Might you expand on that, Mrs. James?"

"First of all," James said, "I know who you are. Everyone in the country who owns a radio knows who Hal Douglas is. Second, Jessie has spoken very often and very highly of you. Third, I've heard your records and think they are quite good. Fourth, Jessie has told me about the tour plans in the UK with this Gene Pitney fellow. Fifth, please call me Jayna. There, is that expansive enough?"

Hal was a bit stymied as he was formulating his reply. He and Jessie never really talked much about her parents. All he really knew about Jayna James was that she was an actress and Tony Winston had tried to rape her. He quickly ascertained that only one of those facts would make for good small talk with Jayna James. He went with it.

"Well, Mrs. James, I know who you are, too," Hal said, trying to figure out where to go next. He decided to parrot her in a cutesy way. "Everyone who's ever been to a movie knows who Jayna James is. Jessie speaks very highly and very often of you and Governor James. I can't wait to see your next movie. I'm very excited about the upcoming UK tour with Mr. Pitney and Jessie. And, by the way, I can't call you Jay…um-m-m…I should call you Mrs. James."

But, before Jayna James could reply, Hal Douglas, in an effort to endear himself to Jessie's mother, blurted out, "Oh, by the way, I'm going to do some movies, and I was hoping you'd give me some advice."

"Here's my advice, Hal, and it's not original," Jayna James said warmly enough. "If you don't already have one, get a lawyer…now. Do you have legal counsel, Hal?"

"No, I don't Mrs. James," he responded quickly. While he was growing in self-confidence every day, he still didn't know what he needed to know, and he felt that Jessie's mother would be a good ally. So he played quasi-dumb to get a lay of the land with her. "My manager, Rick Starr, is taking care of that business for me."

"Oh, dear boy," she said with some anguish in her voice. Then she caught herself. She knew who Rick Starr was and what his reputation in Hollywood was. He made some of Tinseltown's shadiest characters look like beaming rays of sunshine.

Again, Hal didn't know if her three-word response was good or bad. So, again, he asked, "Might you expand on THAT, Mrs. James?"

Jayna James didn't know what Hal's relationship with Rick Starr was. Since she didn't know Hal at all, she wouldn't presume he would take her into his confidence. That was something she would have to delve into with Jessie. She decided to straddle the fence.

"Well, Hal," she said with the trained confidence of a seasoned actress, "I'm in the movies. I don't do TV. I know who Rick Starr is, but I didn't realize that he had branched out into movies. That rather took me by surprise. Have you signed a deal with Rick? Does Jessie know about this? Do you know what the timeframe is going to be? Do you know who is writing, directing, and producing?"

"Well, Mrs. James, if you ever decide to get into television you could sure give that guy on *Meet The Press* a run for his money," Hal said as he chuckled. "That is one long list of questions. Unfortunately, I don't have a long list of answers that don't include the words 'I don't know.'"

"Hal, are you in Los Angeles, or are you at home?" she asked.

"I'm home in Milwaukee, Mrs. James."

"Maybe Governor James and I can talk to you about all this when you come to Los

Angeles," she said. "Are you coming out to see Jessie?"

"I'd love to, Mrs. James, but my, I mean, our schedule is pretty full. If I get out to Los Angeles, it wouldn't be until April. And that's what I was calling Jessie about… our plans."

Motherly concern over Hal's readily apparent naïveté overcame Jayna James. "Hal, I've been in this business for a long time," she explained cautiously. "There are a lot of pitfalls that newcomers often succumb to. You're a friend of Jessie's, and I don't want to see you make mistakes that we can help you avoid."

"Thank you, Mrs. James," Hal said. Then, trying to sound a little more competent than how he was apparently coming off to Jessie's mom, he boldly added, "By the way, Mrs. James, I haven't signed anything with Mr. Starr yet. I told him it would have to wait."

"That's good to hear, Hal," she said, mental relief sweeping over her. "Governor James and I would be happy to give you advice. Look, I've taken up enough of your time. I'll get Jessie. She's out by the pool. It was very nice talking to you, Hal."

"You, too, Mrs. James."

The phone clanked a little bit as Jayna James put it on the kitchen counter and sauntered out to the pool to get Jessie.

December is one of the coolest months in Los Angeles, and it can be rainy. This day, however, was sunny and mild. Jessie lay sleeping on a custom-made, heated chaise lounge, enjoying all sixty seven degrees of warmth.

Her movie star mother couldn't help but notice how stunningly beautiful her daughter was — and how she rocked the black bikini covering only a small part of her body, which was, right now, as white as Ivory Soap.

"Jessie, dear," she said quietly, not wanting to startle the sleeping beauty.

Nothing. No body movement. No flicker of the eyes.

She didn't want to keep Hal Douglas waiting on his long-distance call, so she moved a bit closer and gently touched her daughter's arm while calling her again.

"Oh, hey, Mom," Jessie said. "I must have dozed off. Everything OK?"

"Hal Douglas is on the phone for you," she said. She chose not to allude to any of the conversation she had with Hal, not so much because of what they had talked about but because she didn't want to appear to be a busybody.

On the outside, Jessie appeared happy to hear that Hal was on the phone. On the inside, she had mixed feelings. She HAD to talk to Hal right now, whether she wanted to or not.

"Thanks, Mom. I'll grab it in the kitchen. Could you give me a few minutes alone with Hal?"

"Of course, Dear," her mother said. "I had planned to meet Liz Taylor for lunch. I'll just head over there a little early. Maybe I can find out who her next husband will be before Army Archerd does!"

The two beautiful James women kissed each other goodbye, and Jessie slowly made her way into the house.

"Hal Douglas," she said excitedly into the phone. "Is this America's biggest pop star Hal Douglas on my phone?"

That made Hal laugh, and he responded, "The one and only. Would this be America's brightest female pop star Jessie James on my phone?"

"Oh, no, you must have the wrong number, Mr. Douglas," Jessie said, giggling a little. "You seem to be looking for Diana Ross. She apparently is America's brightest female pop star. Just ask her. My name is Jessie James."

"Nope," Hal said assertively. "I AM looking for the always lovely and truly delightful Jessie James. And, according to a beautiful and legendary Hollywood movie star I just talked to, she lives here."

"Hi, Hal," Jessie said in a soft tone. "It is so-o-o-o good to hear your voice. Did the Douglas family have a great Christmas?"

"It was our best Christmas ever, Jessie," said Hal. "I was able to share my good fortune with my family. I couldn't ask for more. How 'bout you?"

Jessie knew that question was coming. She dreaded what she was about to say to Hal. She decided to give a rambling answer to soften the blow.

"First, I want to tell you what I gave my parents for Christmas, Hal. I'm so excited about it." She explained expansively about the *Jansen and Jayna James VA Home For Heroes*, her $1 million gift, and that Bob Hope, Dean Martin, Jerry Lewis, Johnny Carson, and other celebrities were also kicking in large amounts of money to get it built.

"What an extraordinary gift to give to your parents," he said, smiling. "I am so proud of you, Jessie. My dad is a wounded World War II vet. Those guys deserve all the help we can give them for what they did for us and the rest of the world. They are a great generation of Americans. On behalf of all the vets who will be helped by your gift, I say 'thank you.'"

Then he asked the question that Jessie thought might make her heart stop.

"Might I pry a little bit and ask what you got for Christmas?"

"Oh, Hal, Hal, Hal," Jessie said as she began to choke up a bit. "They got me a TV show. A syndicated variety TV show. It was a dream of mine growing up."

"Wow! That's great, Jessie. I'd cry, too, if my parents got me a TV show" said Hal. "But, I don't know how any of that works. What does that mean?"

"Oh, Hal," Jessie said as she broke down and sobbed. "It means a career change for me."

Chapter Forty Seven

The ride to the Snows of Stowe Resort seemed like an eternity for all three occupants of the Rolls-Royce. All seemed lost in their thoughts as they listened to the radio, talking very little. A heavy snow began to fall, and Gary Ford took the opportunity to break the silence. "Do you ladies like to ski?"

"Never tried it," said Kim Starr. "We just brought the kids here for a change of scenery and to let them experience something different." After she said that, she chuckled to herself, thinking she was now contemplating the same thing in a completely different context. After initially being somewhat mortified by the note Ford had pressed into her hand, she was now flattered and more than slightly turned on by it. Rick Starr was a man of few compliments, and those were reserved for people who made money for him. Kim knew very well that her husband considered her to be "overhead" in his life.

Michele Miller wanted no small talk; she wanted no skiing chatter; she wanted no hotel tour; she wanted Gary Ford. "Oh-oh, the snow is coming sooner than the TV weatherman predicted last night," she said in a very knowing tone of voice. A good display of acting, too, since she made it up on the spot to facilitate her sexual agenda.

Michele then made her move. "Kim, darling, I think we really should get you to your hotel now before the roads get bad. You don't want to worry Rick and the girls, do you?"

Gary Ford wanted to get in between the two ladies — just not in a conversation, especially a conversation that he knew was headed towards an argument. He didn't say anything, but, hedging his bets, he purposely made the Rolls slip and slide on the road a little bit. It was becoming quite clear that Miller wanted sex with him NOW and that she was going to get her way. He figured he'd get the one-night stand with her out of the way and then work on bedding his real desire, Kim Starr. Swerving the car should help Michele's cause.

Kim only had a few seconds to make a decision. For reasons that she neither could nor wanted to contemplate, Ford's note gave her comfort. She no longer feared for her friend's safety. And, she really didn't mind if Michele had sex with the beautiful Mr. Gary Ford. She was hoping, however, that it would be a quickie for them. Gratified and flattered by his sweet note, Kim had decided that she, too, would sleep with him. But she wasn't going to settle for a round of lustful, noisy sex. She would make love to him. Long, sweet, warm, and magnificent love, something she hadn't done with a man since the first year of her marriage to Rick Starr.

"Good idea, Michele," she said sweetly. "I'm not used to this kind of weather, and it's scaring me. Drop me off, and call me tomorrow. Maybe we can go shopping or do lunch. Do you know where my hotel is, Gary?"

"Sure do," he said. "I'll get you there safe and sound." He still made the Rolls slip and slide a bit, just for appearances.

Just then, Gene Pitney's "Town Without Pity" came on the radio. Gary turned it up a bit, saying, "If you don't mind, Ladies, this is one of my favorite songs of all time. I love this guy."

Perfect timing, thought Kim. She reached into her purse for a pen and a pad of paper and quickly but neatly scribbled a note.

"You can screw Michele tonight, but make it short and superficial. Be nice to her. She's a sweetie. Then, you are mine. All mine. I don't like being abandoned and ignored. I like to be taken care of. Can you do that? Eyes talk…silently. I like the way you've been looking at me today. I'm not looking to fall in love with you, but I would like to be in lust with you for the next few days that I'm here. Let's call it a 'sweet distraction.' Can you handle that? I think you can. Don't call me. I'll call you."

It was while she was folding the note that she realized that Gary was singing along with Gene Pitney. And quite well. *"The young have problems, many problems. We need an understanding heart. Why don't they help us? Try to help us. Before this clay and granite planet falls apart…."*

"Wow…that's awesome," Kim said. "Ever thought of a career as a singer?"

"Yes and no," said Ford. "Yes, because I think I could be successful, but no, because I want to be the boss. I want to call the shots. I want to be in charge of my life and destiny. That ain't how show business works, is it, Michele?"

Thinking of the problems she was having on *The Ninja Nurse*, she quietly said, "Nope, that ain't how show business works. But it does give you money and fame — and the allure…" Then with a sly smile on her face and her hand again on his penis, she added, "It gives you many other great opportunities, too, Gary. Do you know what I mean by that?"

While Kim heard Michele's end of the conversation, she really wasn't paying attention to it. Her mind was now reeling with the opportunities that the situation and the conversation had just presented to her.

Ford was an amazing singer; her husband was one of the most powerful men in the music industry. She wasn't sure that Michele wanted anything more than a one-night stand with Gary, but Kim now had a legitimate reason to get together with him. She may never need to play that hand because Miller might be heading back to Hollywood in the next day or two to work out problems on her TV show. Nonetheless, she now had a perfect excuse to see Ford again.

The Rolls pulled up to the Very Vermont Ski Resort. Gary Ford jumped out of the car, first telling Michele to stay put and stay warm, then waving off the bellman. He opened the back door for Kim and told Michele he was going to make sure Kim got into the hotel safely. Michele didn't care what he did right now. It's what he was going to do in about fifteen minutes that mattered to her.

As he walked Kim into the hotel, he said, "I hope my note didn't upset you. I've just never laid eyes on a woman like you before. Can I see you again?"

"You better," Kim said. Then, for appearance's sake, she shook his hand as if they were wrapping up a business meeting and placed her note in his hand.

Chapter Forty Eight

"I don't understand what you're telling me, Jessie," Hal said in a soft, quiet voice. "A career change? What does that mean?"

Her sobbing had subsided a little, but her mind was racing. How was she going to justify blowing up all the career plans she and Hal had been making since summertime so she could have her own TV show?

"Look, Hal," she said in a very loving tone, "this isn't easy. But let me try to explain. Los Angeles or Hollywood, whatever you want to call it, is my home. This is where I live. These are the people I know. These are the circles I travel in."

Hal chimed in, "No one's asking you to move, Jessie. None of this is clear to me, and, I'm starting to get worried about where you're going with this."

"This has nothing to do with moving, Hal," she quickly explained. "I've lived here my whole life. I know how these people think. If you're in the movies — great! If you're on TV — great! But, to them, being a pop star is like being the president of the moon, Hal. It's not on their radar. They don't care. Don't you get it? In *Billboard* and *Cashbox* and on Top 40 radio I'm a star and a huge star at that. Here, I'm nothing. No one cares. Top 40 music is the red-headed stepchild of the entertainment industry. It's not taken seriously."

Nothing but silence emanated from Hal's end of the phone. After a pause of fifteen seconds that seemed like an eternity to Jessie, Hal spoke. And he was angry.

"You're going to throw away your career and all of our plans just so you can impress your friends in Hollywood?" Hal asked incredulously. "What's gotten into you, Jessie? You know this doesn't affect only me. What about Gene and Don Jon? What about the song we wrote? What about Sunshine Records? What about the UK tour? And, most importantly, what about us? This is a side of you I've never seen. This is very selfish."

Now it was Jessie's turn to get angry. "First of all, Hal Douglas, you don't own me. Second, just because something is important to me doesn't make me selfish, Third… shit, Hal…I don't have a third. Please, let's not fight. This is something I've wanted since I was a kid. Don't you understand that? Can't you be happy for me?"

"If I thought you were making a good, sound decision I would be very happy for you," Hal said matter-of-factly. "I can't figure out why you want to walk away from everything you've achieved so far and everything else that you are on the verge of achieving."

"Is that what you think I'm doing, Hal? Walking away from all of it? You couldn't be more wrong. I'm capitalizing on what I've achieved in the pop music industry, and I'm going to roll it over into something even bigger and better. Why would you begrudge me that?"

"That's a load of crap, Jessie," Hal said as if he was spitting something with a bad taste out of his mouth. "You've already told me why you're doing it: status in Hollywood and to impress your Hollywood friends. Right now, in Hollywood, you're the little fish in the big pond. You want to be the big fish in the big pond.

"Think about it, Jessie. First, you're going to hurt a lot of people if you walk away from your recording and touring careers. Second, you have a sure thing going right now in music. And, you stand a good chance to make music history with our duet. Walk away from that and you WILL hurt yourself. I promise you that."

"Stop it, Hal," Jessie yelled into the phone. "You sound like a know-it-all."

"Nope, I won't stop," Hal said firmly. "Third, is your TV show a sure thing? How do you know it will do well in the ratings? It could be an absolute flop. Then what? Fourth…oh dang it, Jessie…I don't have a fourth. Isn't there a compromise? Can't we sit down and discuss this with your mom and dad? Can't we pick their brains?"

"This is important to me, Hal," she said again. "This is something I want. Maybe we should both calm down and talk about it later. Maybe in a day or two. What do you think?"

Hal was never one for tricks or deceit. He was still too naïve to try to manipulate anyone.

"I'll do that for you, Jessie," he said. "But I also think if you walk away from all of this now, you're making the biggest mistake of your life. You're too smart for that. I don't know what's gotten into you, but we'll give it some time."

Jessie was getting angry again but tried to contain herself. "My life is what's gotten into me, Hal. My mother is an Oscar-winning actress. She's respected by everyone in the acting community here in Hollywood. My father is the former governor of California. He is one of the most highly-respected governors this state has ever had. This is where I live. I want the respect of my friends and peers for myself and for my parents. Period."

"Jessie," Hal said very softly, "you are talented and bright and beautiful. The world is your oyster right now." He chuckled and added, "Yeah, I heard that in a movie, and I liked the way it sounded, and it's true. I think you can have it all. It will be a lot of work, but I think you, of all people, can do it all."

Jessie was starting to relent a bit. She was also showing some insecurity. "Do you really think I can, Hal? You think I can do the TV show, the tours, the recording sessions, and everything else that comes my way?"

"On second thought," he said, "nope, I don't *think* you can do it all, Jessie. I was wrong: I *know* you can, and I'm going to help you. Why don't we start like this? Let's go to Connecticut to see Gene and see how he wants us to move forward with the duet. Then, we'll do his UK tour. And, Jessie, notice I said 'we'll do his UK tour.' I'm going to suggest to Gene that he add you to the tour. I'm not really ready to play hardball with anybody, but in this case I will tell him I'll only do the tour if he puts you on it."

Jessie interrupted, "I appreciate that, Hal, but how does that really solve my problem? I really, really want that TV show."

"Connect the dots, Jessie," Hal said patiently. "I've thought about this a lot in the last couple of days. If the record becomes as big as we all think it will and if we do well on Gene's UK tour and establish ourselves there, then we will be the biggest pop stars in the world."

Hal paused a bit to let that sink in, then he continued with a smile in his voice, "OK, maybe not as big as The Beatles and The Stones, but we'll be huge. Then you start your TV show. The whole world will want to see it. Don't you see how your music career is, as they say, setting the table for your TV career?"

"How can you be sure?" Jessie asked quietly. "You used the word 'if' two times talking about our future. What 'if' you're wrong? What 'if' the record flops? What 'if' England hates us? Then what?"

"You're smarter than that, Jessie," he said. "And where did your self-confidence go? What happened to you in California?"

"It's just different here than in the rest of the country," she said. "If you're a movie star or a TV star then you're somebody. Pop music — that's a whole different world. It barely registers here. I want to be SOMEBODY. I want to make my parents proud. I want their friends to think I'm somebody. There's nothing wrong with that, is there, Hal?"

"Jessie, you've gotta trust me," Hal implored. "You will be somebody. You'll be a bigger somebody than most of those other stars in Hollywood are because you're going to be a pop star, a TV star, AND a movie star. You're gonna be a triple threat."

"Whaddya mean?" she asked impatiently.

"Jessie, we're teen idols now, and with Gene's help we're going to go into the music stratosphere," Hal explained. "You won't just be a pop star…you'll be a music superstar. Then you're going to start your TV show and become a TV star. Then you're gonna be a movie star."

Jessie was getting peeved. "Hal, you're talking through your ass now," she said. "You have no idea how any of that works."

"I might not have the practical knowledge," Hal said curtly, "but, I've been thinking a lot about what Gene said when we were at his house. You know, about our being in the driver's seat, about our taking control of our careers and getting what we want.

"I'm ready for that Jessie. Are you? I'm ready to get what I want and to do what I want and to do it with who I want but — in a fair way. Are you? This is our moment, Jessie. We could become the biggest team in show business history. I've got a plan."

Jessie was relenting in the face of Hal's optimism. And, she knew, in fact, she had come this far with Hal helping her career. She decided to hear him out.

"Spill the beans, Machiavelli," she said with a giggle.

The reference wasn't lost on Hal. "Um-m-m, maybe Machiavelli, Jr.," he said with a laugh. "I think Gene's the man with the plan. I know exactly where I want to go with our careers. I'm convinced Gene's the guy to get us where we need to be on the first leg of this journey."

"What are you thinking?" asked Jessie.

"Look," he said. "First, the record can't flop. The timing is right on it for both of us. It's a great song, and, with Gene's involvement, it'll be a great record. This is a #1 song just waiting to be recorded and released.

"Second, Gene is still huge in England, and his tours sell out. Plus, my song 'My Only Girl' went to #1 in England earlier this year, so I have some cache. And, remember, because I was touring the US when the record went to #1 in England, I didn't have a chance to go to there to do any TV or radio promotion, so there has to be some pent-up demand there.

"I wish Rick Starr had released 'Sundown Never Comes' there, but he didn't think it was right for that market. I'm gonna ask him to put out 'On The Street Where You Live' immediately. That'll set the stage for the tour with Gene.

"Third, when we come back from the UK you can go right into production for your TV show, maybe get it on the air for the summer. And who do you think will be the first guests on the first episode of your first TV show? Gene and me. And we won't do any other TV until after your show, even though everyone from Ed Sullivan to Merv Griffin to Johnny Carson will want us.

"And fourth, and this is the kicker, Jessie: Rick called me before Christmas and said Family Films is offering me a $6 million, six-movie deal. I told him I would call him after Christmas with my answer. He got a little pushy with me, Jessie, and I didn't like that. So, I've decided I am gonna take the deal, but I'm gonna take it on my terms."

"And those terms are?" Jessie asked.

"And those terms are," Hal paused for dramatic effect, "Jessie James is my co-star in those movies, and they have to up the money. I'm letting Rick Starr know that you're gonna be my co-star or there'll be no movies. You're gonna be a movie star. Whaddya think?"

"I think I'm crazy in love with the cutest, most talented, most courteous, and most generous teen idol in the world," Jessie answered quickly. Then she began to weep.

"Those better be tears of joy," Hal said.

"Of course they are, you nincompoop," she said, still crying. "You're making all of my dreams come true. I wouldn't have any of this if it weren't for you, Hal. I was a beauty-queen-who-wanted-to-be-a-singer, and you're making me a star."

"Well, now, Jessie," Hal interrupted. "Don Jon Ross should really get the credit for that."

"Yeah, but, if it hadn't been for my getting added to your tour and your making such a big fuss over me, my career would have been over after 'Take Me Now' fell off the charts. A one-hit wonder. Don Jon had no clue how to get me another hit.

"'Yes! No! Yes!' and 'Love Me Now' only became hits because I was on your tour. Then you take me up to Connecticut to meet Gene Pitney, and next thing you know we're working on plans to solve our career issues, fix my Tony Winston problem and your Rick Starr problem, and potentially create one of the biggest hit records in the history of pop music."

"I think a lot of it was luck and fate, Jessie," Hal added quietly.

She either didn't hear him or chose to ignore him. "Then I make a rash decision and decide to turn our lives and careers upside down for selfish, tunnel-vision reasons, and you take it in stride and patiently show me how I can have it all…music, TV, and movies.

"Hal, you've come so far and grown so fast. You are a budding genius and a gracious, kind, and generous man — a man I am madly in love with. Count me in for your plan, Hal. Let's conquer the world."

"Jessie, my next call is to Gene to tell him what our game plan is. I'll buy us a little more time to get back to Connecticut. Enjoy some more time with your family — and enjoy that warm California sun. Don't talk to Don Jon or anyone else about anything until I call you back. I love you, Jessie. You're the girl of my dreams. Stay warm and safe and dry. I'll call you soon. Bye."

Chapter Forty Nine

"This Don Jon Ross really knows how to treat a guy," Tony Winston was telling his friend Steve "Shortstop" Alioto on the phone from Las Vegas. "Maybe I was wrong about him. He's putting me up at the new Caesars Palace hotel. Just opened last year. Everything that doesn't smell like smoke still smells new."

"See, Tony," Alioto responded. "All that bullshit carping you were doing was wasted time. You're a star, and this guy with the rhyming name knows it and wants you real bad. I think this is gonna work out for you. But, Tony, keep yer eyes open. You know how shifty those show biz people are."

"You're not funny, Shortstop. By the way, it's sixty three degrees here today…and sunny. How's Kenosha?"

"Well," Alioto said, "it's windy, ten degrees, seven inches of snow. Go fuck yourself."

Winston laughed. "Hey, I have a meeting with Don Jon in about an hour. We've been kicking the record deal around, and he wants me to sign it today. You'll be the first one to know what happens."

Winston's problem was that he didn't know what the deal was. He had been so thrilled — and desperate — to get a deal that he didn't ask a lot of questions when Ross offered it to him over the phone a month before. But, Winston figured he had to be smarter than a guy with rhyming first and middle names who owned a two-bit record company with the Shirley Temple-like name of Sunshine Records.

Before leaving Kenosha, Winston told all his long-time, non-show business friends that he was working out a "huge" deal with Sunshine Records that was going to put him back at the top of the charts and probably running the record company because "Don Jon Ross was the Babe Ruth of chumps."

The bragging was Winston trying to feel good about himself and convince himself that he was helping Don Jon Ross and Sunshine Records more than Don Jon Ross and Sunshine Records were helping him.

A small part of him, however, still felt he was a big star with a lot of sway and influence. Tony Winston was trying to foster and grow that part of his ego and persona. He had to believe it first before he could sell it to anyone else.

Don Jon Ross was confident Tony Winston could get back in the charts…not the Top 40, but he could be a staple of Easy Listening radio stations around the country. In the radio industry, they were known as M-O-R stations, middle-of-the-road.

The off-the-top-of-his-head plan that Ross had concocted for Winston now seemed like a brilliant idea: a Christmas album, an album of WWII standards, and two albums of songs that Don Jon Ross picked and controlled the publishing on. He could see each of those albums selling a minimum of 100,000 copies each. Ross also planned to re-establish Tony Winston as a top-level nightclub attraction and put him out on the road.

Ross knew he could pay Winston $40,000 per album and still make a small fortune off Sunshine Records' new star, especially after expenses were factored in. Ross figured $10,000 in expenses for each album was not only believable but also somewhat legitimate. Of course, there would be some padding that would benefit Ross.

His plan all along was to make Winston think he was low-balling him and then let the singer come up with his own counter offer that would likely still fall below the $40,000 plateau; thus, Ross set up his scheme: a manila folder on the table and a pressing phone call to take in the hotel bedroom. He just hoped Tony Winston would take the bait.

"Praise the Lord, and pass the ammunition," Tony Winston muttered to himself as he was getting ready to disembark from the elevator on the fourteenth floor — the top floor — of Caesars Palace. He was meeting Don Jon Ross in his suite to sign the contract for his two-year, four-album deal with Sunshine Records. Meanwhile,

Ross was enjoying his beautiful and expensive suite at Caesars, hopefully courtesy of Winston. While waiting for him, Ross downed a room service breakfast of bacon, eggs, steak, and champagne.

Bracing himself for the unknown, Winston knocked on Don Jon's door. He was two minutes early for their one o'clock appointment. Don Jon Ross opened the door, and Winston was taken aback by the blast of cold air that blew out of his suite.

"Tony Winston, I presume," Don Jon said with a big smile on his face. "Son of a bitch, you look good. C'mon in, c'mon in. I've got money in the bank, a pen in my hand, and your contract on the table."

Winston walked in laughing, "Good thing I wasn't a hooker. Good morning, Don Jon. Got any more of that champagne?"

"Sit down, Tony," Don Jon said with a big smile on his face. "I'll have more sent up while we finish this deal. Son of a bitch, you look good. You look like a star."

Don Jon Ross was conservatively dressed in a powder blue shirt under a navy blue crew neck sweater, black slacks, and Converse All Star Chucks — black and white tennis shoes. He wore them with everything except a business suit.

"Hey, Don Jon, nice to finally meet you," Winston said with slight hesitation in his voice. "Are you storing beef up here in your room?"

"Nah," Ross said quickly. "Big guys like me sweat a lot so we gotta keep it cool. You know what I mean?"

That was only half the truth. The room was uncomfortably cold for another reason. Don Jon's plan was to keep Tony Winston a little uncomfortable and distracted as they commenced contract talks. The meeting in his over-air conditioned room was Ross' plan to keep an unfair advantage over Winston. Don Jon could control everything that happened, and he immediately began to put his plan into action.

"Tony, a little problem came up with my other Sunshine Records star, Jessie James, and I gotta call her right now. Do you mind? There's a nicely stocked bar in the corner by the window. Get what you want, and have a seat by the table over there. That yellow love seat is ver-r-ry comfy. I'll need about ten minutes with her."

In the refrigerator-like atmosphere of Don Jon's room, Winston would have really preferred a cup of hot black coffee, but he decided to check out the bar. "Nice-ly-stocked indeed"; he whistled as he took a look at the three shelves filled with the best liquor money could buy.

Tony was a Jack Daniels Green Label aficionado. It was lighter and much less sweet than the Black Label. It worked great in cocktails, but Tony also loved it straight with just a little ice. Staring at him from the first shelf was an unopened bottle of his whiskey of choice. Tony poured himself a drink and headed to the "ver-r-ry comfy" yellow love seat to await Don Jon.

As he dropped on to the love seat, he noticed a manila folder sitting on the table with his name on it. He could not believe his luck. It had to be Don Jon's contract offer for him. "I've gotta take a sneak peek at that," he said quietly to himself. He remembered his dad always telling him that "forewarned is forearmed."

If he knew what Don Jon was ready to offer him, he would not be taken by surprise. He could have a counter-offer ready without missing a beat. It was important to Tony that he didn't look like he was desperate or stupid. Winston wanted to be able to act the part of a supremely confident star who was going to do Don Jon Ross and his little record company a favor.

He could hear Don Jon talking in the bedroom, which was a good one hundred feet away from where he was sitting in the massive suite. Tony knew he'd be able to close up the folder quickly if Don Jon came out while he was looking at it, and the record company owner wouldn't know the difference.

Tony opened the folder and saw a typed Sunshine Records contract for the two-year, four-album deal that Don Jon had offered him over the phone. What gave Winston a jolt was the money figure that Don Jon had scribbled into the contract. $10,000 per album, half up front in cash, the balance when each album was record-ed, pressed, and shipped to radio stations and record stores and all expenses had been paid.

There were a couple of lines spelling out that Sunshine Records would be solely re-sponsible for finding, producing, and releasing all the songs that Winston would re-cord. All expenses incurred by Sunshine would be split 50/50 with Winston before the final balance per album was paid out. In addition, there was a line about excess expenses from a preceding album being charged against any current album in production.

Tony could barely control his anger. But, he did. He now knew the game that Don Jon was playing. The Sunshine Records owner was going to try to lowball him, get him for a fire-sale price. Tony Winston was going to have none of it. He was mad, and he was cold. He would make Don Jon, at a minimum, double the offer, or he would threaten to walk. Little did he know that he had walked right into Don Jon's trap and was doing exactly what Don Jon had hoped he would.

Don Jon finished his phone call with Jessie James and returned to the table where Tony Winston was seated.

"Did you get everything worked out?" Winston asked, just to feign interest in someone other than himself.

"Yeah," said Ross, "I love Jessie, but she makes my ass tired."

Tony Winston realized that Don Jon Ross didn't know that he and Jessie James had been man and wife for a short period of time, and he wasn't going to share that information with him just yet. He decided, just for fun, to go fishing with Ross.

"I hear that Jessie can be problematic," Winston said, "really full of herself, you know, with the movie star mom and the governor dad. I've heard that she's quite the little minx, too."

Don Jon wasn't going to be caught up in any backstabbing, name calling, or gossiping about Jessie James. He felt that Jessie could sometimes be difficult, but that's only because she wouldn't always do what he wanted her to do. Nope. He wasn't going to play whatever game Tony Winston wanted to play.

"Jessie is a star, a gifted singer, and my friend," Don Jon said in a very matter-of-fact tone of voice that was meant to send a warning to Winston. "Now, let's get down to business, Tony. In my book, you're a star, too. Don Jon Ross and Sunshine Records want to put you back in the charts and make you rich. So, whaddya think, Tony?

Tony Winston had a lot riding on this conversation: his ego, his career, and his bank account were front and center in his mind. "Of course that's my goal, too," Winston said. "How are we gonna do that?"

"Well, Tony," Don Jon said in as serious a tone as he could muster, "I think you're great, and my brother Jim Tim thinks you hung the moon. As a matter of fact, he's already written a bunch of songs for you."

Winston couldn't believe his ears. Don Jon Ross had a brother whose name rhymed, too? But, he didn't want to interrupt Ross while he was spelling out the terms of the record deal.

"Here's what I'd like to offer you: $10,000 per album, 50 percent of that up front in cash, then a 50/50 split on the back end money after expenses."

Ross saw Winston wince ever so slightly, so, to stay on the offensive, he decided to sweeten the pot right then and there. "That's $5,000 per album in cash, up front. And Tony, I'll give you all the upfront money for all four albums right away. That's $20,000 cash. Whaddya think?"

That offer threw Winston off his game. If Ross were only going to offer him the $5,000 now for the first album he felt he could bitch about it. But $20,000 now for product that would be delivered over a two-year period threw a little wrench into the works. It made Don Jon Ross look like a generous guy who was willing to work with his new star.

Still, Winston mustered up the courage to counter. "That's very big of you, Don Jon, but how about $20,000 per album with 50 percent up front when we go into the studio? Your cash outlay will be smaller, which is better for you now and better for me in the long run. How's that for a compromise?"

Tony took a sip of his Jack Daniels Green and summoned up even more courage. "We need to respect each other if this deal is gonna work, Don Jon. I really think ten grand per album looks like you're pegging me as a has-been who you're trying to pick up at a fire-sale price. Yup. That's what it looks like to me. A little disrespectful, Don Jon."

Both men were silent…for different reasons. Both were trying to outplay the other. "You know, Don Jon," Tony added in a bit of a hushed tone, "MGM paid me and my sisters $5,000 to record 'London Lady Falling Down' and the flip side. Two songs, five grand. And, we won an Oscar."

Don Jon Ross also had a lot riding on this conversation: his ego, his record company, and his bank account. He wanted to be in the driver's seat, and he didn't want to come across as an opportunist while doing so. He had given this moment a lot of thought before arriving in Las Vegas. Thinking that the fading star needed the money, his plan was to low-ball Winston with a small, guaranteed advance fee in cash as a negotiating ploy to keep his attention away from the gray areas of the contract. Don Jon Ross was a schemer at heart.

"C'mon, Tony," he implored. "MGM is loaded. They're huge. They've got Herman's Hermits, The Animals, Connie Francis, Lou Christie, The Cowsills, and The Osmonds. They've even got Conway Twitty. I'm a little family record label. I have one act: Jessie James."

"Oh cry me a fucking river, Don Jon," Winston said in a tone that came out far more belligerent than he intended it to be. "Your 'one act' is one of the two hottest pop stars in America today. Let's make a deal we can both live with so we go into this with positive attitudes."

"Ah-h-h Tony, you're making my ass tired. Look, you're a star. And, you're a star I want on Sunshine Records. C'mon, let's make some hits together," Don Jon said with a big frown on his face.

Then, for dramatic effect, Don Jon stood up and started to pace. He hoped he was making Tony Winston nervous. After what he thought was enough time where he hadn't said anything, Don Jon walked over to the love seat where the aging singer was sitting, looked straight at him, stuck his right hand out, and said, "Goddammit, Tony, you're right. I only have one star on Sunshine Records, and I need another one. I really need another one. I need Tony Winston. I was taking the short view with that $10,000 per album offer. I was looking to make a quick buck. You have the long view. We do have to respect each other for this to work over the long haul. I'll take your counter offer, and I'll go you one better. I'll still pay you the fifty percent upfront money for all four albums right away. That's $40,000. That's how much I like you, respect you, and want you on Sunshine Records. Deal?"

Winston couldn't believe his luck — or — his moxie. He made Don Jon Ross double his offer, and he guilted him into paying the $40,000 upfront. "I'll take that deal, Don Jon. And, I'll make you glad you signed me."

"Great!" Don Jon said. "Let's make some hits and some money."

Sunshine Records' expenses and artful accounting would see to it that Tony Winston never saw more than the upfront $10,000 cash per album, and, if the accounting were artful enough, he might even have to give some of that back to Sunshine Records. But, at this point, only Don Jon Ross knew that. His business philosophy was given to him by his Harvard-educated attorney, Brian Williams, who always said, "We didn't create the system. We simply work within it!" This meant that all the expense manipulation would be legal…and in Don Jon's favor.

Well, that was easy, Tony Winston thought to himself. One bullying comment, and Don Jon Ross doubled his offer. Tony Winston already saw his name back at the top of the *Billboard* charts and on neon signs in front of big Las Vegas casinos. While mentally taking that all in as the big picture he had hoped for, he forgot to look at the small print…just as Don Jon Ross had planned.

"I think that's a deal we can both live with," Winston said with a grin. "Let's get Tony Winston and Sunshine Records some hits. Let's get Don Jon Ross some #1s."

Pleased that his con had worked and that he got Tony Winston for half the price he would have been willing to pay, Don Jon wanted to keep the moment light, so in his best Humphrey Bogart voice, he said, "Tony, I think this is the beginning of a beautiful friendship."

The two men laughed, and Don Jon threw out another impulsive idea to Winston. "You know what else I was thinking, Tony? Maybe we could pair you up with Jessie James on a song or two for the label. Think about how heavy that would be! Two superstars from different generations introducing each other to their fans, their generations."

That caught Winston off guard, and there was a moment of stilted silence. Don Jon sliced through that moment quickly. "Think about that. I'll have the contract papers drawn up and sent to you in Kenosha next week, but why don't you and I shake on it."

As the record company owner reached over to shake hands, Tony Winston dropped an unexpected bombshell: "Don Jon, did you know that Jessie and I used to be married?"

Then, in a one-two punch, Winston jammed another stick in the spokes: "So, Don Jon, you and I agree on the details and the numbers, but now I gotta run it past my lawyer."

Winston had no lawyer. Still a bit uneasy with his gut feelings on Don Jon Ross, he just wanted to buy a little time.

"Good idea, Tony," Ross responded immediately. "You got forty eight hours, and the clock is ticking." Ross hadn't been expecting this but felt he needed to sound confident, look confident, and act confident. He also had an inkling that there was no lawyer…that Winston was just stalling.

"And you gotta tell me about you and Jessie. What the hell?"

Chapter Fifty

Gary Ford ducked into the public men's room to read the note that Kim Starr had pressed into his hand. "Bingo!" he said louder than he had intended. Ford then ripped up the note and flushed it down the toilet. He didn't want Michele to accidentally find it nor did he want any evidence of his forthcoming tryst with the stunning Kim Starr to fall into the wrong hands. Then he washed his hands.

As he climbed back into the Rolls, Miller flashed her breasts at him. "That took a little too long, Mr. Ford," she griped. She flashed him again. "Maybe this will get you to the Snows of Stowe quicker!"

"I had to pee," Ford lied. Michele smelled his hands. "At least you have good hygiene," she chuckled. "Let's go."

Gary smiled as he made his way to Michele's hotel. Not only was he going to bag a cute Hollywood starlet tonight, but soon he was also going to have sex with possibly the most beautiful woman he had ever laid eyes on.

As the Snows of Stowe came into sight, Michele began to massage Ford's penis through his pants. "I'm starting this, Gary," she said looking straight at him. "If you want to finish it, this is what we have to do. There are too many busybodies at a place like this. I don't need any scandal. Drop me off by the shuttle bus stop over there, then drive around to the parking garage at the back of the hotel. Give me twenty minutes to walk to the hotel, make some small talk at the front desk, sign some autographs, take some pictures, and play 'Hollywood star' with everyone. You come up the back stairs to my room. It's 333 on the third floor. If no one is in the hallway, knock three times on my door. If someone is in the hallway, head to the main staircase and go down to the lobby for a few minutes, then come back up. Knock three times. Got it?"

"I hope the sex isn't this complicated," he said with a smile as she jumped out of the car, flashing him one more time.

Twenty minutes later Gary Ford was knocking on the door to room 333. Michele Miller pulled him into the room and immediately began to suffocate him with kisses as her hands prowled his body. "Get your clothes off, and get into my bed," she ordered.

Ford had anticipated good sex, but now he was thinking it could escalate into GREAT sex. Two hours later an exhausted Ford thought to himself, "What's the next level up from GREAT?"

Michele came bounding out of the bathroom with a gigantic red shower towel wrapped around her pert, lithe body. "That was fabulous, Mr. Ford," she said, leaning over him and giving him a peck on the cheek. "If you ever get to Hollywood, you'd better look me up. I could handle more of that. But now, I've got phone calls to make and some problems to take care of for my TV show. And it looks like I have to head out of here earlier than I thought. I'm probably leaving tomorrow."

Gary got out of bed and looked around for his clothes. Miller just stared at his naked body as he walked the ten feet to where they were draped over a satin love seat.

Nothing was said as he got dressed. Michele grabbed his coat and took it to him. "My home phone number is in the pocket." She led him to her door. As she put her hands around his neck to bring his face to hers for a final kiss, she said gently, "You were fabulous. When you fuck Kim, be nice and be careful. She's a sweet, sweet lady married to a dangerous, dangerous man. Goodbye, Gary."

Michele looked out into the hallway, then pushed Ford out. Ford walked down the hallway with a smirk on his face, whispering to himself, "So FABULOUS is the next level after GREAT."

As he got off the elevator in the lobby of the Snows of Stowe Resort, he found the nearest wastebasket and threw away the piece of paper holding Michele Miller's phone number. He had no intention of ever seeing her again.

He wanted Kim Starr. Gary Ford was a man who was best friends with lust. He knew lust as well as he knew himself. Lust was what he had — and all he had — for the likes of Michele Miller. However, his brief encounter with Kim Starr had him reeling. It was nothing he had ever experienced before. He didn't know what was going on in his head or his heart, but he couldn't wait to find out.

Michele Miller's warning was now rolling around in his head, *"When you fuck Kim, be nice and be careful. She's a sweet, sweet lady married to a dangerous, dangerous man."* The next thought that bounced around in his head was one that he had never had before. He didn't want to *fuck* Kim Starr. Nope. You *fucked* a woman like Michele Miller, someone who was only in your life for a moment. Someone whose body — and body alone — you wanted to savor for a night of lust but in the cold light of day be on your way.

He wanted to *make love* to Kim Starr. There was something magical that set a woman like Kim Starr apart from the rest. Yes, he'd only known her for all of maybe sixty minutes, but he sensed it. He had known only one other woman like her in his life. A woman he had made love to many, many times. A woman of great dignity and class. A woman he had been ready to marry and spend the rest of his life with. But it was not to be.

He got into the Rolls and sat behind the wheel, staring out into the falling snow. He started the car up and said very loudly to himself, "It's gonna be alright, Gary. It's gonna be alright."

Chapter Fifty One

Gene Pitney was on the phone with Al Kooper, who was making all the recording session arrangements Pitney had asked for. Kooper was especially excited about the Black church choir he had lined up for the recording session, The Harlem Gospel Choir.

"Gene, they'll make you weep," Kooper said dramatically. "They will make you fucking weep. You can take that to the bank. And, I got 'em for $250, but you gotta credit them on the record. Are you cool with that?"

"I am, Al, but I'm singing with them. With the choir. It's the only way I can get my voice on the record without getting in the way of the Hal and Jessie duet. So I'm gonna have to be up in front of the choir."

"Um-m-m, not quite sure what you're talking about there, Geno," Kooper said with a question in his voice. Kooper was in the dark because Pitney had purposely not told him who the recording session was really for and what was going to be recorded.

Pitney laid out the whole scenario for Kooper and said, "I HAD to mislead you and keep you in the dark, Al. Nothing personal, but a lot of futures and a lot of money is riding on this. I couldn't afford to have it sidetracked by a slip of the lip."

"So are Hal and Jessie the Hal and Jessie I think they are?" Kooper asked politely.

"Hal Douglas and Jessie James," said Pitney. "The two biggest teen idols on the charts right now, and they've written a duet that they want me to produce and sing on. You've just written the third verse of that duet. After this record comes out, Al, you'll never have another financial worry in your life. Now, your next mission, should you decide to accept it, is to figure out how to get me on the record without, like I said, getting in the way of the duet."

Kooper was silent. He was thinking as fast as he could. "Weeeeelllllllll," he drew out, "first things first. I don't think it's gonna be a problem with the choir, Gene. They're thrilled to death to be on a record with the legendary Gene Pitney. And, when they find out who else is on the record, they might pay you to be there! But, I'll explain it very clearly to them."

Pitney interrupted, "What about my third verse, Al?"

"Got it right here; I knocked it off in about an hour the other night. You'll love it. Now I gotta hope Hal and Jessie do, too. I didn't know who I was writing for, but I think it's pretty damn good."

Pitney said, "Let me hear it, Hotshot."

Kooper liked to sing but was only passable as a singer. Before he sang the third verse over the phone, he explained to Pitney, "I was a bit limited in what I could do because of what was already written. With all due respect, the verses you gave me were pretty much moon-June stuff. Very touching but pretty simple. But, I think I pulled it off and brought terrific closure to the song. Here it is. First up is what would be Hal's part."

Magic was THAT day
You walked into my life
Magic is THIS day
You will become my wife.

He let the simple but eloquent words sink in, then he began what would be Jessie's part.

When we first met
I WANTED it all
On this magical day
I HAVE it all.

"Then they join together for the chorus again," Kooper said.

If you walk with me

Down this aisle

A lifetime of love

Is what I'll…I'll

I'll promise you

So, promise me

End my fear

A lifetime of love

Is oh so near.

"Love it," said Pitney sincerely. "Nice job, Al, wrapping it up with past and present tense in both their verses. Now, where do you figure the choir and I come in."

Kooper fell silent again, then it dawned on him. "Where else but on the chorus?" Kooper said, matter-of-factly. "It's heaven-sent for you and the choir, especially that little stutter step on 'I'll…I'll…I'll promise you.' That's where Gene Pitney almost steals this record. Here's what we'll do. I'm gonna double track you but not the choir. I'll lay you in over and on top of the choir. You'll sound like you're floating above Hal, Jessie, and the choir. It's gonna be awesome. I think we'll need that croaking 'Town Without Pity' voice of yours."

"I can croak with the best of them. You're a genius, Al," said Pitney with real warmth. "You're a genius."

Getting caught up in the excitement of his last minute ad hoc plan for "A Lifetime of Love," Kooper blurted out, "I can't fucking wait to record this."

"That's two of us, Al," said Pitney. "But we have to wait a little bit longer, and we've gotta keep it under our hats."

Kooper heard him, but he was too excited to have anything Pitney was saying really register in his head because he had another idea for the record. "Hey, Gene, you've done me enough favors on this already what with getting me writer credit on the song for that third verse, but can I ask you for one more?"

"Fire away," said Pitney.

"I'd like to add a 'Like A Rolling Stone' organ to it," Kooper said, referencing his own spectacular organ playing on the iconic Bob Dylan record.

Pitney let those words hang in the air longer than was comfortable for Kooper, and he began to feel a bit self-conscious, thinking that maybe he had pushed his participation in the project a bit too far.

He broke the short silence with a question. "Whaddya think, Gene?"

"Great idea, Al," said Pitney. "Who are we gonna get to play that organ part?"

Kooper pulled the phone away from his ear and banged it on the table a couple of times, then picked it up and said very quietly, "You're a real prick, Pitney, but I think I may just know someone who can play it."

Laughing, he said goodbye to Pitney, saying he would see him in New York for the recording session, and hung up. Kooper was feeling a little smug. He had added a third verse to what could become one of the biggest-selling pop records of all time so his name would be on the label as a writer, and he had just talked himself onto the record as a musician. He needed this boost of self-confidence because he knew that his new band, Blood, Sweat & Tears, was suffering from infighting. Even though he was a founding member, he already felt he was being shunted into the background. He didn't think he was long for the group.

Al Kooper felt that "A Lifetime of Love" could be the crowning achievement of his still young career. The upcoming recording session looked like it was going to be a very important milestone in pop music history, and he was thrilled to be a part of it. The bigger thrill, however, was that he was a key player in the whole deal, a very key player. He loved that. He loved that his friend Gene Pitney had so much faith and confidence in him.

Chapter Fifty Two

The phone rang at 2574 N. Oakland Avenue in Milwaukee. Having just picked up their new car — a Christmas gift from Hal — Rita and Frank Douglas had walked in the door only moments before.

"I'll get it," Rita said. "You go soak your foot in some Epsom salts." Frank Douglas had suffered a serious leg injury when he was hit by Nazi machine-gun fire during World War II. The Epsom salts brought some soothing relief to the foot of his badly damaged right leg. Cold weather was especially rough on the war injury.

"Douglas residence, this is Mrs. Douglas speaking. How may I help you?"

"Good afternoon, Mrs. Douglas. This is Gene Pitney."

"Well, Mr. Pitney, isn't this a nice surprise. And you know what? We just heard that cowboy song of yours on WOKY as we were driving home in our new Ford Country Sedan. We needed that."

"Um-m-m, you needed to hear '(The Man Who Shot) Liberty Valance'?" Pitney asked, somewhat mystified.

"No," Mrs. Douglas said firmly. "We needed a station wagon. My husband Frank wanted a white one with the luggage rack. We were lucky they had one on the lot."

While Pitney was getting a kick out of talking with Hal's mother, he really wanted to talk to Hal and get all the arrangements made for him and Jessie to fly to Connecticut to get down to work.

"I've seen pictures of that car," Pitney said. "It's a beauty. I think you'll enjoy it. Say, Mrs. Douglas, is Hal around right now?"

"He is just coming in the door with Pepper," Mrs. Douglas said. "Not the condiment, the dog," she added with a chuckle in her voice. "Here he is, Mr. Pitney. Very nice speaking with you again. By the way, we really like that cowboy song. You should sing more of them."

Hal jumped on the phone as soon as he realized who was on the other end. "Hello, Mr. Pit...I mean...Gene. How are things in Connecticut?"

"Everything is coming together for the recording session, Hal," Pitney said. "Al Kooper wrote a terrific third verse, he lined up a fabulous Black church choir, and he's going to play organ on the record. He also came up with a brilliant ploy to get me on the record without getting in the way of your duet. Now, all we need is you and Jessie."

"That's all great news, Gene," Hal said, still finding it difficult to call his musical hero by his first name. "I have some great news, too."

Hal went on to give Pitney a long, detailed version of the conversation he had with Jessie about the recording session, her new TV show, and her joining him in the movies. He regaled Pitney with his plans to make Jessie a triple threat. Then he hesitated and summoned up all his courage to tell Pitney what the linchpin of his plan was.

"Gene, I want...let me rephrase that...I would very much like Jessie to join us on the UK tour. I'm hoping you'll say yes."

Gene decided to play with Hal a little bit. "Are you kidding me, Hal?"

"I'm not kidding you, Gene. I'm serious."

"You interrupted me, Hal," Gene fired back. "I was saying...are you kidding me? I never thought you'd ask! I wanted to throw that out as an option, but I didn't know how you two felt about it or what plans Jessie might have. But we do have to talk about money, Hal."

"Jessie and I haven't even discussed that, yet," Hal pointed out. "I don't want to sound naïve or like I'm a goody-goody, Gene, but the money isn't important to me at this point. That will come later. I want this to happen because I think it will be good for Jessie's career, my career, our career, and your career. I'm still not the brightest guy in show business, but I've been paying attention, and I see how one thing leads to another."

"You've become very wise very quickly," Pitney said.

"Thanks," said Hal. "I think the record will lead to big success on the UK tour, and that will lead to big success for her TV show. Put that all together, and it'll lead to big success for us in the movies. Colonel Parker proved that already with Elvis. Then it all goes around again, you know? More hit records for us, tours, TV shows, movies. I'm very excited for us, but this UK tour is the first step, and it's an important one."

"Great," said Pitney. "How soon can you two get back to Connecticut?" We'll rehearse the song here so as not to waste expensive studio time, and we can talk a little bit more about Tony Winston and Don Jon Ross. We also have to come to an agreement about who's gonna pay for the session."

"What do you suggest, Gene?" Hal asked. "The business end of show business is something I still need to learn."

"Well, we have at least five options," Pitney said. "First, we could pay for it and own the master, you, me, and Jessie. We'd split the session costs three ways. Second, you could pay for it and own the master. Third, Jessie could pay for it and own the master. Fourth, we could offer it to Don John Ross or Rick Starr and have one of them pay for it — or have them share the costs — and then they own the master. Fifth, I could pay for it and own the master."

"Wouldn't it best if we — you, me and Jessie — owned the master, regardless of the costs?" Hal asked. "It seems to me like it's going to be a pretty valuable master. If we own it then we decide what happens with it. We're in control, right?"

"Now you're thinking, Hal," said Pitney with a knowing smile in his voice. Hal Douglas was getting shrewder about the music business more and more every day.

"Can you give me a ballpark figure on what it's gonna cost to do this?" Hal asked.

"Rick Starr has always taken care of my records, and Jessie has Don Jon Ross. We're both novices in this aspect of our business."

"Depends," said Pitney. "What are we going to bill to the session? Are we going to pay me as producer and arranger? If so, how much? Can we rehearse and know the two songs so well we can get them recorded in one day to keep studio costs to eight hours? Right now, the only set costs we have are the travel costs, the studio time, the session musicians, the church choir, and Al Kooper. I think we're looking at maybe $5,000."

"Dang!" Hal virtually screamed into the phone. "I need to own my own record company. Those guys must make a fortune."

"They do quite well, Hal," said Pitney with more than a little chuckle. "You and I and Jessie do well, financially, as singers, but the real money is in songwriting, publishing, owning masters, and selling records. It's fun to be performing in front of audiences, but the real money is behind the scenes. That's the direction I'm moving in."

"Jessie and I want to go there, too, Gene. Where you lead, we will follow. See you soon. Bye."

Chapter Fifty Three

Kim Starr was just getting ready to jump in the shower after dropping her kids off for their two-hour ski lesson when her hotel phone rang. She was alone in the room. Her husband, Rick, had come down with a bad toothache overnight and was off to see a dentist.

She wasn't really sure she wanted to answer it because she was looking forward to a long, hot shower in peace and quiet, but she picked up the phone and gave a cursory "Hello."

"Hey, Kim, it's Michele. Can you talk?"

"Of course, Michele. I was just getting ready for a shower, but that can wait. Is everything OK?"

Michele Miller started sobbing. "No, nothing is OK, Kim. I just got off the phone with my agent. He says I need to 'suck it up' and shrug off how they're treating me on the TV show. I'm heading back to LA this morning to fire him and walk off their ninja fucking nurse show."

"Hey, Michele, are you sure you want to do that?" Kim asked, trying to be consoling yet sensible. "What else do you have going on or lined up? Do you really want to walk away from a network-TV hit show?"

Michele's sobbing had relented and had turned into anger. "Those sons-a-bitches treat me like crap because they think they have me over a barrel. What they don't know, Kim, is that Family Films wants to sign me to a six-film deal. I've heard they signed that kid singer, Hal Douglas, to a deal, too. I think they want to fashion these films after the Mickey Rooney *Andy Hardy* series. It's lightweight stuff, I know, but the money is good."

"Well, Michele, did you call for advice or just to vent?" Kim asked.

"A little bit of both, I guess," she answered.

"Are you done venting?" Kim asked in a very respectful tone of voice.

"I just want to kick their fucking nuts up into their fucking throats, every fucking one of them," Michele yelled into the phone. "There, now I'm done fucking venting," she added with a little laugh.

"Then," Kim said, "before you kick any nuts, fire anyone, or walk off a hit TV show, call your lawyer. You do have a lawyer, Michele?"

"Five Percent Freddie Steinberg's my guy," Michele said with another laugh. "Everyone gets a piece of the action when you're a star."

"Call Freddie and get his advice — then take his advice. Don't do anything rash or stupid that could get you blackballed in Hollywood. Promise me?"

"Alright, alright, I'll call Freddie when I get back to LA," Michele stipulated. "You're no fun, Kim. I really want to kick some balls into some throats. That's what a ninja fucking nurse would do. I gotta get to the airport now, but I'll call you tomorrow. I'll be good. Promise. Bye."

Kim shook her head at how irrational some people could be. Michele was ready to throw away a small fortune and her career because her feelings were hurt. Speaking to the empty hotel room, Kim said, "Your agent's right, Michele. Suck it up, and shrug it off. A million other talented actresses out there would give anything to be in your position. I was one of them. You're the lucky one who is. Suck it up, and shrug it off."

Then, she stripped naked and picked up the phone again. She placed a call to the Presidents Residence. When the hotel clerk answered, Kim asked to be put through to Gary Ford's room.

Ford picked up the phone and sleepily said, "Hi, it's Gary."

"Gary, it's Kim Starr. I'm standing naked, alone in my hotel room, just getting ready to take a hot, steaming shower. And I'm thinking about you."

Ford had been awake all of five minutes and was trying to get acclimated to the cold light of day. "Either I'm asleep and dreaming or that is the least subliminal thing anyone has ever said to me while I was awake," Ford responded with a hearty laugh.

"It wasn't meant to be subliminal," Starr said. "It was meant to paint a clear picture for you. I'm offering myself to you; I'm here for the taking. I just want to make that perfectly clear to you, but it will also be on my terms. I will call you at noon tomorrow. Goodbye, Gary."

Chapter Fifty Four

Don Jon Ross and Tony Winston needed each other. They kinda liked each other. And each of them thought that he had one-upped the other in the contract they had just agreed on — but had not signed. Still, Ross was wondering why Winston hadn't even mentioned the fact in any of their previous conversations that he'd been married to Jessie James. So he asked.

"Tony, what's the deal? Why did you keep that top secret?"

"Well, Don Jon, it's a bit of a long and somewhat sticky story that I don't want to get into right now. Or ever. But, suffice it to say, there won't be any duets with Jessie James and me. Can we leave it at that?"

"Well, I guess it really wasn't part of the contract," Don Jon said, "so I can't really hold you to it, but you sure are making me pretty curious about this."

Winston was not going to tell Don Jon about the stipulations he had agreed to with Jessie's parents — Jansen and Jayna James — so he could keep his career afloat. He was embarrassed about it and was trying to let the whole thing die on the vine. No one needed to know. It could only hurt him.

Winston felt a cold chill go up his spine, and it wasn't from the freezer-like atmosphere in Don Jon's room. "Look, it's all resolved between Jessie and me," he explained. "There is some bad blood, but it's resolved. You've gotta accept that, Don Jon."

Don Jon didn't like to be told what he "had to accept," but he decided that this was not the time nor the place to hold an inquisition. And he surely was going to remember this conversation and look into it — for two reasons. First, he was nosey, and this seemed like it was ripe for some real juicy gossip. Second, he wanted to make sure he wasn't signing either a slug or a criminal to his record label.

While he was perturbed with his newest star, he decided he was going to act cool about the whole thing. "I'm OK with that, Tony, if you assure me that it's all resolved between Jessie and you. She's my future. She's single-handedly keeping Sunshine Records afloat. I gotta keep her happy. Got it?"

"All you have to do," Winston said, "is tell Jessie that we will never record together, we will never tour together, and we will likely never be in the same city together."

"If that's the resolution then so be it," said Don Jon. "Hey, can you come back to LA with me to meet my brother, Jim Tim? He was going to come with me, but he had a last minute change of plans. I told you he's a huge fan of yours, and he's written at least four great songs for you to record. I'd like you to hear them. And, as long as you're there, I'll introduce you to my sister, Fay Kay. She's the accountant at Sunshine Records. She's the one who will be signing your checks."

Once again, Tony Winston's brain was spinning inside his head. Not only could he not go to LA, but Don Jon had a sister with a rhyming name, too? "Son of a bitch," he muttered under his breath.

"You really gotta hear these songs," Don Jon said. "They're brilliant."

"Don Jon, I can't step foot in LA. Part of the resolution. Can your brother come here?"

Now Don Jon's irritability status had ratcheted up from being simply perturbed to getting very pissed off. "Tony," he semi-screamed, "now you are seriously making my ass tired. You may not want to tell me what happened between you and Jessie, but if I keep hearing you can't do this, you can't do that, you can't go here, and you can't go there I'm gonna start thinking something bad happened. And, speaking as the owner of Sunshine Records, that bothers me about one of my artists."

"C'mon, Don Jon," Tony yelled back. "LA isn't the only place I can record. We can do it here or in New York or even Chicago. You gotta let me and Jessie keep the peace the way we want to and have to. Can you do that? What's the difference where we record?"

Don Jon was getting ready to blow his top and give Tony a piece of his mind. Then it dawned on him that the seemingly very uncomfortable position that the singer was in opened up a big window of financial opportunity for Don Jon Ross and Sunshine Records. The lightbulb went on in his head. Not using the Sunshine Records studio to record meant they'd have to pay for a studio and studio time and hire musicians who weren't friends with and loyal to Don Jon for the work he gave them. Expenses. Lots of expenses. Lots of opportunities to pad the expenses at Tony Winston's expense, pun intended, thought Don Jon.

He decided his best gambit was to play along with Tony…agree that it was no big deal where they recorded. Shrugging his massive shoulders and throwing his pudgy arms in the air, Don Jon said, "You're right, Tony. We can make hit records any-where. Let's do it where you're most comfortable. Do you want to record here or in New York or Chicago?"

"Me and the girls recorded all of our early hits in Studio A at RCA in New York," Tony said very excitedly. "I would love to go back there and record these albums there."

With dollar signs in his eyes and the thought of an all-expenses-paid trip to New York, courtesy of Tony Winston and his contract, Don Jon stuck his hand out and said, "It's a deal, Tony. We're gonna get you Studio A at RCA in New York, and we're going to make magic again."

Chapter Fifty Five

"We're gonna call the album *World-Wide World War II Winners*," Don Jon Ross told his newest recording artist. "Whaddya think?" Like most things in both his personal and professional life, the Sunshine Records owner pretty much made up the title on the spot without much thought or research.

It was nine o'clock on a Monday morning, and Tony Winston was elated to be back in Studio A of the RCA Recording Studio on East 24th Street, between Lexington and Third Avenue in Manhattan. He was momentarily lost in the memories of those years when he and his sisters topped the charts with songs recorded in this very studio. He heard Don Jon, but the words didn't register. He was remembering his glorious past and wondering if it really could happen again. Could lightning strike again and put him back at the top of the charts?

Don Jon Ross took Winston's silence as disapproval and said, "Well, then you come up with a better title."

Winston snapped out of his reverie and dropped back into the conversation. "I'm sorry, Don Jon," he said. "It's just so exciting to be back here. I was daydreaming there for a bit. Title? What title are we talking about?"

"Your first Sunshine records album, *World-Wide World War II Winners*," said Don Jon.

Tony was more than a little worried that the title Don Jon had dreamed up would pigeonhole him as a washed up singer who wasn't contemporary or relevant. But, he had to be careful. He had signed the Sunshine Records contract that Don Jon had drawn up, which called for the World War II album. He also didn't want to insult or upset Ross who, essentially, was salvaging his career

"Yeah, I like it, and so will my fans." He secretly hoped he was right and that Don Jon's idea would work. To get his mind off his insecurity he decided to change the subject.

"Don Jon, did you know that Elvis recorded 'Hound Dog' and 'Don't Be Cruel' right here in this very studio? How cool is that?"

"Your fans don't want to hear that crap," Don Jon said. He realized his tone of voice was a little too defensive, so he quickly added, "They want to hear their favorite crooner from *Teddy Griffin's Talent Jamboree* sing sentimental songs that let them relive their youth. They want to be taken back in time to when they were young and attractive and getting laid!"

"I know, Don Jon," said Winston, explaining himself. "Sometimes I find it hard to believe that a schmuck like me from Kenosha, Wisconsin, recorded hit records in the same studio that Elvis did. That's all I meant."

Even though, in general, Don Jon didn't much stand on tradition, he was impressed to be in RCA Studio A, and he let his artist know that.

Just then the producers of Tony Winston's World War II album walked in. Don Jon wanted a great record, as well as an expensive one, so he had hired the hit-making team of Hugo and Luigi.

Hugo Peretti and Luigi Creatore were cousins who produced hits for Perry Como, Elvis Presley, Sam Cooke, and a host of other RCA Victor recording artists. Their hits included Cooke's "Twistin' The Night Away" and "Another Saturday Night" as well as "I Will Follow Him" for Little Peggy March and "Shout" for The Isley Brothers. They became seriously wealthy after co-writing Elvis Presley's smash "Can't Help Falling In Love."

They were a surprise that Don Jon wanted to spring on Winston. Tony looked at the famous pair then looked at Don Jon Ross and said in astonishment, "You seriously got Hugo and Luigi to produce my album, Don Jon? I'll be a son of a bitch."

Winston headed across the room to shake hands with his producers but stopped and hugged Don Jon on his way.

"Awkward," the bulky and not so touchy-feely record company owner shouted. "Leave me alone! Go say 'Hi' to the boys."

"Hi, I'm Tony Winston," he said as he introduced himself to the famed producers. "I can't tell you how thrilled I am to work with you on this project."

"We're pretty excited about it, too," said Hugo Peretti. "Who's the Gene Pitney fan?"

Both Winston and Ross just stared at the producer, who was casually dressed in a Perry Como-type cardigan sweater. Neither one knew what he meant by the comment.

Don Jon offered up a quick answer. "I love Gene Pitney. Wish I had him on my label. But, where'd that come from?"

"The album title," Peretti said. "Pitney put out an album a few years ago titled *Gene Pitney Sings World-Wide Winners*. Thought maybe that's where you got it."

"Nah," said Don Jon. "I just thought it up and liked the sound of it. Whaddya think?"

"I think Gene Pitney might be looking for a label," said Luigi Creatore, avoiding the album title discussion and steering the conversation into shoptalk. "That's what we hear on the street. We've also heard that he's booked time for a recording session at Bell Sound, but it's all kind of mysterious. No one is really sure what's going on because Pitney — not his record label — is paying for the session."

"You really think Pitney might be available to sign?" Don Jon asked as the wheels started turning in his head. "He really hasn't had a big hit for a while. Hm-m-m. That's an interesting prospect."

Peretti wanted to get to work. "What time are the musos coming?" he asked Don Jon, using the insider nickname for musicians.

"The studio will be set for them to come in at eleven," Don Jon said. Then, looking at Winston, he added, "Tony says his voice is best in the afternoon. We've got the studio all day. No one else is booked. Do you think we can cut twelve songs in eight hours?"

"We can," Luigi Creatore said. "After you sent us the song list we put together the charts, so we're ready to go. I presume you hired the usual suspects for session work. The question is, can Tony do twelve songs in one session? That's quite a workload."

Winston, who was drinking hot tea to get his vocal chords lubricated, said, "Not trying to sound cocky fellas, but I can do most of these songs in one or two takes. Don Jon picked 'em. I like most of them so that makes it easier."

Hugo Peretti then made a stunning suggestion for the session: "Why don't we try it live, you singing with the orchestra instead of recording separate tracks? Are you up for that, Tony?"

"Great idea," Tony said. "Don Jon, do we have background singers coming in?"

"I hired Cissy Houston, and she's bringing in some girls with her."

Hugo explained that he and Luigi had worked with Cissy Houston before, and they felt she could and would love to do the session live with the orchestra. Looking at his watch, Peretti said, "OK, it's 10:30; let's get into the studio so we can set the orchestra up the way we want. And, can we change the title to *World-Wide Winners From World War II*? It trips off the tongue better, I think."

"Done," said Don Jon. "What else can you guys tell me about Gene Pitney?"

Chapter Fifty Six

Everything and everybody was working unbelievably well. They were only three hours into the session, and eleven songs were done, five of them done on the first take. "I'll Be Seeing You" was the final song of Tony Winston's recording session with Hugo and Luigi. Winston asked them to keep that song until the end because he wanted his voice to be a little strained.

"I'll sound very broken-hearted," he said with a laugh. "This is the one that will make 'em weep."

What he hadn't given any thought to was what his reaction would be to the song as he was singing it. He was only ten years old when President Franklin Roosevelt asked Congress to declare war on Japan, so he didn't have the WWII connection to the song. But, as he was recording it, his mind began to conjure up memories of his beloved sisters.

Growing up in a warm, close, and loud Italian family in Kenosha; winning *Teddy Griffin's Talent Jamboree*; soaring to undreamed of heights in show business. It was a great life with great memories…until the accident that took his sisters' lives.

I'll be seeing you in every lovely summer's day…in everything that's light and gay…I'll always think of you that way…I'll find you in the morning sun…

That verse crushed him. Tears rolled down his cheeks like raindrops. The pain of the lovely memories cracked his voice in anguish, but he kept on singing, almost whispering the lyrics. The orchestra kept on playing, and Hugo and Luigi kept the tape rolling.

In the control room, Hugo turned to Luigi and Don Jon and said, "I've never seen or heard anything like this. We're using THIS take. This is extraordinary. I think Tony might have a #1 on his hands here."

Don Jon Ross couldn't believe his ears. A #1? Could it be possible that he had just signed another hit maker to little Sunshine Records? And he got him for a song, pun intended.

Tony Winston, shoulders sagging, heart breaking, and tears streaming, finished the song, took off his headphones, and just stared into space. The entire orchestra stood up and applauded the performance. Winston walked out of the studio and began to weep. He had no idea what reaction Hugo, Luigi, and Don Jon had to what had just happened in the studio, and he didn't care. He just knew he couldn't record the song again. He may not, he thought, ever be able to sing it again.

Don Jon found Winston in the anteroom to the studio. "That's all I've got, Don Jon," Winston whispered. "I can't do it again. If it didn't work for you or Hugo and Luigi, you're gonna have to come up with another song."

"Tony," Don Jon said, beaming, "Hugo and Luigi could not believe their ears. They think you have a #1. You wanna hear the playback?"

"I can't do that today, Don Jon. Maybe tomorrow. I gotta go." With that, Tony grabbed his cashmere overcoat and headed out to the street to hail a cab. It was snowing, and the Christmas decorations were still up all over the city. Only three cabs passed him before one picked him up.

He hopped into the back seat and said, "Plaza Hotel, 5th Avenue and 59th Street."

"Do I look like a tourist?" the seasoned cab driver asked sarcastically. "I've been driving cab in Manhattan since 1951. I know where the Plaza Hotel is."

Not in the mood for any kind of pissing match or small talk with a cab driver, Tony simply said, "Sorry. I have a lot on my mind right now."

The cab driver turned around to face his back seat passenger to accept his apology. "Hey, you look very familiar, Do I know you? My name's Charlie. They call me

Charlie Mumbles cuz I don't always speak so loud and so clear, ya know? But, I know you from somewhere. What's your name?"

Tony was torn. Should he introduce himself to the now suddenly loquacious cabbie as Tony Ranzunno or as Tony Winston? Did he want to talk to someone now to take his mind off his sisters…the sisters he adored? Or did he want to be left alone in his thoughts?

As he was mulling his decision over in his mind, Charlie Mumbles forced his hand. "Hey, wait a minute," the cabbie said. "That's RCA. You're a singer — a famous singer. Wait, wait, don't tell me. It's coming to me. You sang with them three girls. That's it. Tony Winston and the Churchill Sisters. You're Tony Winston. Son of a bitch. I've got the great Tony Winston in my cab. You doing another record?"

"Hi, Charlie. I am Tony Winston. And, yes, I am doing another record. Thanks for asking."

"Tony Winston. How 'bout that?" Charlie said more to himself than to Winston. "Me and my mom, God rest her soul, used to watch you on that *Teddy Griffin Talent Jamboree* TV show. She loved you. She thought you were better than Sinatra. I loved all those records you made with the girls. What was that last one you did? You know, from that movie? The one with that British bombshell. I can't think of her name right now. Man, she was a dish."

"'London Lady Falling Down,'" Tony answered. "That was our last hit. Jenny Cobb starred in that movie with Steve McQueen. But, I gotta be honest with you, Charlie. I've never seen the movie. They did screen it in Hollywood the night before the Oscars, but I was stuck at the airport in Chicago."

"Did you ever get to meet those two? Steve McQueen and Jenny Cobb?" Charlie asked in wonderment. Charlie loved going to the movies and watching TV. He couldn't get enough information on his favorite stars.

"I did get to meet them both at the Oscar show and at an Oscar party afterwards at Jayna James' home. Steve McQueen wasn't talking to anybody at the party. He looked pretty sullen. I got to say hello to Jenny Cobb and chat with her about five minutes. She was stuck to that husband of hers like a stamp to a letter. She said very nice things about our record. And, Charlie, I gotta tell you, she is far more beautiful in person than she is on the big screen. I heard that she just signed to do the next Elvis movie."

"Hey, Tony. I gotta ask you a question, if you don't mind?"

"Fire away," said Winston.

"Really, how did that song win an Oscar?" Charlie asked, and without waiting for an answer, he started to sing it: *Walking along the Thames…one of London's gems…in her Audrey Hepburn gown…London Lady falling down…by the light of Big Ben …it was plain to see…I had fallen for her…and London Lady had fallen for me.*"

Winston laughed out loud, almost snorted, listening to Charlie Mumbles' version of his Oscar-winning song. "Our version was much better than that pathetic attempt," Winston said, giving Charlie a little punch in the shoulder. "And, when you put strings and horns on a song, a lot is forgiven. It was written by a guy who wrote a bunch of Top 40 hits in the 1950s, and it needed a 1950s feel, you know, because the Steve McQueen character was an aging 1950s pop star. As long as it rhymed, everyone was happy. It sure beat 'Mairzy Doats'!"

"I hear ya. So how come I haven't heard you on the radio lately?" Charlie asked innocently enough.

"The British groups kinda killed our careers," Tony said politely. "And a lot of others', too. But I'm not looking back, Charlie. Moving forward. I'm recording again. Got a big deal with Sunshine Records. Gonna get some more hits."

"I hope so," Charlie said. "Most of the music the kids are listening to today ain't all that bad, but it ain't what we had in the '50s. You know, Sinatra, Como, Clooney, Crosby…Tony Winston."

"Thanks, Charlie," Tony said. "You got kids?"

"Two teenagers…twins," he said. "Good kids. I hope they go to college and make something of themselves, unlike their father."

"Don't put yourself down like that, Charlie," Tony said. "A job's a job. And driving cab in Manhattan is one tough job. What kind of music do they like?"

"My boy Warren likes those bands that you say put you out of business," Charlie said with a subdued laugh. "You know, The Beatles, The Rolling Stones, The Dave Clark Five, and that Herman guy. His twin sister Wanda loves the boy singers like Hal Douglas, Neil Diamond, Bobby Vinton, and Gene Pitney. And, she's really crazy about that girl singer, Jessie James. All she sang last summer was that 'Yes! No! Yes!' song, and now all she plays on her record player in her room is that new one 'Love Me Now.' Do you know her, Tony? Do you know those songs?"

"I've heard of her," Tony said, somewhat chagrined and not offering up any information at all about his short-lived marriage to the pop star.

"Here's The Plaza, Tony. Front door, OK?" asked Charlie.

Tony pulled two $50 bills out of his pocket and gave them to Charlie Mumbles. "It's yours, Charlie. Thanks for the ride and the conversation. And Charlie, thanks for remembering. Do me a favor?"

"If I can I sure as hell will," said Charlie.

"Call The Plaza and give the front desk your name and phone number, and tell them to give it to me. When I do a show in New York I want you and your family there."

Tony Winston jumped out of the cab and disappeared inside The Plaza.

Charlie "Mumbles" Carson decided to call it a day and go home to take care of his ailing wife. She had been diagnosed with cancer earlier that year. The $100 Tony Winston had given him was about what he earned in a month traversing the streets of Manhattan in his cab. He decided that he would stop and pick up her favorite pizza and surprise her and the twins. Hell, he decided to splurge and get two pizzas, a six-pack of Coke, and a gallon of ice cream for dessert. It was going to be a party at the Carson house that night, courtesy of Tony Winston.

Charlie rolled down the window of his cab and yelled to anyone on the streets of Manhattan who would listen, "God bless Tony Winston!"

Chapter Fifty Seven

"I've gotta move to Las Vegas," Tony Winston mumbled to himself as he heard Irene Buri Nelson on WLIP Radio say, "Right now…ten degrees below zero in downtown Kenosha…that will shiver your timbers!"

Just then his phone rang. He really didn't want to get out of his warm bed to answer it, but he thought to himself that it would be a good way to get motivated and get going on this icy January morning.

He glimpsed at himself as he passed by the mirror on the huge dresser next to his bed. "I make Professor Irwin Corey look good right now," he said to his image as he ran his hand through his wavy locks of graying hair drifting in all four compass directions.

He got into the living room and picked up the phone, "Hey, it's Tony."

"Tony, it's Frank."

Tony Winston was shocked. He recognized the Chairman of the Board's voice instantly. He was rattled and didn't know what to say, so he just said, "Hey, Frank."

"I just heard William B. Williams play your record 'I'll Be Seeing You' on WNEW," Sinatra said. "I hate your guts."

"Jeez, Frank," Tony said, not knowing if Sinatra was serious or kidding. "I did it in one take. I didn't know they were going to release it as a single." Tony hoped that statement was innocent enough and would bring something out of Sinatra that would clarify what he meant.

"I recorded that song a couple of times," Sinatra said, laughing, "and I could never get it fucking right. How did a jamoke like you from Wisconsin make one of the greatest records I've ever heard? Crosby's gonna slash his wrists when he hears it."

Even though it was ten degrees below zero outside his living room window, Tony Winston was sweating and shaking. His heart was racing at Indy 500 speed. He didn't know what to say or how to react.

"You gotta come to New York and do Ed Sullivan's show," Sinatra said. "Are you still working? What's going on with you? I haven't seen you in ages. What label are you on? RCA? Capitol?"

Tony decided quickly that he was going to be straight with Sinatra. The two had been great pals in the late '50s and early '60s, before Tony's career faded. Now, Sinatra was SINATRA and Tony Winston was a footnote. "I'm helping out a guy who owns a small record company, and I signed a four-album deal with him. And, I gotta be honest, Frank. No one else was knockin' on my door, even after my record won an Oscar."

"C'mon, Tony," Sinatra said, "That 'London Lady Falling Down' was a bullshit record. It won because that movie was such a blockbuster. And that dame in that movie, Julie Cobb, now that's a dame."

"Her name is Jenny, Jenny Cobb, Frank. She just signed on for the next Elvis movie," Tony said. "She's gonna be huge. And, hey, it may have been a bullshit song, but they gave us five grand to do it," Tony added a bit defensively. "And, that Cushman guy, the movie producer, he almost begged us to do it. Plus, the girls wanted to."

"Speaking of the girls," Sinatra said with some sadness in his voice, "very sorry about your loss. I loved your sisters, Tony. You know that."

Neither one knew what to say so there was a short silence that seemed to last an eternity. Then Sinatra said forcefully, "You shoulda called me. I've got my own label, you know. We could have put together a deal for you on Reprise. I would have loved to have this song on my label, but you give it to a small label schmuck. I don't know what's wrong with you, Tony. Why didn't you call me?"

"C'mon, Frank," Tony said, starting to clench his teeth. He didn't want to piss Sinatra off, but he wanted him to know that he had felt abandoned after his recording career crashed. His voice slowly got louder and angrier as he addressed Sinatra. "The Beatles come, and all of a sudden people like me and my sisters are persona non grata, both with the public and the record industry. My recording career died, AND my sisters died. No one called me to be on their TV shows; no one called me to open for them on a nightclub tour; and certainly no one called me to be on their record label. Not even a pity call from any of my old 'friends.'"

Sinatra was uncharacteristically quiet on the other end of the phone.

"Then, one guy calls," Winston said quietly. "One small label schmuck named Don Jon Ross at Sunshine Records. He calls and offers me a deal. A four-record deal. I'm gonna say 'No, I don't need you. I'm just waiting here for RCA or Capitol to call. You have a nice day Mr. Small Label Schmuck. Thanks for calling'?"

There was complete silence on Sinatra's end of the phone line.

"That guy showed me respect, Frank," Tony said, talking a bit too loudly. "He wanted me on his label. So, really, the question is, why didn't YOU call ME? You're the Chairman of the goddamn Board. Why didn't YOU call ME with an offer?"

Sinatra, who knew the ups and downs of show business better than anyone else did, let Tony's rage sink in before saying anything. Thoughts of how he had humbled himself to get his Oscar-winning role as Maggio in *From Here To Eternity* were running through his head. He recognized the bitterness and anger that Tony Winston was venting.

While he was more than a little taken aback by Tony's shouting and finger pointing, Sinatra shrugged much of it off to Tony's Italian bravado, but, in the pit of his stomach, he knew that Tony was right. Frank Sinatra, the biggest star in America in the 1940s, knew how humbling the rejection of your former peers could be ten years later in the 1950s. Frank Sinatra knew how crushingly embarrassing it was to pick up a phone and call someone who once worked for you or was one rung below you in the show business pecking order and ask them for a job.

Frank Sinatra knew exactly where Tony Winston was coming from. "I'm calling you now, Tony. You're right; I shoulda called you when you really needed me, but I'm calling you now. 'I'll Be Seeing You' is one of the greatest records I've ever heard. Whatever you want or need from me, you've got. Let's make that record #1."

Chapter Fifty Eight

One month later, Frank Sinatra had stayed true to his word. He had told Tony Winston "'I'll Be Seeing You' is one of the greatest records I've ever heard. Whatever you want or need from me, you've got it. Let's make that record #1."

After that, Tony got calls to be on all the major talk shows and variety shows including Ed Sullivan, Merv Griffin, Johnny Carson, Andy Williams, the Smothers Brothers, and many more. They all wanted him to sing "I'll Be Seeing You."

Radio stations coast to coast were playing Tony's new record and dusting off some of his old hits to play, too. And, the icing on the cake: Tony was now headlining New York's famed Copacabana nightclub at the unheard of salary of $15,000 per week.

His face was on the cover of the big music magazines, *Billboard* and *Cashbox*, as well as *Time* and *Newsweek*. Tony Winston's comeback was being heralded as the "story of the year," and the new year was barely two months old.

Tony Winston could not believe his luck. Less than three months ago he was in a hotel room with Don Jon Ross just trying to salvage his career. Now, he was the hottest property in show business. But, Tony Winston wasn't thinking about his career at all right now. He was ensconced in his luxurious suite at The Plaza Hotel, recovering from a raucous Copacabana show the night before when two members of the Rat Pack — Frank Sinatra and Dean Martin — had joined him on stage, and his ninety-minute late show went on for almost two and a half hours.

Winston was relaxing by watching his favorite TV game show, *Concentration* starring Hugh Downs. The phone rang, and it both startled and irritated the singer. He really loved *Concentration* and prided himself on usually solving the puzzle before the contestants. Now the damn phone ringing was ruining his concentration. He didn't want to abandon *Concentration*, but he was always interested in who was calling and what offer they were making because he acted as his own agent.

Grabbing the receiver from the cradle of the phone, with a bit of an edge to his voice he said, "This is Tony Winston…how did you get my number?" On the other end of the line, Rick Starr said, "One little fucking hit record, and all of a sudden you're gonna be a dick?"

Tony Winston didn't recognize the voice and certainly didn't like the attitude he was hearing. But, after many long and quiet conversations with Frank Sinatra about career ups and downs and how to weather those storms successfully, Tony calmed himself down quickly and said, "Let me try that again. Hi, this is Tony Winston; what can I do for YOU?"

"Ah-h-h, I was just goofing around, Tony. This is Rick Starr. Do you know who I am?"

"Everybody in the free world knows who Rick Starr is," Tony said, sounding profoundly impressed that Rick Starr was calling him. "I watch your TV show all the time."

"That's what I'm calling about, Tony. I want you on my TV show, *Starr Power*. What do I have to do to get you on? Who do I call? And, by the way, what's your contract like with Sunshine Records?"

"Let's take those one at a time," Tony said. "I'd love to do *Starr Power*, and I'm my own manager, so let's consider that done. My deal with Sunshine Records calls for four albums in a two-year period. That's it. It's pretty clean and simple."

Rick Starr liked the sound of all of that, especially that Winston was his own manager. Starr didn't hold artists in high regard either for their talent or for their business acumen. To him, singers were a dime a dozen, and he never met one he thought could outsmart him.

He knew of Tony Winston's past career and figured this new run of success was a flash in the pan, but he still wanted a piece of it if he could get it. And he wanted it now — before it fizzled out.

"Listen, Tony, I'm a power broker in music, TV, and movies. You probably already know that. I've got my own record label and music publishing company; I've got the TV show; and I'm starting to make movies. I can get you into the show business stratosphere before you can say 'Rick Starr is my hero.' We should be working together. What is Sunshine Records doing for you?"

"Whoa, whoa, whoa, Rick. Slow down," Tony said. "I've got a record deal with a guy who showed me respect when no one else did, and he signed me to a pretty nice deal. Why would I leave him? We got a #1 with our first record, and I'm guessing there could be more to come. I'm sitting very pretty right now."

"You've been in show business a long time, Tony," Rick said, trying to set Winston up so he could go in for the kill. "You know how much money the big labels like Capitol, RCA, and Starr Records can spend promoting an artist's career and working on longevity for that artist. How much is Sunshine spending on you?"

"Fuck if I know," Winston said, wondering to himself IF he should know.

"Probably not a lot, if anything," Starr said quickly. "I haven't seen any ads in the trades for you, and I'm guessing you got yourself on all those TV shows using your own contacts. You're heading for burnout, Tony. You can't do it all. You need to concentrate on the performing part of your career and let someone like me handle the business end of it. Is that something you're interested in talking about?"

Much of what Rick Starr had just said sunk in quickly with Tony. After all, he himself thought Don Jon Ross was a chump. But, he was a chump who gave Tony his second shot at fame and fortune. Tony was interested in becoming a superstar again. Maybe he could work out a deal that benefitted all three of them — Rick Starr, Don Jon Ross, and himself — so he agreed to talk to Rick Starr about his career.

"OK, Rick. I'm interested," Tony said "but I won't do anything unless Don Jon Ross and Sunshine Records get a square deal. Can we agree on that?"

"I'm sure we can," Starr said. "How soon can you come here and tape my TV show? That's when we can talk about it all."

"Where do you tape *Starr Power*?" Tony asked, as he was quickly getting excited about what working with a media magnate like Rick Starr could mean to his career.

"We tape in LA," Starr said.

"Oh shit," Tony said to himself. Then, regaining his composure, he said to Rick Starr, "Throw some dates out, and I'll check 'em against my calendar and get back to you."

Chapter Fifty Nine

Rick Starr was having sex with his wife, Kim, as the kids were sleeping and the sun was rising on another gorgeous Sunday in Pacific Palisades. There was about as much passion in their lovemaking as there was in the reading of a will. Kim surrendered herself to him so he wouldn't be able to justify a possible wandering eye. Rick always bragged to anyone who would listen how he liked to "bang my babe."

He still found his thirty-two-year-old wife beautiful and desirable, and he enjoyed their little fifteen-minute trysts every Sunday morning. Rick was only interested in his sexual satisfaction. He was not a very involved or creative lover, and that worked to Kim's benefit this particular Sunday morning.

As Rick was thrusting away, trying to reach his sexual fulfillment, he didn't notice how distant and uninvolved his wife was. There was no way he would realize that she wasn't really engaged in what was going on in her bed. Her life was flashing by her as she accepted Rick's gyrations. She thought of what a wonderful — if not over-ly-loving — life he had given her; she thought about the thrilling week of exquisite and passionate lovemaking she had shared with Gary Ford in Vermont; she thought of her kids; she thought of what the downside for them and her would be in leaving Rick; she thought about the kind of life she and the kids could have with Gary Ford in Chicago; she thought about the possibility of Rick having her killed if she left him; she thought about the possibility of Rick having Gary Ford killed if he found out about the affair.

She was startled out of her reverie, and Rick was stymied in his sexual conquest by the phone ringing.

"Son of a bitch," he said as he rolled off Kim. "I was almost there. Who the hell is calling me on a Sunday morning?"

Kim, trying to play the part of the loyal and loving wife, grabbed her husband's hands, put them on her breasts, and said, "You don't HAVE to answer it, you know. You can talk to these."

"C'mon Kim," he snarled back at her. "I can talk to your tits any time I want. This could be someone offering me a deal. I'm gonna take this call. I'm done with you. Go take a shower."

Rick's callous dismissal of his naked, gorgeous wife was a relief to her. Remembering her glorious sexual escapades with Gary, Rick's robotic sexual machinations left her cold, dispirited, and unmoved. Gary had made warm, sweet, passionate love to her night after night. Rick Starr simply "banged my babe," as he liked to brag.

As she headed for the shower that was connected to their huge 40x40 master bed-room, she heard Rick answer the phone. "It's Rick…it's early…this better be good."

"Hey Rick…Tony Winston. I know it's early, but I'm just getting back to the hotel after my Copa show, and I wanted to get something cleared up with you. Can we talk?"

"Well, Tony, just for the record, I was banging my babe when you called. So, again, this better be good. Talk to me."

"I was talking to Frank Sinatra, Dean Martin, and Jules Podell after my show to-night, and they gave me an idea. Jules wants me to extend my gig at the Copa. We're breaking records that were set in the 1950s by Dean and Jerry. It's incredible."

"Hooray for Tony Winston," Rick said in a semi-mocking tone of voice. His sense was Winston was angling for some sort of deal and was going to try to fleece him because he was so hot right now. "So, you're calling me at 6:30 in the morning to impress me with a head count from all of your shows at the Copa?"

"No, you'll read about that AND how much money they're paying me to extend my stay in *Daily Variety* on Monday," Winston shot back with more than some minor irritation. He was getting tired of Starr's condescension but was careful to not get mad about it. "It's about your TV show, Rick. I wanna do *Starr Power*, but with this new deal and some other stuff I've got going on in New York, I don't have any time to get out to LA. But, Frank, Dean, and Jules said it would be a great idea if you came to the Copa and taped a 'live' segment for your show. Jules said he would even cover your production and talent costs. Whaddya think?"

Rick Starr loved the idea, but he didn't want to accept it right away. That would take some of his bargaining power away. He wanted to hold the upper hand with Winston, who he still thought was going to be a flash in the pan on his second round of stardom.

"The Copa will pick up my production costs?" Starr asked. "Well, that's a good start."

Starr was thinking on his feet. He quickly saw this as an opportunity to get his current teen heartthrob, Hal Douglas, on stage at the Copacabana and introduce him to an older and richer audience. This could open more doors for Starr and his teen star, and someone else would be footing the bill. Starr was hatching a plan, but he didn't want to lay it out — incomplete and underdeveloped — on the phone with Tony Winston.

"I like it," he said to Tony, "but I gotta work some things out with my people here in Los Angeles, and I gotta talk to Jules. I've got his number, so I'll call him later this afternoon — at a more reasonable hour."

"Thanks, Rick. That's great to hear. Sorry I bothered you and your wife so early. I'll buy you guys dinner when you're here in New York."

Because he still wanted a part in whatever success Tony was going to have, Starr decided to use his parting remarks to massage Winston's ego. "Tony, I wanna help you out here. I like you. I think we can work well together. I'll make this deal happen one way or the other. Can you make sure Jules will cooperate with me?"

Winston was also eager to make the deal happen. He couldn't believe his luck when the Copa offered to extend his contract. That saved him the embarrassment of making up some flim flam story of why he couldn't go to LA to tape *Starr Power*.

Because of the agreement he signed with Jayna and Jansen James following his attempted rape of Jayna, he couldn't step foot in California. But, as his career was soaring again, he did not want that information to be made public. He did not want to be dragged through the mud by the gossip magazines.

"I'll make it happen, Rick," said Tony. "This is going to be exciting. Let me talk to Jules first. Can you call him on Monday? That'll work better."

"I'll call him on Monday afternoon. Make sure he's in his office at 1 p.m. I don't have time to waste."

"I'll take care of it, Rick. Talk to you later."

After he hung up, Tony Winston breathed a sigh of relief and said to himself, "I'll take care of it even if I have to pay to get most of it done."

Chapter Sixty

Rick Starr really wanted to package teen idol Hal Douglas with the now-resurrected 1950s star Tony Winston. On completely opposite ends of the demographic spectrum, nonetheless, they were the two biggest male pop stars in the country right now. As he relaxed by the heated pool in his Pacific Palisades compound, he was calculating what he had to do, who he had to deal with, and what it would cost him to get Hal Douglas out on tour with Tony Winston.

The first step was easy. He would take his *Starr Power* TV show to New York to tape the special episode at the world-famous Copacabana. Tony Winston and Hal Douglas would co-headline the program. It was, after all, his show, and Hal Douglas was, after all, his act. Tony Winston had already agreed to do the show. Hal would do what he was told to do, Starr thought to himself. And, Jules Podell, who owned the Copacabana, would pay for the entire production plus talent fees for Winston and Douglas.

"It's looking pretty good for Rick Starr," he said, sotto voce as he reached for his ice-cold bottle of Mountain Dew. His phone rang, but he ignored it, knowing his wife would get it. He was still struggling with how to get the two stars to agree to go out on a package tour, how he would get promoters to buy a May-September show like that, and, more importantly, how he was going to make the most money on it.

As he was jotting down notes and ideas on his ever-present legal pad, his wife, Kim, came trotting out to the pool. "Rick, Gene Pitney is on the phone for you. Do you wanna take it?" she asked.

"Gene Pitney," he muttered. "What the hell does Gene Pitney want? A record contract? Does he want to do my show? Tell him I'm busy right now, but I'll call him right back in a few minutes. And don't forget to get his number."

Always needing to be in control, Starr made Pitney wait twenty minutes before he plopped down in his over-sized chair in his over-sized office and called him back.

"Hello," said Pitney in his cheery voice.

"Where the fuck am I calling? Where is this 203 area code?" Starr asked in a gruff tone of voice. He wasn't used to calling people back — he had people who did that for him — so he had no intimate knowledge of what the major area codes were around the country.

Always congenial, Pitney said, "Well, some people call this the Constitution State, and some people call it the Nutmeg State. You're Rick Starr, you're busy, you can just call it Connecticut."

Not knowing what Pitney wanted — and always looking for the next deal — Starr quickly adjusted his attitude and his ego. "Sorry, Gene. I'm home today, and I'm not used to making calls. I have girls who do that for me. I thought I was calling Yugoslavia or somewhere like that," he said with a bit of a forced laugh.

"So, what can Rick Starr do for the legendary Gene Pitney?"

"Well, it's the other way around," Pitney responded. "It's what I'm going to do for you."

"Fire away, Gene. I'm all ears."

As Pitney laid out his complex offer, Rick Starr thought that Pitney had read his mind.

"I produced a duet for your guy, Hal Douglas, and Jessie James. I'm sure you know THAT will be the biggest hit record of the year. And, Rick, I guarantee you it will be one of the biggest hits in the history of pop music."

Rick Starr was listening intently. He wanted to interrupt and take charge of the conversation — and the deal — but he decided to let Pitney play out his hand.

"Here's how I see this working where everyone is going to make a lot of money," explained Pitney. "Hal and Jessie wrote the song. It's called 'A Lifetime of Love.' They get songwriting credit and songwriting money. It needed a third verse — and I wanted to get my friend Al Kooper some money — so I hired him to write it. He gets songwriting credit and songwriting money, too. I'm producing AND singing on it. And, it's going through my publishing company, Pitfield Music. That's where some of my money comes from. And, there will be a Black gospel group on the song, too.

"I picked up a second-rate song that my friend Johnny Tillotson wrote for the flip side. I owed him a favor. So, he's getting songwriting credit and money. I changed some words in the song, as part of the deal with Johnny, so I get songwriting credit and money on that song, too."

Starr couldn't control himself anymore. "Alright, stop right there," he semi-yelled into the phone. "I know you're GENE PITNEY, but that doesn't mean squat to me. OK? I'm RICK STARR. How do you think you are dictating all these terms to me on a deal for a guy I own? Hal Douglas is my act. I own him. What the fuck?"

"Can I finish?" Gene asked politely. "I think you'll like what you hear next."

"This better be good or you and I are done, and you'll be hearing from my legal counsel."

Starr's bluster didn't faze Pitney. "We'll run the flip side, the Tillotson-Pitney song, through your publishing company," explained Pitney. "So you get the same pub-lishing money I get for the A side. And, the icing on the cake is that you get to distribute the record on Starr Records in the UK and other countries we mutually agree on."

Now fuming, Rick Starr spoke very firmly to Pitney through clenched teeth, "Imag-ine my fucking excitement getting to distribute the record in the UK," he said in a not-so-cheery manner. "Whaddya figure, Gene? Forty seven people live there and maybe, just maybe, thirteen of them will buy the record? This is so much bullshit…"

Pitney interrupted the now very angry and seemingly implacable Starr. "Jessie James is on Sunshine Records, and they will distribute it in the US. No ifs, ands, or buts about it."

Then Pitney fell silent to let it all sink in with Starr. Pitney wanted the next few moments to be full of drama and very memorable because this was going to be the biggest deal of his life not directly related to his own singing and recording career.

Only two words tumbled out of Rick Starr's mouth. "Says who?"

"Says me," said Pitney very matter-of-factly. Then, just half a beat later, he added, "And Jansen and Jayna James."

Hearing the names of the Oscar-winning movie star and her husband, the former governor of California, introduced into the conversation threw Starr for a loop. He was silent as he was trying to forge a riposte.

Pitney quickly filled the void. "But, I am going to do you one more favor," he said. "I'm asking Don Jon Ross to sell Tony Winston's contract to you. I'm sure you know that Tony is back at the top of the charts, and he's on Sunshine Records. But he can't be on Sunshine Records, so he's gonna sign with Starr Records.

"So, you see what a great deal this is for you, Rick? You will have two of the biggest recording stars in America on your label. Does it get any better than that?"

Starr, still fuming, was a bit taken aback by this last part of the deal that was being run past him faster than a jet plane. While it would make it much easier for him to get Hal Douglas and Tony Winston out on a package tour, he still wasn't sure how all the pieces were fitting together.

Compromising his own ego, Starr decided to be accommodating and ask questions in a polite way. Part of this tactic was that he hoped it would put Pitney off guard until he could get to the bottom of the deal. However, the bigger part of the deal, the part that made him control every ounce of his ego and power, was that it was how this deal, falling out of the cornflower blue California sky and into his lap, was seemingly too good to be true.

"I'm sorry, Gene," he said a little sheepishly. "This is all coming fast and furious at me, and I haven't really been able to digest all of it. So, my first question is: what do Jansen and Jayna James have to do with this other than being Jessie's parents?"

"Rick," Gene said, "I'll give you that answer, then we'll discuss my fees for writing songs and producing records for your label's next star, Tony Winston."

Chapter Sixty One

Pitney recounted for Starr the story of Tony Winston's attempted rape of Jayna James nearly word-for-word from what Jessie James had told him about the sordid incident.

Starr was at a loss for words. Nothing would come out of his mouth. He sat in his over-sized chair in his over-air-conditioned, over-sized office and just shook his head.

"And, another tidbit for you, Rick," Pitney said with a chuckle. "You probably didn't know that Tony Winston and Jessie James used to be married."

Slowly, Starr regained his composure and his jaded sense of humor and said, "I've stepped into *Peyton Place*," he said, alluding to the seedy and hugely popular prime time TV soap opera.

"Now I get it," Starr thought to himself as the real reason why Tony Winston couldn't come to California to appear on *Starr Power* dawned on him.

"I see how it's all gonna work," he said to Pitney, "but, what I don't get is why you said Tony CAN'T be on Sunshine Records. The guy is red hot right now. Any label would kill to get him."

"That's very simple, Rick," Pitney said. "Jessie James is on Sunshine Records, and she and Hal Douglas are the hottest teen stars in the country. When this duet comes out, the two of them will become pop royalty in the same league with Elvis and The

Beatles. What Jessie wants, Jessie gets. She doesn't want Tony Winston anywhere near her, and that's something you're gonna have to make sure she gets."

Starr wasn't exactly sure what that component of Pitney's deal would mean to him, and it wasn't something he was going to ponder right now. But he did want to be very clear about what Pitney had told him about Tony Winston's contract.

"So, you're telling me that Sunshine Records is going to willingly sell me the contract of one of the biggest stars in America right now?"

"That's right," said Pitney quickly. "To make it all work Don Jon Ross has to get Tony Winston off his label or he'll lose Jessie James. And, if he loses Jessie James, he loses his biggest star — AND this duet — which means he could lose his record company."

Rick Starr took a quick sip of his Mountain Dew, then interrupted Pitney in a harsh tone. "You're sitting there in Connecticut telling me that Jessie James is so big she can push around the owner of her record label? That's out-fucking-rageous. Nobody on Starr Records pushes Rick Starr around. And you can take that to the bank."

"What I'm telling you, Rick," said Pitney, very slowly and meticulously, "is that Sunshine Records is so small that Jessie James can push them around. She is Don Jon's meal ticket. She knows it, and he knows it. She's a smart one, Rick."

"She wouldn't last a day on my label," Starr muttered.

"Don't take it personally, Rick," Pitney said with a smile in his voice. "She doesn't need you. Your other artists might need you, but Jessie James doesn't."

Pitney pointed out that Don Jon Ross and Sunshine Records were in line for a huge windfall when the duet hit the market. "It's gonna be huge," he declared. "My guess is pre-orders for the single will surpass a million copies, so it will be a gold record in the US immediately. We're timing the UK release to coincide with Hal and Jessie joining me on my upcoming UK tour. So, Rick, you'll easily sell a quarter-million copies in the UK. Does that work for you?"

That number eased Starr's mind a bit, but something else Pitney said had him troubled. In the back of his mind, he had an uneasy feeling that Gene "Mr. Nice Guy" Pitney was trying to outsmart and outmaneuver him.

But, he continued to play nice until he could figure out what the Pitney scam might be. In Rick Starr's world, everyone was trying to scam him. He didn't believe there were people who were honest and forthright and willing to cut everyone in on a good deal.

"Gene," he said, "I know you're engineering this deal so everyone wins, but you're telling me that you're giving me Tony Winston, one of the hottest singers in the country right now, but you're taking the other hottest singer, Hal Douglas, away from me on your tour. And you're taking him away from me without my permission and apparently not cutting me in."

That comment seemingly forced Pitney's hand. He really wanted to discuss terms of his writing and production deal for Tony Winston on Starr Records before he addressed the Hal Douglas-Rick Starr relationship. But, when Starr indicated it was up to him to give Hal Douglas permission to go on the Pitney UK tour, the latter became more important than the former.

Just then, Kim Starr walked into her husband's office to tell him she was heading out to meet some friends for lunch. She asked if she could get him anything before she left.

More than a little rattled by what was taking place in his phone conversation with Pitney, Starr lashed out at her. "Can't you see I'm on an important fucking phone call?" he screamed. "Yeah, you know what you can get me? A wife who knows when I'm on an important fucking phone call and doesn't interrupt me. And, maybe, just maybe, you or her could get me another cold Mountain Dew — and set the air-conditioning for sixty seven. It's getting hot in here."

Most of Starr's employees, friends, and relatives were easily nonplussed by his quick temper. Rick knew — but didn't care all that much — that most of his employees didn't really like him. What he didn't know was that they called him "Rick the Prick" behind his back. However, his verbal flare-ups didn't faze his wife. She turned on her heel without saying a word and headed to the kitchen, turning the AC down to sixty seven as she passed by the temperature control box outside the office.

Kim shook her head, remembering the pleasure she had derived during her time with Gary Ford, but that was over, and she was determined that this — Rick the Prick and his tirades — were her cross to bear for the life he gave her. She'd be the good wife…while she could stand it.

Pitney was used to doing business with brutish cutthroats like Rick Starr. And, after all of his successes and failures, all of the different personalities he had encountered along the way, and all of the people who had tried to screw him during his career, he had learned how to turn outbursts from the Rick Starrs of the music world to his advantage.

Without commenting on Starr's verbal abuse of his wife, Pitney used the little temper tantrum and quickly turned the conversation back to his writing/production deal. "Rick, let's hammer my deal out with you first," he said.

"Remind me," Starr said flatly as his wife delivered his fresh, ice-cold Mountain Dew. He didn't even look at or acknowledge her. "What fucking deal is that?"

"Since I'm the one delivering Tony Winston to your label, here's the deal I want," Pitney proffered. "He has to deliver an album of WWII cover songs, a Christmas album, and two albums of new songs over the next two years to fulfill his deal with Sunshine Records. I want to write and produce one song on the Christmas album and a minimum of three songs each on the two new albums. And Starr Records has to guarantee to release and legitimately promote a minimum of three of those songs as singles."

Starr's agitation was growing. He realized that Pitney had spun the conversation away from Hal Douglas, and Rick wanted to get that situation sorted out pronto. But, knowing that Pitney knew how to write hit songs, he was willing to discuss his terms. Starr figured it was a good move. After all, Pitney had written "Rubber Ball" for Bobby Vee, "He's A Rebel" for The Crystals, and "Hello Mary Lou" for Ricky Nelson.

"What's that gonna cost me, Gene?"

"$2,500 per song to write and produce, plus chart incentives," Pitney answered quickly. "Another $10,000 if the single sells a million and/or goes to #1 on the *Billboard* or *Cashbox* charts. And, I want five cents for every 45, and twenty cents on every LP sold. Plus the accounting has to be verified by my people in New York."

Starr didn't want to embrace the figures that Pitney tossed out at him. He really wanted to argue and negotiate them down. He did like the idea of having Tony

Winston on his label and Gene Pitney writing and producing for him, but there was still something gnawing away at him, something that was unsettling him. Pitney kept pushing and pushing him. He wasn't offering a deal; he was demanding it.

That was it. Starr realized that Pitney was talking as if he was in the driver's seat, as if he had Starr over a barrel. Starr realized that Pitney was negotiating from a position of unbridled swagger. But why? He took a big swig of his Mountain Dew and tried to process everything that was coming at him.

"This ain't fucking happening," were the next words that tumbled out of the mouth of the now furious Starr. "Hal is my act. I made him what he is. He owes me his whole career. This ain't fucking happening."

A steadfastly calm Pitney said, "Well…it is, Rick, but we're not cutting you out. This was an extremely hard decision for Hal to make, but he wants more control over his career. He wants more say in what he does, when he does it, where he does it, and who he does it with. He still feels very loyal and grateful to you, but he wants to make more of the decisions."

Silence on both ends of the phone line.

"And Rick," Pitney said, as he broke that silence and readied the final dagger, "you don't have a signed deal with Hal. You never signed him to a contract."

At that point, Starr knew he was defeated. He now had to make the best out of a very bad situation. He decided to play nice and a little coy, starting with the deal that Pitney was negotiating for himself. "That sounds like Lennon-McCartney money, Gene. I might be able to pay it if you can deliver some great hits like you've written in the past."

"I've been sitting on some songs for a while," Pitney responded. "I've got a Christmas song that could become a standard. It's called 'Send Me A Little Home For Christmas.' I'll send you a demo tape. You'll weep."

"Great," said Starr impatiently. "But I gotta get Tony into the Top 40 and keep him on the middle-of-the-road charts, too. Can you guarantee me some hits, Gene?"

"C'mon, Rick. You know there are no guarantees for hit records. It's a crap shoot."

"C'mon, Gene," Starr shouted. "You want guaranteed money, but you tell me there are no guarantees. What the fuck?"

"Here's your guarantee, Rick," Pitney said, as he was setting Starr up for the coup d'état. It was something he had hoped he wouldn't have to use. He was hoping that Rick Starr would have been happy with a good-sized part of a big deal and not been greedy and pushy. He was hoping they could make a verbal deal, figuratively shake hands, and be friends and partners in an extraordinary venture. That's evidently not the road that Rick Starr wanted to go down.

"After we agree to ALL the terms of the deal," Pitney said very calmly, "and there are a few more to discuss, like getting Tony Winston on Starr records ASAP, I guarantee you that nobody from my team goes to the press with the story about Tony Winston's attempted rape of Jayna James."

Chapter Sixty Two

Gene Pitney's plate was full. After selling millions of records worldwide as a pop star, he was now enjoying — actually thriving on — being a behind-the-scenes musical architect with ethics.

He had just finished the first move in the musical chess game he was involved in with some of the heavy hitters in the music business. He forced multimedia mogul Rick Starr into accepting all of his terms regarding Tony Winston, Hal Douglas, Jessie James, Don Jon Ross, Sunshine Records, and Starr Records. Pitney's plan was brilliant in its simplicity and that it worked to the advantage of everyone involved. He had crafted a plan where every player was a winner. His parting comment to Rick Starr was simple. "Don't try to thank me with words, Rick." Starr was contemplating what that might have meant on any number of levels.

The two hottest pop stars in the country would soon be heading to Pitney's Connecticut home to put the finishing touches on a duet they recorded in New York under Pitney's tutelage and production wizardry. Hal Douglas and Jessie James had written "A Lifetime of Love" while stuck in a motel in New Jersey during a blizzard. Pitney helped the young pop stars flesh out their B+ effort at songwriting by getting the great Al Kooper to write a third verse, by hiring the best session musicians in New York for the recording at the best studio in New York, by having a Black gospel group sing on the record, and by agreeing to sing on it himself. Pitney had quickly turned "A Lifetime of Love" into an A+ song that would surely top the charts around the world.

His next move, perhaps the easiest of them all, was to inform Don Jon Ross, the owner of Sunshine Records, that he would have to sell the contract of the suddenly hot again 1950s star Tony Winston to Starr Records. Pitney's leverage was going to be the Jessie James-Hal Douglas duet. James was on Sunshine Records, but Douglas was not. Pitney's plan was, again, brilliant in its simplicity. There would be very little arm-twisting necessary. Jessie and Hal were the biggest pop stars in the country. They could literally fart on a record and sell a million copies. Everyone in the record industry conceded that. In the deal that Pitney had concocted, Don Jon Ross would get the US release of the duet for Sunshine Records in exchange for selling Winston's contract to Starr Records.

As he was sitting in his office making notes following his phone conversation with Rick Starr, Pitney's wife Lynne came padding down the stairs with the mail. "Here you go, Gene," she said. And she put five rubber-banded stacks of fan letters on his desk along with the latest copy of *Billboard*.

"This is going way too well," he said to her, setting the fan letters in a box at the side of his desk to be dealt with later. "Rick Starr agreed to everything. He'd be stupid not to, but he's quite a bully, and I thought he'd try to put up a big fight just to show me how powerful he was. He didn't."

"What's next?" she asked. It's not that Pitney kept her in the dark about his business dealings on purpose; he just had so many irons in the fire that he oftentimes just forgot to tell her what he was up to.

"Jessie and Hal will be coming here shortly, and we'll finish up pre-production on the duet," he explained. "Then it's on to New York to record it. I'm not quite sure when I'm going to deal with Don Jon Ross on the Tony Winston deal."

His wife looked at him, shook her head, and said, "I know who Tony Winston is, but I have no idea who the guy is with the rhyming name."

After Gene explained the scenario to her, including Winston's attempted rape of Jayna James, Lynne plopped down in a chair across from her husband and said, "You're making all this up just to impress me…right?"

"No, my darling," he said with a smirk on his face, "it's the truth, the whole truth, and nothing but the truth. And, as Jack Paar used to say, I kid you not."

"Who all knows about the attempted rape?" she asked him. Gene told her who the players were, and she quickly surmised that Don Jon Ross wasn't in on that information. "So, let me get this straight," Lynne said as she sat up straight in the chair. "One of rhyming guy's two biggest stars used to be married to his other star and attempted to rape the movie star mother of that other star…and that star doesn't want to ever be anywhere near the first star. And so that first star — Tony Winston — can never step foot in California or the parents of the second star — Jessie James — will ruin his career. And rhyming guy doesn't know any of this?"

"Jessie never told him," said Gene.

"Are you gonna tell him?" she asked.

"Not if I don't have to," Gene replied. "Look, I certainly don't condone what Tony Winston did, but he's being punished and penalized for it. I'm not in the game of piling on. What happened is between Tony, Jessie, and her parents. If they're OK with the deal then it's fine with me."

Lynne Pitney was now VERY interested in what her husband was up to. "How are you going to get rhyming guy to give up Tony Winston's contract? He just had that huge hit with 'I'll Be Seeing You.' Ick. I'm feeling a little dirty now because I loved that record. The guy's on a roll. Why would rhyming guy want to sell his contract?"

"Because I'm going to give the Jessie-Hal duet to his label, Sunshine Records," Gene explained, "and he'll likely sell two million copies of it or more. Sunshine Records becomes a major player in the record business, and it positions him to attract other artists to his label. I won't tell him about Tony's poor choices if I don't have to."

He then explained the deal he made with Rick Starr about the UK and worldwide release of the duet, as well as his own production deal with Starr Records for Tony Winston product.

"Gene Pitney," she said. "You're a Genius! With a capital G!"

"I AM," he said with a laugh.

"Just keep that pig Tony Winston out of this house," she said without a smile on her face.

Chapter Sixty Three

Mary Pat MacGregor was a cheerleader-beautiful blonde; more petite than eye-poppingly buxom; pathologically shy; quietly brilliant; deeply religious; and cunningly motivated. Her parents had died in a house fire when she was a junior at Riverside High School in Keokuk, Iowa. She and her twin brother, Michael, were shipped off to live with their aunt and uncle in Sherman Oaks, California. Michael suffered from muscular dystrophy, and he had a severe level of intellectual disability. Mary Pat was his caretaker and protector. Her whole life centered on taking care of Michael.

Mary Pat was not naïve. She knew she was beautiful; she knew she had a sweet body; she knew that boys wanted to be around her; she knew that all the boys wanted to have sex with her; she also knew that she would only have sex with the man she would eventually marry.

She even knew that her aunt and uncle did not want to be burdened with her brother so she would be his caretaker for life. But the swiftness of it all came as a surprise. At a small birthday party for Michael and her, her aunt and uncle gave her an ultimatum. After the little party held at their modest home ended and her friends had left, Mary Pat's Uncle Skip took her outside.

"Mary Pat," he said, "Aunt June and I are looking at retirement soon. We love you and your brother, but we need to take care of ourselves now. You two can stay here for one more year while you get established in whatever career you choose, and then you have to move out of the house. You and Michael. We can't take care of him."

Mary Pat knew she would have to quickly find a career where she could make a lot of money with little education or training. With her fetching looks and body, Mary Pat thought she would give acting a shot. She was only thirty minutes away from Hollywood via the 101, so the hotbed of the entertainment industry was conveniently nearby.

A short while after moving in with her aunt and uncle and after adjusting to life as a senior at Notre Dame High School, Mary Pat went to a cattle call audition for models for a pilot of a new TV game show called *Over The Top*. Mary Pat was excited because the job would pay $50 per week. She didn't get the job, but the photographer hired to do the photo shoot for the show befriended her. And, over coffee two weeks later, he made her an offer.

"I do some of the *Playboy* photo shoots, too," twenty-eight-year-old Parker Gramza told the budding actress. "If you're interested, I could get you an audition there. Hef likes your girl-next-door look. Playmate of the Month gets $2,500 and a lot of modeling offers. Interested?"

Mary Pat was stunned. The money was an eye-opener, but the idea of being naked not only in front of a male photographer but also millions of men around the world shook her to her core.

She didn't want to say no, but she didn't want to say yes either, not without considering all the ramifications of either answer. And, she was even wondering if it was just a come-on from the photographer. They had shared coffee a few times at a small coffee shop/bakery on Sepulveda Boulevard, but that was all up to this point.

"That's very nice of you, Parker," she said haltingly, "but if you want to go out on a date, you could just ask me that."

"A date," Parker chirped quizzically. "Oh, Mary Pat, aren't you just as cute as Christmas! You're beautiful, but you're not my type. I'm gay. My partner and I have been together for three years now. He works as an ad salesman for *Playboy*. He's my in with Hef."

They both laughed. Then, Mary Pat explained her living situation to Gramza. She told him about the ultimatum from her aunt and uncle; she told him about her brother; she told him about her religious beliefs and her flat out "no way" attitude to pre-marital sex. She had absolutely no interest in getting naked for the whole world to see.

Parker listened politely. He had heard it all before from countless women he had photographed for *Playboy*. He looked around the quaint little retro coffee shop to make sure no one was eavesdropping and, with no condescension he said, "Look, Mary Pat. That money is on the table. Countless beautiful women are paid handsomely every month to be stapled in the middle of Playboy. Then you know what happens? Those millions of guys who buy the magazine will look at them, likely beat off fantasizing about making it with them, then completely forget about them when next month's tits and ass come out. Sorry, Mary Pat. In the world of monthly girlie magazines, even an unforgettable girl like you is forgettable when the next issue comes out."

"Parker, you're trying to make it sound like it's just so anonymous," she said. "I wouldn't get undressed in this coffee shop then strut down Sepulveda for anyone and everyone to get a good look. Why would I pose naked for *Playboy*? "

"I'll tell you why, Mary Pat: for your future and your brother's future. It's a great foot in the door. Many of the Playmates go on to become actresses or models; some end up marrying wealthy men who fall in love with the idea of marrying a Playmate; some marry actors. Some of them even use that money to go to college and pursue their dreams of becoming lawyers or doctors. Mary Pat, in this town, being a Playmate is like having a reserved, front row seat in life."

A week later she called the photographer and said, "I'll do it." She had one and only one stipulation. "I want my brother with me at all times."

After the photo shoot she went to church and prayed for forgiveness. And after that, she never looked back and never regretted it. She also never looked at those nude photos, and she told herself she never would. She was glad she did it, but she wasn't proud of it.

She also vowed that the first prayer she said every morning, for the rest of her life, would be, "Forgive me, God. I did it for Michael."

Two months later, Mary Pat MacGregor wore a cheerleader's outfit on the November 1965 cover of *Playboy*. She wore just her glorious cheerleader's smile on the inside pages of the magazine. She was stunningly beautiful, and the camera adored her. For the first time in *Playboy* history, the centerfold Playmate was featured over twelve pages of the magazine.

Within days of the magazine hitting the newsstands and finding its way to mailboxes around the country, Mary Pat MacGregor was inundated with phone calls, job offers, and requests for dates. Some of the latter came from some of the biggest TV and movie stars in the world. She knew they wanted to use her for her looks and her body. She had to think long and hard about that. It's not the route she wanted to follow, but there was always Michael to consider. She had compromised once to ensure his future. Would she do it again? Would she need to?

Then she met Rick Starr.

Chapter Sixty Four

Even though he was born in the Bronx, Rick Starr hated being in New York. He hated the weather; he hated the congestion; he hated the New York attitude; he hated staying in hotels; he hated not having an office nor his people doing his bidding; and he hated having to tell everybody all the time why he hated being in New York.

But the Copa was in New York, Tony Winston was in New York, and his next big deal was in New York. So New York would be his home for the next two weeks.

Rick set up shop at the five-star St. Regis-Sheraton. While most of the other show biz movers-and-shakers preferred to stay and schmooze at The Plaza, Rick wanted to be left alone so he could get his business done. He was in New York to make money, not friends.

With his briefcase in one hand and his ever-present yellow legal pad tucked under his other arm, Rick was on Madison Avenue hailing a cab and getting pissed off. He was used to doing business California-style — shorts and a T-shirt from his home office. Now, in order to get all the necessary components in place for the live broadcast of his *Starr Power* TV show from the famed Copa, he had to go there and be there every day for a two-week run-up period before the show hit the air. This did not make him happy.

What did make him happy was Mary Pat MacGregor. She was a former *Playboy* centerfold and now the Executive Producer of *Starr Power*. She had wanted to be an actress, but when she met Rick Starr at *The Grammy Awards* in 1966, her career path took an unexpected turn.

Starr had been introduced to Mary Pat MacGregor by his friend, Billy Breiling, an ad salesman for *Playboy*. Starr was at the awards ceremony solo that night because his wife, Kim, had come down with the flu. Breiling thought Mary Pat MacGregor, who was also his friend, would look good in that empty seat, and, more importantly, he thought that Rick Starr could help her career. Matchmaking, homewrecking, or sexual trysting never played into the equation for Breiling. He was just trying to be helpful.

Rick Starr was immediately taken by the innocent beauty of MacGregor, and, for the first time since he had been married, he wanted a woman other than his beautiful wife Kim; he wanted Mary Pat MacGregor. He also recognized her as a recent *Playboy* Playmate, but he didn't let on. He thought this was going to be his lucky night.

Not shy in his small talk, Starr let her know whom she had just met. "I am exactly what I appear to be," he said. "You are sitting in the second row of *The Grammy Awards* because I am a rich and powerful man in the music industry and TV and, soon, movies. And I think you are the most bewitching woman in this auditorium tonight."

More than a little taken aback by his bluster and bragging, Mary Pat simply but nicely said, "A pleasure to meet you, Rick."

The Grammy Awards were great fun from that second-row seat. Just about anyone who was anyone in the music industry had come by to pay homage to Rick Starr, and he introduced each and every one of them to her. She realized she could get used to this. Mary Pat MacGregor knew she had to be careful. Very careful. Rick Starr could help her, but at what cost?

She discovered the potential cost that night at the Grammy party they attended at the home of a famous rock 'n' roll producer. Her head was spinning from meeting Frank Sinatra, Barbra Streisand, Henry Mancini, and many other stars. She also might have had just a little too much to drink.

"Let's go for a walk in the garden and get some fresh air," Starr said to her. In the crisp air of a beautiful California night, Starr stopped her underneath a tall palm tree, wrapped his arms around her, and gave her a long, passionate kiss. "I haven't been able to take my eyes off of you since Billy introduced us," he said as she pulled away from him. "I have to have you…tonight. You owe me."

"I don't know if I should call you Rick or Mr. Starr right now," she said while on a slow burn. "I didn't go to the Grammys looking for a one-nighter with someone rich and famous nor did I go looking for a career. I went because a friend, a friend of ours, Billy Breiling asked me to go. I don't owe you a thing. Now, if you want me to tell Billy that you hit on me I can do that. Or, if you act like a gentleman the rest of the night I can forget what just happened."

"Oh, c'mon, Mary Pat," Starr said in a bit of a bemused tone of voice. "We had a great time at the Grammys, and I introduced you to a bunch of stars, so I thought you might want to top it off, that's all. I saw you in *Playboy*, so I just figured…"

"Well, you figured wrong," she said sternly. "Here's what I owe you. 'Thanks, Rick. That was fun.'"

Starr just glared at the winsome blonde glaring back at him.

She continued. "There, that's what I owe you. Now, what you owe me is an apology for your primitive and relatively buffoonish attempt to get laid. You need to watch more romantic comedies and hone your come-on more than just a little bit. Or do the starlets around here fall for that oafish crap? Look up the word Neanderthal when you get home. And, by the way, when you get home, apologize to your wife, too."

In his professional life, people always said "yes" to Rick Starr, so in his first extra-marital gambit, Mary Pat's "no" surprised him more than a little. After his anger over her refusal and her lecture subsided, he looked at her in a different light. In that moment, he realized that Mary Pat MacGregor had morals, integrity, character, and honesty. She could have succumbed to his unctuous sexual entreaties to perhaps endear herself to him and get herself a job, if, in fact, that's what she was looking for. Rick Starr was a career-maker.

Most other women in Hollywood would have jumped at the chance to have sex with the powerful Rick Starr and hopefully advance their careers. She didn't. Now he KNEW he wanted her but in a different meaning of the word. Call it luck or call it fate, but he realized, in that moment, that he had perhaps found his right hand…woman.

This Mary Pat MacGregor woman was both angelic and trustworthy at the same time. She appeared not to be intimidated by him and not to be someone who would sell her soul to the devil to be in show business.

Rick Starr was looking for someone just like that, someone he could trust implicitly. Mary Pat MacGregor might be that person. So, taking the measure of this beautiful and extraordinarily ethical woman — a rare quantity in show business — Rick told himself if he couldn't have her sexually then the next best thing would be to have her join his company. She was beyond compare to everyone else he knew in show business. That's an advantage he wanted; he wanted her on his team.

He decided to take a chance.

"Mary Pat," he said quietly and respectfully, "you have humbled me. I apologize."

He took her by the arm and led her back into the party. "I want you to come work for me. I need someone with your backbone and your integrity."

"Look, Rick, if this is another come on…"

"It's not, Mary Pat. Can you come to my office on Monday? Billy Breiling will be there. We'll make a deal. I want a person like you working for…I mean…with me."

Mary Pat looked at him and decided she would give him a chance to give her a chance. "Two things," she said quickly. "I did the *Playboy* shoot because I needed the money to take care of my brother. Second, what time should I be at your office, Mr. Starr?"

"Be there at nine o'clock. And call me Rick."

Chapter Sixty Five

"$25,000 a year, a car, and an apartment," said Rick Starr as he sat in his Beverly Hills office decorated to tell anyone who entered "I am important." "That's the offer, Mary Pat. You will be the Vice-President of Starr Entertainment and the Executive Producer of *Starr Power*."

Mary Pat, dressed stylishly but demurely, couldn't believe what she was hearing. The money was in the stratosphere; the titles were unbelievable; the responsibilities were frightening. But what she heard next truly stunned her.

"The most important thing you will do here at Starr Entertainment," Rick said slowly and pointedly, "is speak truth to power. And that means to me and to anyone who works here. Anyone who works with and for us.

"Mary Pat, you are untouchable here at Starr Entertainment. I am still the boss, but I know my frailties. I know my weaknesses. I know my faults. I'm arrogant. I'm pompous. I'm self-important. I'm self-centered. I'm impressed with myself.

"Until I met you I had never met someone who I knew would or could keep me in check and balance me out. The other night, after *The Grammy Awards*, you made it perfectly clear what kind of person you are. I don't necessarily always appreciate that kind of person being in my line of sight, but I'm cognizant of the fact that I need it more than anything else in my life. Oh, shit, this is way too introspective for me.

"Anyways, that's what I need from you. I won't always accept it, and I will get pissed off at you, but that's what I am asking of you. Can you do it?"

"My goodness, Rick," Mary Pat said with a teasing smile on her face, "when did you introduce all this humble pie into your personality diet?"

"Great," said Rick laughing, "you're starting with the truth-to-power shit already. I was just testing you. By the way, you look very fuckable today; now get the fuck to work."

She stared at him. Glared at him.

"Kidding, just kidding," he said.

"OK," she said. "But, Rick that's the last time you'll ever use the 'F' word — or any derivation of it — in my presence. Also, you will never take God's name in vain in my presence."

Silence.

"And, I want a stake in the company."

More silence.

For a brief, comic moment, Rick Starr was having second thoughts. In his head, he started to talk to himself as he paced in his office, "Fuck is my favorite word. I like to fuck; sometimes I don't give a fuck; I work with people who are stupid fucks; I like to fuck over people who try to fuck me over; my wife's a great fuck; I really DID want to fuck Mary Pat, but she wouldn't have one fucking thing to do with it and essentially told me to fuck off and don't fuck with her — literally and figuratively; I'm incredibly fucking rich and talented; how the fuck does she expect me to never say the word fuck or any derivative of it in her presence; should I give a fuck that she doesn't want me to use the word fuck or any fucking derivation there-fucking-of?"

Then, out loud, he said, "OK. I won't say f-f-f...that word...and how 'bout five percent, which is negotiable — up and down — every year on your anniversary?"

She rose elegantly from her chair, offered her hand, and said, "Miss Mary Pat Mac-Gregor will accept your very generous offer...when you put it in writing and sign it."

Then with a sly grin on her face, she added, "Might Mr. Rick Starr tell Miss Mac-Gregor exactly where the fuck her office is?"

Starr just looked at her and threw his hands in the air.

It was the first and last time she ever used that word. It pained her, and she would have to go to church to ask God's forgiveness. But, she thought, it was well worth it at that moment in time.

Chapter Sixty Six

Over the years, Rick Starr found out that Mary Pat MacGregor wasn't just a good hire. She was a brilliant hire. She took to the job of Executive Producer of the *Starr Power* TV show like bees to the honey.

While he was full of himself — and angst — about being away from his turf in Southern California to prepare for the New York taping of his TV show, Mary Pat was putting it all together as if she were a twenty-five-year TV veteran.

Starr rushed into the Copa thirty minutes later than he had planned because he had trouble getting a cab. "You know, I don't have this kind of trouble in LA," he said to Mary Pat as she greeted him in the cramped room that was serving as their production office for the show.

She had been there since 7:00 a.m. and had arranged for a continental breakfast for everyone involved with the show. There was fruit, cereal, and pastries along with three different types of fresh fruit juices.

"What trouble?" she asked. "Getting to work on time?"

That rankled Starr, and he was ready to blow a gasket. However, he had discovered, much to his chagrin, she was never fazed by his mercurial temper

The media mogul took off his coat and threw it at the table full of food. The juices spilled all over the floor, food went flying in all directions, glasses and pitchers shattered. Mary Pat picked up the jacket and handed it back to him.

"There's a coat rack in the corner, Jackass. The bill for the breakfast is going on the Copa's tab. We'll take care of the second bill for all of this mess. Now, tell me what kind of trouble you don't have in LA."

Embarrassed by his third-grade temper tantrum, Starr began to calm down. "Cabs. I can't get a cab. That's my problem. A million cabs in this stinkin' city, and they all drive past me like I'm invisible."

"Well," Mary Pat said with a sweetly smug look on her face, "maybe if you told me what you needed I'd have gotten it for you. Just like I got Dean Martin and Frank Sinatra to appear on *Starr Power* this week."

"You got who to do what?" Starr asked in disbelief.

"Frank and Dean want to do the show, and they both want to sing duets with Tony, and they want us to write a song for the three of them to sing," she explained quickly. "They'll even do it for union scale if we come up with a special song for the three of them."

"Can we do that?" he asked with a hint of fear in his voice. "Can we get a song written specifically for the three of them in four days?"

"When you say 'we,' exactly who do you mean?" Mary Pat said, laughing.

Starr stammered a bit and said, "You know…we…you and me. Can we get that done in four days?"

"Yes, WE can," she said with a lilt in her voice. "I happen to know that Paul Anka is in town recording a new album over at RCA. I got in touch with him at his hotel. He'll have the song done by tomorrow afternoon. The song is ours for free if you put him on *Starr Power* to promote his new album when it's out. He said he can't get Dick Clark to make a promise to put him on *Bandstand*."

"What do you think?" Starr asked his Executive Producer.

"WE already said 'yes.' I've already talked to Frank, Dean, and Tony this morning. They're all fired up. Frank and Dean weren't that thrilled about talking to me at 7:30, but I turned on my Midwestern charm. Starting tomorrow, they're at our disposal for the rest of the week. Tony Winston is thrilled to death. He'll do anything we ask him to do."

"Mary Pat, you are f-ff-f…fabulous. You are a fabulous Executive Producer," Starr said, catching himself before he uttered his favorite word. "But, now that we got Mom, Dad, Grandma, and Grandpa covered with those three, I still need Hal Douglas."

"I was about to get to that, Rick," she said with a hint of caution in her voice. "I called the number you gave me for Hal, and his mother answered the phone. Very nice lady. Rita is her name. I didn't know Hal was from Milwaukee. My grandparents were, too. After talking with his mom for about five minutes I discovered Hal was raiused about a mile from where my grandparents lived."

"Yeah, yeah, yeah. Blah, blah, blah," he said, lapsing into his normal pompous tone. "Go and have the Milwaukee reunion on your time. Do I have Hal Douglas for this show?"

"Well, Hal's mother gave me another number to call," Mary Pat explained. "I called it. It was Gene Pitney's house. Gene wants to talk to you…this morning."

Rick Starr said to himself, "Oh, shit."

Chapter Sixty Seven

"Get Pitney on the phone for me," Rick Starr snapped at his Executive Producer.

"Oh, Rick," said Mary Pat MacGregor with a heavy sigh, "we've been making so-o-o much progress with your manners and now this. Let's try that again, and this time use your nice words."

Even though she was brilliantly competent, thorough, and already more capable than many of the grizzled TV veterans he employed at Starr Entertainment, she pissed him off on a daily basis by constantly pushing him to alter his behavior, language, and temper…among many other things.

Reining in his ego and anger — yet again — he politely rephrased his demand as a polite question. "Hey, Mary Pat, might you get Mr. Pitney on the phone for me?"

She had already started dialing as the words were falling out of his mouth. "My pleasure," she said. "Be nice. I'll bring you a Mountain Dew."

Gene Pitney answered the phone in three rings.

"Gene," he started in before Pitney could even offer a pleasant greeting, "I want Hal for my TV show in New York on Saturday. We have a deal on everything else. Don't fuck with me on this."

"Calm down, Rick," Pitney said quickly. "Hal's at my house right now with Jessie. We'll be recording the duet in New York next week. How many songs do you want from him, and when do you want him for rehearsals? Also, I will have to present the idea to Jessie, the former Mrs. Tony Winston. I'm not sure how she'll like Hal working with Tony."

Mary Pat walked in with his Mountain Dew, and he put his hand over the phone and mouthed "Thank you." He was learning.

"It's business, Gene," Starr said in a very animated tone of voice. "Tell Princess Jessie this is business, and it's good business for Hal."

"As soon as we hang up I will have that conversation with her and Hal," Pitney responded.

With Pitney's assurance that he would try to get Hal Douglas to do *Starr Power* with Tony Winston, and with an ice-cold bottle of Mountain Dew in his hand, Rick Starr's demeanor changed.

Leaning back in his chair, he politely asked, "Can he give us three songs? Three of his biggest hits? He can pick 'em."

"I'll discuss that with them as well," said Pitney. "And, Rick, we have one more thing to discuss. Hal has agreed to go out on my next UK tour to establish a fan base there. You need to know that. For planning purposes."

That didn't sit well with Starr. He wanted to throw his bottle of Mountain Dew at the wall but then realized he'd face Mary Pat's wrath. The longer he worked with her, the fonder he was getting of her. Not a romantic fondness. Just a fondness for the great qualities she had and was teaching him.

"C'mon, Gene," Rick said. "I've got plans for Hal. After this TV show hits the air, people will be begging to see Tony Winston in concert again…across the country. I want to team him up with Hal on a US tour. Hal will bring in an audience that doesn't give a rat's ass about Tony Winston and vice versa. They both pick up a new audience, sell more records and more concert tickets, and everyone is happy. Hal can't be a teen idol forever. He's gonna have to think about the future. I think pairing him with Tony right now exposes him to the audience he'll need in the next two or three years. Plus, I got him a movie deal. He can't fuck around singing to those dopey teenagers much longer. It's too risky."

"Rick, you're jumping the gun" Pitney said definitively. "We don't know that he'll even do the TV show with Tony. That's going to come down to Jessie's decision. What do you think those odds are?"

Rick Starr was almost beside himself with rage. "I know this fucking business inside out," he screamed. "I just laid out Hal Douglas' future in this business for you very accurately and succinctly, and you're telling me all of this can be blown to fucking smithereens by one spiteful blonde bitch?"

"Rick," Gene said adamantly, "I never want to hear you talk about Jessie James like that ever again. Got it? She has every right in the world to despise Tony Winston. So, if you want to make this grand scheme work you might want to go on a charm offensive. And Rick, I need Hal on my UK tour. I'm in a bit of a career slump right now, and I can open the door to success in England for him. This is a win-win for him and me. And, you might as well know now: he looks to me as a mentor…almost as a father figure. I'm taking over his management. We've signed a deal. I don't need to remind you that you neglected to sign Hal to a contract, do I?"

Rick Starr sat in his chair stunned. He had made Hal Douglas a star. He had called all the shots. He had taken him from a small-town nobody to superstardom. He had made him a millionaire.

"Don't play this fucking game with me, Pitney," a very angry Rick Starr screamed into the phone. That outburst brought Mary Pat back into the office, staring at her boss who was livid with rage.

She quickly grabbed the phone from him and said, "Hi, Mr. Pitney. This is Mary Pat MacGregor. We talked earlier this morning. Can we call you back in a few minutes?"

"I'm here all day," Pitney said. "Talk to you later."

"Good night, nurse," she said, staring at her boss. "The entire crew could hear you, and I think they heard you in New Jersey. Get hold of yourself."

"Not now, Mary Pat. I cannot take your goody two shoes shit right now. Gene Pitney is yanking my biggest star right out from under my nose…and there's nothing I can do about it. I screwed up with Hal Douglas. I'm gonna get him. I'm gonna get even with both of them."

"Is there a way to make a deal with Mr. Pitney and Hal where you can stay in the picture?" she asked. "After all, you did make him a star. Can they really be successful without you?"

"Of course they can," Rick shouted. "Do you know who Gene Pitney is? He's sold a trillion records around the world. He's written hits for everybody and their chicken. Hal's close to the top of his game, and Pitney knows exactly how to get him to the very top. And he has a plan already in motion. Mary Pat, I'm screwed."

"Can I take a shot at this?" Mary Pat asked demurely, not wanting to hurt Starr's ego any more than it already was. "Let's not throw this away, Rick. Let's see what we can salvage. I am a five percent stakeholder in this company. Give me this chance. Please?"

Calming down slightly, the media mogul simply said, "Shit…why not. But, there is an elephant in the room, Mary Pat." He slowly explained the Tony Winston attempted rape story to her.

Chapter Sixty Eight

Mary Pat grabbed Starr's yellow legal pad and said, "Rick, please give me the *Reader's Digest* version of your relationship with Gene Pitney and any deals you have with him. I also need to know what you want from him going forward."

Twenty minutes — and three pages of notes — later, Mary Pat asked her boss to give her twenty minutes alone on the phone with Gene Pitney. Reluctantly, Starr grabbed his ever-present Mountain Dew and left the room.

Just before ducking out of the room he turned back and said, "Mary Pat, whatever happens next will change our business relationship. Don't doubt me on that."

The room was now deadly quiet. The breakfast mess was still decorating the floor and walls. Mary Pat, who had learned to think on her feet following her parents' deaths in a fire when she was still very young, paced the floor for about a minute. The plan came to her quickly.

She placed the call to Pitney's Connecticut home. Pitney was in the driver's seat, so she was simply going to be honest with the singer and get the best deal she could for her boss. That was not really a plan she had conceived on the spot. It was her way of life. Integrity and principle always ruled the day in her life. Win or lose with them, she reflected, you always felt good about yourself.

Pitney's wife, Lynne, answered the phone and, after exchanging pleasantries with Mary Pat, got her husband on the phone.

"Gene, this is Mary Pat MacGregor again. I'm Vice President of Starr Entertainment and Executive Producer of *Starr Power*. Can you and I talk?"

"Love to," Pitney said quickly.

Throwing caution to the wind, she said, "Gene, Starr Entertainment accepts all the terms of all the deals that you and Rick have previously discussed concerning Tony Winston, Don Jon Ross, Sunshine Records, and your personal involvement in all of them. We'll have our legal team draw up all of the documents and have them sent to your home for your approval, consent, and go-ahead.

"We understand the concern and worry that Jessie James has about Tony Winston and all of their implications in these deals. Starr Entertainment will guarantee that Tony abides by all of the restrictions currently in place regarding him and Jessie.

"We understand that Jessie may have qualms about Hal working with Tony Winston. I would like to talk to her about that."

Pitney, feet up on his desk, couldn't stop himself from smiling as he listened to her.

"Starr Entertainment is ready to move quickly on all of this. We will not drag our feet, put up roadblocks, or create legal hassles. We ask only two things of you, Gene. Two things."

"What's that?" Pitney asked, more than a little puzzled because they had agreed to everything in his plan.

"Set up a phone call or in-person meeting with me and Jessie, give us Hal for a three-month spring tour with Tony, and schedule your UK tour for the fall" she said quickly. "That's what we need. Please give us those three months."

That came as a surprise to Pitney. He hadn't even thought of that as a possibility where everyone could benefit. Then, even before he had a chance to say "yes" or "no," Mary Pat added the frosting to the cake.

"Do that for us, and Starr Entertainment will offer you a record deal on Starr Records with mutually agreed upon terms. And, of course, when you're on our label the door is always open to appear on *Starr Power* to promote your records."

"Mary Pat, you're a pleasure to deal with," Pitney said. "I'm going to tentatively accept that offer. I will speak with Jessie as soon as we hang up, and I've gotta call my UK promoter Arthur Howes and clear it with him. Shouldn't be a problem. He's got tours going out twelve months a year. Can I get back to you a little later today?"

Not leaving anything to chance, another trait she acquired after the death of her parents, she said, "Can you give me an approximate time on that, Gene? I've gotta go back to Rick with this."

Pitney got more than he bargained for. Not only was he going to get both Hal and Jessie on his UK tour, he just landed a deal with Starr Records, a major player in the recording industry. He could chuck his plan to get himself a deal with the smaller-than-small Sunshine records. "I'll have an answer for you in three hours," Pitney told her. "Please call me. I don't want to talk to Rick again."

Chapter Sixty Nine

Mary Pat MacGregor realized she had just done the first real "deal" of her professional life. Getting Frank Sinatra, Dean Martin, and Paul Anka involved in the TV show had more to do with Sinatra's loyalty to Tony Winston than her negotiating skills, despite the fact that she realized that her skills were pretty good. Her first "deal" was a big one, too.

As arranged, three hours later she called Pitney back. Pitney gave her the news she wanted. "You've got a deal," he said. "Jessie will talk to you on the phone tonight. Arthur Howes was able to move things around, and the new time frame of my tour opened up another dozen venues for us. That is easy money for him. But, before we close it I need to know what the record deal offer for me is?"

"Thank you for being so accommodating," Mary Pat replied. "A grateful Starr Entertainment is prepared to offer you a two-year, two-album deal with $25,000 up front and industry-standard royalties on the back end. Each album will contain twelve songs. We will accept your song choices for six of those songs; we reserve the right to place six songs of our choice on each album so we derive publishing money; we require that you use Starr Entertainment in-house producers; we also require that any singles released from either album be debuted on *Starr Power*. This will all be written up in legalese and submitted to your lawyer."

Pitney countered, "In that legalese, please insert that I will record only at Bell Sound in New York, and I want veto power over any producer I don't like. I'll stick with

Starr Entertainment's stable, but I want a producer I like. And please include standard language for arranger, producer, publishing, and songwriter fees. I get ten songs on the albums; Starr Entertainment gets two. Also, in any and all matters regarding Gene Pitney vis-à-vis Starr Entertainment, Starr Records, and *Starr Power,* I deal with Mary Pat MacGregor, no one else."

"I'll sign off on the deal if you give Starr Entertainment four songs per album," she shot back.

She found Rick Starr sitting at a table in the nightclub. Just sitting there. Not doing anything. Staring into space. Starr had a look of apprehension on his face as she approached. Just for the fun of it, she kept a poker face. Then she said, "I am talking to Jessie James tonight. I think I can talk her through this. If I do, and that is still an if, you've got Hal for the TV show and a three-month tour with Tony in the spring. Gene will schedule his UK tour to accommodate us."

She emphasized the word "us" by moving her left hand back and forth pointing at Starr and herself. She would give him the devilish details of her "deal" later on. She really wanted him to enjoy the moment.

"Son of a bitch," he yelled out. "Mary Pat MacGregor, where have you been all my life?"

She looked at him with that little demure smile of hers and said, "In grade school and high school." She broke out in a hearty laugh, and the two of them embraced.

"Mary Pat, we're going to rework your deal with me when we get back," he said. "I'm going to give you a Bob Hope/NBC deal. I'm going to sign you to a lifetime deal with me. Let's get this TV show done and get back to LA."

"Let me talk to Jessie, then we'll get everything done and get back to LA."

"Also, Mary Pat," Rick added, "I need my star employee working that tour. That's you. We'll discuss it later."

Mary Pat took umbrage with part of that statement. The other part confounded her. "First of all, Rick," she said matter-of-factly, "I am not your employee. I am your business partner. Secondly, I have no idea how tours work."

"You sell Jessie James the idea on the tour, and I'll teach you. Discussion over."

Chapter Seventy

Mary Pat was sitting in her dark hotel room…praying. She had turned all the lights off so she wouldn't be distracted.

She knew Rick Starr could be impossible. He was brazen; he was audacious; he was presumptuous. He was also her business partner, and she felt that they were actually becoming friends. She knew Rick wanted this deal badly.

She knew that Jessie James had every right in the world to hate Tony Winston and say no to the deal. She also knew it would be a great opportunity for Hal to expand his career. The timing was right, and it might never come again.

In the quiet solitude of her unlit room she prayed to God for wisdom, prudence… and a plan. Five minutes before she was to call Jessie James, her prayers were answered. God sent her a plan.

She steeled herself for what could be an awkward and stiff conversation. She made the sign of the cross and dialed the phone.

"Hi, it's Gene."

"Hi, Gene, it's Mary Pat. Would you put Jessie on the phone?"

The two women greeted each other cordially. "Jessie, I want to tell you a story about me and something I did that I hated doing. I did it because it was the best thing to do for me and someone I loved."

As Mary Pat divulged the story of her nude *Playboy* photo shoot to Jessie, she felt like she was going to confession. "I needed the money to take care of my brother and get us a place to live. I hated myself for awhile, but, in the end, I knew I did the right thing for us. I asked God for forgiveness then, and I ask Him for His forgiveness every day."

She broke down in tears. "I know He has forgiven me, Jessie; I believe He delivered His forgiveness to me in the form of Rick Starr and my job."

Then she laughed. "I don't really think it was a quid pro quo from God, but I believe He put me into Rick's life to do good and maybe straighten Rick out a little bit. My job has put me in a position where I can help a lot of people. So, in the end, posing for *Playboy*, something I really didn't want to do, opened the door for me to do so many good things for my family and other people."

"Mary Pat," said Jessie. "Thank you for calling. It was very brave of you, knowing the circumstances. Gene explained all the benefits to be derived from Hal doing the TV show and touring with Tony."

Then a protracted silence.

Jessie then sighed and said, "My friend Katie McGrath always says, 'If you got one, you are one.'"

A protracted silence again as Mary Pat was perplexed. She had no idea what Jessie meant.

Jessie broke the silence again. "A dick, Mary Pat. If you got one, you are one…a dick."

Both women erupted in laughter.

"I've screwed up a lot in my own life," Jessie volunteered. "And I've needed forgiveness. I know how much I regret some things that I've done, and I hope the people involved forgive me. Still, I am NOT ready to forgive Tony; not yet."

Mary Pat's heart dropped. She started crying again.

"But, my love for Hal and Gene trumps my hate for Tony. Gene explained everything to me. He didn't try to talk me into anything. He said it was up to me to say 'yes' or 'no,' and he would abide by my decision.

"I also talked with Hal. He agreed with Gene. These are two people I love, and they have given me the power of making a decision that will affect so many other people. That is humbling, Mary Pat. But, I still hate Tony Winston."

In the dark, quiet isolation of her hotel room Mary Pat could feel and hear her heart start racing.

"I need three things from you, Mary Pat, if I am going to agree to this."

"What do you need, Jessie?"

"Gene said you were the producer of the TV show. Do you know who will be the tour manager for Hal and Tony?"

"I am the TV show producer, and Rick just asked me to be the tour manager," said Mary Pat. "But…"

Jessie interrupted her. "Perfect. I need you to watch over Hal on the tour. He's a star, but he's really only just a boy yet. Promise me that."

"You have my word, Jessie. I will be Hal's Guardian Angel."

"Number two. Please tell Tony I have not forgiven him yet, but someday I will. Also let him know that my family will be starting a sexual assault center in Los Angeles. Rick Starr will donate the first $250,000 to get it off the ground. Tony Winston will be the voice and face of men supporting female victims of sexual assault in our TV ads. We won't implicate him in anything at all. It will look like he is doing it out of the goodness of his heart."

"I will talk to both of them tomorrow and share all that," Mary Pat said earnestly.

"The third thing, Mary Pat. Tony has to write a letter of apology to my mother, and I want it delivered here within the next forty eight hours."

"I will tell him that, as well, when I talk to him tomorrow. And, Jessie, I will personally deliver that letter to you. I'd like to meet you."

"I'll be taping my TV variety show those three months Hal is on tour with Tony. I will miss him, but this'll keep him out of my hair (laughter). I look forward to meeting you, Mary Pat." And Jessie hung up.

Chapter Seventy One

The *Starr Power* TV show broadcast live from the Copacabana came off without a hitch. Everyone involved walked away extraordinarily happy and made promises to the show's easy-to-get-along-with-but-always-in-command Executive Producer Mary Pat MacGregor: Frank Sinatra promised to do *Starr Power's* upcoming anniversary show; Dean Martin promised he would go on a future *Starr Power* and sing with his son's band Dino, Desi & Billy; Tony Winston promised to take second billing to Hal Douglas on their upcoming tour. To pump up Winston, Rick Starr had told him about the tour with Hal Douglas about an hour before the show started.

The special song that Paul Anka wrote for Frank Sinatra, Dean Martin, and Tony Winston was funny, melodic, and clever. Anka simply wrote new lyrics to the lilting melody he had written for "It Doesn't Matter Anymore," a song that had been a hit for the late Buddy Holly. It proved to be one of the high points of the show. Anka was going to ask the three stars if they wanted to record it in a studio and release it as a single.

Frank Sinatra and Tony Winston dueted on "I've Got You Under My Skin," and Dean Martin and Tony Winston teamed up on a raucous version of "Hello, Dolly!" Also on the show were Gary Lewis & The Playboys who'd been booked both because they were a very hot band and because Gary was the son of Jerry Lewis, an interesting touch considering the fact that his dad and Dean Martin were not talking to each other. Dean and Gary, however, hugged and chatted with each other for a good half hour after the show.

Hal Douglas, thrilled to be on the show with so many of his idols, brought the house down with three of his biggest hits, including "On The Street Where You

Live," which he dedicated to his mother Rita. After his star turn, Hal returned towards the end of the show to do a duet with Tony Winston on, of all songs, "London Lady Falling Down." That was the Oscar-winning song that Winston had recorded with his sisters.

Del Shannon, Sam Cooke, and Johnny Rivers each sang one song to fill out the bill on the show. Mary Pat MacGregor kept them — and their egos — all happy and — more importantly — in line.

Tony Winston closed the show with his heart-wrenching version of "I'll Be Seeing You." The staff and crew, as well as many of the other entertainers and the audience in the club were weeping. As he sang the last line of the song…*I'll be looking at the moon…but I'll be seeing you*…a huge black and white photo of his beloved sisters was lowered behind him. He walked over and kissed each of his late sisters, then walked quietly off the stage.

Everyone in the nightclub was stunned at the dramatic finish. After a moment of silence, the crowd roared its approval, and the orchestra began to play the song again as the stage went dark and the credits rolled on the screen. The devastatingly sad but lovely closing was Mary Pat's brainchild. She had discussed it with Tony, and he loved it. He knew the sentimentality of it would go straight to people's hearts.

Backstage, alone in his dressing room, Tony Winston could not believe his luck. The TV show was done in New York simply because he couldn't go to Los Angeles due to his agreement with his ex-in-laws, Jansen and Jayna James. A very poor decision on his part in his personal life led to one of the biggest moments in his professional life.

He popped open an ice-cold Coke as he thought about his future. He knew it; he felt it. This TV show would catapult him back into superstardom. The upcoming tour with teen idol Hal Douglas would introduce him to a brand new audience and help to solidify his renewed career.

Then, suddenly, a sadness set in. Tony Winston, on the verge of surpassing the huge success of his earlier career, realized he had no one to share it with. No one to call; no one waiting for him backstage. His short-lived marriage to Jessie James had ended up in a very bitter divorce; his cherished sisters were dead; and he still didn't have enough trust in anyone involved in his career to call him or her a friend.

He didn't hear the door to his dressing room open as he muttered out loud, "Wow, have I screwed up my life."

It was Mary Pat MacGregor. "I don't know what's going through your head now, Tony," she said quietly, "but I've learned it's always better to count your blessings and not your losses. After my parents died in a fire when I was a kid I looked everywhere to try to make sense of it. I couldn't find it anywhere, but then I saw a quote in a magazine from Albert Schweitzer, and it put my whole young life in perspective. I memorized it: *At times our own light goes out and is rekindled by a spark from another person. Each of us has cause to think, with deep gratitude, of those who have lighted the flame within us.*"

"Is there anything you can't do, Mary Pat?" he said with a smile starting to spread over his face.

"There probably is," she answered quickly with a laugh, "but I'm just grateful for everything I CAN do. If you need a couple more minutes, I'll come back. There are a lot of people who want to see you now and share tonight's success."

"Let me get out of this suit, and I'll be out to see all of them in five minutes. I'm looking forward to meeting anyone who wants to be met. And, Mary Pat...thank you for everything you've done for me since we met. I miss my sisters so-o-o much, but I am exceedingly grateful I met you."

As she closed the door, she glanced back at him and said, "Glad to meet you, too, Tony. I thought of my parents when you sang 'I'll Be Seeing You.' I would have been here sooner to get you, but I was sobbing."

Chapter Seventy Two

Back in Los Angeles, Rick Starr was going to make the most of the three months he had been given to tour Tony Winston and Hal Douglas together. His plan was to book large arenas, mid-sized venues, and smaller clubs.

Normally, Starr would have his staff book a concert tour. He didn't like getting bogged down in the details of ticket prices, contract riders, and so on. But this tour was his baby. His plan was to set a music business record for tickets sold and gross sales.

"Fuck the Beatles," he said to himself ver-r-ry quietly. His business partner Mary Pat MacGregor had outlawed THAT word.

"The larger the venue, the smaller the ticket price," he explained to her.

She looked more than a little puzzled. Mary Pat knew TV. Concerts were all new to her. "I thought the whole tour was supposed to be a cash cow for you," she said.

"The larger arenas will attract the kids," he explained, taking a swig of his ice-cold Mountain Dew. "It's all about asses in seats for me, but the kids want that common bond of being with other kids who enjoy the same music they do. They don't care about comfort. We'll charge 'em $3.00 and pack 'em in; 10,000 tickets in Chicago is a $30,000 gross. That one show covers about a quarter of what I'm gonna pay Tony Winston for the entire tour. This is gonna be sweet."

"If it's all about numbers, why then would you bother with a small club some-where?" she asked. "I don't get it.

"We gotta give Tony's fans a place to go once in a while, too," he said. "Most of them don't want to be in an arena with a bunch of screaming, creaming teenage girls and pimply-faced teenage boys. They want to be in a nice club where they can drink and have a chair with arms and a back on it. I can charge them $20 for that privilege."

In less than a week, Rick Starr, using all the clout he had in the entertainment business, had booked Hal Douglas and Tony Winston for sixty dates over a three-month period. Thirty six arenas, twelve mid-sized venues holding between two thousand and three thousand people, and twelve nightclubs.

Mary Pat ran the numbers and shook her head in disbelief. She ran them again just to make sure her figures were right before she reported them to Starr. She walked over to his office, knocked on his door, then walked in without waiting for a response.

Starr was sitting with his feet up on his desk reading *Billboard*. "Whaddya got, Mary Pat?"

"What I got," she said, mocking his use of the vernacular, "are numbers that show if we sell out all the dates, all 513,000 seats, we will gross nearly $3 million, Rick. I'm stunned. I didn't know teenagers had that much money."

"They don't, Mary Pat," he answered, "but their parents do. And soon, we'll get it from them."

"That's a lot of money, Rick. Can we pull this off? Really?"

"I've been thinking about that, Mary Pat," he said. "I've been running concerts around this country for a lot of years but nothing this big. I need the best tour manager in the free world, and that's gonna be you. I need someone who is in total control. I also need someone with ethics who is watching out for us, watching out for our company...keeping an eye on everything, making sure everything runs smoothly, making sure no one drops the ball."

"Me?" she said with a faux quizzical look on her face. "Let's focus on this very cogent fact: I've only been to one concert in my life and that was in the audience for a Bobby Vinton show. Let's keep that in mind."

"I need you on this one, Mary Pat. I'll run *Starr Power* for those three months."

The two business partners just stared at each other. Rick Starr said it again. "I NEED you on this. You are the only person I trust. There is a lot of money and ego at stake here. If we pull this off it'll set a precedent in the industry. It will make us the go-to promoter for all the major tours."

He jumped out of his chair and walked over to where she was standing. "You can do this, Mary Pat. You can do it."

She just stared at him as he finished off his bottle of Mountain Dew, walked back to his desk, then turned to her and said, "I'll make it worth your while. "

Mary Pat was almost petrified as to what he would say next.

"Twenty-five percent of the company," he said. "That's what this tour is worth to me. I will make you a twenty-five percent owner of this company if you pull this off for me. We'll come to mutually agreed upon terms. I'll teach you everything I know, and I'll give you daily phone support during the tour."

Her petrified look turned to shock. Her head was spinning. Rick Starr was offering her the chance of a lifetime. Not only would she be a part of one of the biggest tours in music history, she would also become a twenty-five percent owner in one of the most successful entertainment companies in the world.

All that came out of her mouth was, "I think I'm going to throw up!"

Chapter Seventy Three

The recording session for "A Lifetime of Love" ended in a standing ovation from the musicians for the singers.

"Never saw anything like that before," Al Kooper said to Gene Pitney as the performers all took awkward bows to the musicians. Brooks Arthur, the studio engineer, bounded out of the control room and triumphantly announced, "That baby's a #1!"

Pitney took Hal and Jessie aside and simply said, "Follow me." He proceeded to thank each member of the gospel choir individually and introduce each one of them to the two biggest pop stars in the country. The members of the choir were over the moon. A lot of laughing, crying, and hugging ensued. Hal and Jessie looked at each other and couldn't believe how much fun they were having nor how grateful the members of the choir were to meet them and share their joy.

They didn't quite understand that Pitney was teaching them how to be stars that fans would love and embrace. He then sent them another signal. After the informal meet-and-greet he called the room to order. "I have recorded a lot of hits here with Brooks Arthur," he said, "but that cranky son of a bitch never ran out of his control booth telling me they were 'a #1.' So, congratulations to each and every one of you. This has been the most exciting recording session of my life. And recording with The Harlem Gospel Choir was one of the greatest moments of my life.

"When this record sells a million copies, each one of you will get a gold record to put on your wall. You will always remember your part in pop music history. My friend Al Kooper over there, raise your hand Al, will get your names and addresses. You WILL get a gold record. I promise you that."

The party broke up shortly after, and Gene, Hal, and Jessie left the studio and jumped into a waiting — and warm — limousine. Gene waited to break all his big news to Hal and Jessie until they were having dinner at Luchow's, a favorite restaurant of his in the East Village. Luchow's carried Gene's favorite Australian wine.

He offered up a toast to the two young stars, then got down to business. "Everything is going to move at lightning speed in the next few months. I've ironed out everything, professionally, for the two of you. If you want it all to work, you two have to iron out your personal lives and demons."

Hal looked at Jessie and said, "I'll do whatever it takes to make all these dreams come true. Will you?"

"Could you expand on that word 'whatever' for me?" Jessie asked.

Pitney didn't sense any anger or annoyance in Jessie's question so he just crossed his legs, picked up his wine glass, and sat back and listened, although for a brief moment he did consider excusing himself because he felt he was eavesdropping on some pillow talk.

Hal reached for Jessie's hand. Pitney was now really feeling awkward. "I talked it over with my parents," Hal said, "and I am going to move to Los Angeles. I'm going to take the six-picture deal that Rick got me from Family Films, and you're going to co-star with me in them. He wanted that TV star Michele Miller, but I said no to that. I will learn to fit in with your friends, your parents' friends, and their lifestyle. I will plan my touring and recording schedule around the schedule of your TV show. I'll even arrange to have Danny Harmon end up in the trunk of a Buick on Topanga Beach."

That comment made Jessie giggle and Pitney almost spill his wine.

"See, I'm even learning my LA geography," Hal chuckled.

While he had her hand in his, Hal blurted out an unplanned "Jessie, God wants you to marry me!"

"Oh, dear Lord, Hal Douglas," she said with a hearty laugh. "I haven't heard a proposal that lame since Don Jon Ross first offered me a record deal. Let me think it over."

A surprised and chagrined Hal said, "Wh-wh-what?"

"OK," she said quickly, "I thought it over. I'll only marry you if you marry me."

Gene Pitney simply said, "This sounds like one of those cheesy Family Films."

Chapter Seventy Four

Even Gene Pitney could not believe it. He was sitting in his office at his home in Somers, Connecticut, reading about the record-breaking UK tour with Hal Douglas and Jessie James. His copy of *Billboard* had just arrived in the mail, and it showed that "A Lifetime of Love" by Hal Douglas and Jessie James featuring Gene Pitney with The Harlem Gospel Choir was at #1 for the thirty sixth week in a row.

A front page story quoted Sunshine Records owner Don Jon Ross as saying the single had surpassed sales of one million copies in the US and was approaching three and a half million copies worldwide. "I told her she should do it," he told the magazine triumphantly and erroneously. "I told her it would be the biggest hit we ever had."

Gene Pitney was back on top. He was part of a huge worldwide #1 record; he was managing the two biggest stars in the music world; he had a new, big-money record deal with a major label; and he had engineered a multi-million dollar, multi-faceted deal that would change the face of pop music.

In California, Hal and Jessie looked at the same *Billboard* over lunch by the pool at Jessie's parents' home. After the exhausting fall UK tour with Gene Pitney, they were enjoying a two-week break before getting back to work. They were getting ready to shoot their first movie for Family Films, *You've Got To Be Kidding*. After the six-week shooting schedule for the movie, Jessie would start production on her new TV show, and both stars would record new material for their respective labels. Hal would also fulfill another commitment to a Starr Entertainment tour with Tony Winston.

Reading the front page *Billboard* quote out loud, Hal asked Jessie, "Why would Don Jon lie like that? He was against this project the whole way. He wanted you to do his song 'You've Got The Right.'"

"I know," Jessie said with a smile on her face. "If he tells the truth he looks like the biggest dope in the music industry. Let him have it. I love the guy. He's the only one who would take a chance on me, Hal. I owe so much of this to him. Without him there would be no us."

Rick Starr was in New York with Mary Pat MacGregor, taking the recent addition to Starr Records, Tony Winston, out to lunch. Starr, in his typical acerbic mien, said, "Tony, we both know you're not on Starr Records by my choice, so let's skip the twaddle. Did you see the new *Billboard*? Hal Douglas is at #1 for week number sixteen. And he's at #1 all over the world on Starr Records. He's driving ticket sales for this upcoming tour, not you.

"But, I think I can get a couple more hits out of you before you're washed up…again."

At that point, Mary Pat MacGregor jumped in and grabbed the now deflated Tony Winston's hand. After working with him on the *Starr Power* TV show from the Copacabana, she liked him and considered him a friend and vice versa.

She didn't like the demeaning way Starr was talking to him, and she was never afraid to speak truth to power. "Tony, Rick's ire is not really meant for you," she explained. "He's mad at me because Gene Pitney got the best of him, and I had to cut the deal that made this happen. Made ALL this happen…for Rick.

"I'm going out as the tour manager again with you and Hal. You will be treated as the star you are. I've been told that Hal is a big fan of yours so this should be great fun. This time, I'm going to suggest to Gene that you and Hal alternate opening and closing the show."

"I've gotta make a phone call," Starr said and marched angrily away from the table.

"He's still upset that Gene Pitney is managing Hal," Marty Pat explained to Winston. "It seems Rick never signed a contract with Hal after he discovered him in Milwaukee. That put Gene in the driver's seat, and let's just say that Gene Pitney has better manners and social graces than our friend Rick.

"Having explained that, here is your contract for this tour. Rick said you handle your own management. $125,000 plus air, hotels, meals, et cetera. We've booked the flights and hotels. I'll need receipts for meals and any other reasonable and ordinary expenses. Don't go crazy on me. This contract should set you up for the rest of your life if you invest it well.

"I'm very grateful, Mary Pat. I won't. I don't think Rick was too far off saying this is likely my last hurrah, so can I ask a favor of you?"

"Shoot," she answered quickly.

"My oldest friend from Kenosha is in failing health. I wanna bring him on the tour with me so he can see the country before…you know…before he dies. His name is Steve Alioto. We call him "Shortstop." Can you arrange that?"

"Give me his contact information, and I'll take care of it. Starr Entertainment will cover all costs. That's a sweet thing to do, Tony. I will be going to Mass every Sunday no matter where we are. You're welcome to join me. Go to confession first. Hal will be going to Mass, too. See you on the tour."

"Mary Pat," Tony said with a warmth he had previously reserved only for his beloved sisters, "you are a star…with one R."

Don Jon Ross was having lunch with his brother Jim Tim and his sister Fay Kay, and they were all enjoying the chart success of "A Lifetime of Love" on Sunshine Records. Don Jon was enjoying the cash windfall dropping into his bank account from US record sales surpassing two million on their way to three million. He could now fulfill his lifelong fantasy to run with the big dogs in the music industry. "Now they can all really suck my ass," he said to his brother and sister with a snort.

Fay Kay, the company accountant, was keeping Don Jon happy by expertly manipulating the money for tax purposes. Jim Tim, who had been writing songs for his musical hero Tony Winston, had been irate when he learned that Don Jon had sold Winston's contract to Starr Records, but Don Jon mollified him by getting his superstar Jessie James to hire Jim Tim as the musical director for her syndicated TV show.

Back at the home of Jansen and Jayna James, Hal Douglas finished lunch, put on a Gene Pitney T-shirt, and got on the kitchen phone; Jessie James wrapped a towel around her bikini-clad body and got on the extension. They were calling Gene Pitney. It was a call they had planned the night before, just before they fell asleep following a night of exhausting sex.

Pitney answered his phone in two rings. Hal spoke first, "Hey, Gene…it's Hal." And Jessie then piped in "…and Jessie."

"Hey, Guys. What's up?" Pitney asked.

"You answered that phone kinda like you were waiting for us to call," Hal retorted.

"I was in the kitchen getting a sandwich, and the phone's right here," Gene explained.

In her excitement, Jessie forgot the "script" she and Hal had written for this call and blurted out, "We're gonna do it, Gene. We're gonna get married, and we're hoping you'll be our Best Man."

Pitney, after just the right amount of dramatic silence, simply said, "I amend my previous statement. I have been waiting for this call."

.

www.ingramcontent.com/pod-product-compliance
Lightning Source LLC
Chambersburg PA
CBHW021036090426
42738CB00029B/170